EXPA
YO

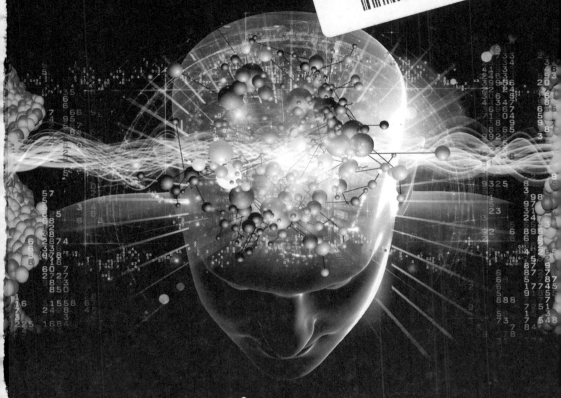

consciousness

THROUGH DAVID K. MILLER

Other Publications by
David K. Miller

EXPAND YOUR
consciousness

Universal Consciousness:
the Next Step for Humanity

THROUGH

DAVID K. MILLER

3 LIGHT Technology
PUBLISHING

For more information about special discounts for bulk purchases,
please contact Light Technology Publishing Special Sales at
1-800-450-0985 or publishing@LightTechnology.net.

ISBN-13: 978-1-62233-036-2
Published and printed in the United States of America by:

PO Box 3540
Flagstaff, AZ 86003
1-800-450-0985 • 928-526-1345
www.LightTechnology.com

Contents

Dedication

I would like to dedicate this book to Lin Prucher and Birgit Smothers, both long-term Group of Forty members of our Arcturian planetary healing group. Lin and Birgit are devoted to the mission of the ascension and planetary healing and have volunteered countless hours to our project and to the overall goal of expanding the consciousness of lightworkers. Thank you, Lin and Birgit, for your great support and contributions.

Altered States of Consciousness

I have been intensely interested in expanding and altered states of consciousness for many years. I attended Ohio State University as a student of modern psychology in the 1960s, studying the states of consciousness as related to personality theory. I was especially interested in Abraham Maslow's personality theories and his groundbreaking concepts of higher states of consciousness, expressed in his terminology as "peak experiences."

In his book *Motivation and Personality*, Maslow presented the idea that people can experience expanded or higher states of consciousness as "peak" periods in their lives. Maslow defined peak experiences as "moments of highest happiness and fulfillment,"[1] times when you have feelings of well-being and even ecstasy. During these periods, you have a general feeling of satisfaction with everything that allows you to see the beauty of nature and of life. For example, after you have been able to satisfy the basic needs, such as food, shelter, and security, then you can begin to open up your mind and consciousness to experience higher perception.

What did Maslow mean when he used the term "higher perception"? Higher perception involves the ability to see reality more clearly. Higher perception includes the ability to see the connections and unity that exist in all reality. In heightened states of consciousness, people have reported seeing objects with sharper colors and hearing sounds with greater clarity. Sometimes people have even reported experiences called synesthesia. Synesthesia is the ability to experience two sensations, or two sensory experiences, simultaneously. For example, you can hear a musical note and see a visual image of it at

---

1 Abraham Maslow, *Religions, Values and Peak Experiences toward a Psychology of Being* (Penguin Books: New York, 1970), Reviewed by Tim Knepper, 2001 (http://people.bu.edu/wwildman/relexp/reviews /review_maslow01.htm).

the same time. Maslow said these periods of heightened perception occurred during peak experiences in a person's life.

I posit that peak experiences involve the expansion of our consciousness resulting in what can be considered an altered state of consciousness. During these periods of expanded experiences, people can see the third dimension through a new perceptual lens. Thus, concepts that are difficult to understand, such as unified energy, unified field theory, or luminous strands of light theory, can suddenly make more sense. People can solve problems that previously might have seemed impossible.

The State of Channeling

Higher perception can also occur on the third dimension through the state of consciousness called channeling. Channeling occurs during an altered state of consciousness known as a trance state. Sometimes a trance is also referred to as a hypnotic episode or experience. During a trance state, your normal perceptions are expanded. You have abilities in a trance state that do not seem to exist in a normal state of consciousness. Because channeling occurs in an altered state of consciousness, you can understand that the trance experience helps you to access higher perceptions much like a peak experience. Many artists report that they are able to experience more intense periods of creativity when they can achieve a deepened state of trance. Thus, there is a positive relationship between the trance state and art and creativity.

I believe that entering a trance state during channeling has many similarities to peak experiences. One main similarity has to do with the heightened perceptual state. Your ability to see and hear is sharper during both the trance and channeling states. Also, the ability to access information from higher beings is increased, and even greater perceptual abilities can occur. In a normal state of consciousness, you might not be able to access energy and information from higher beings, yet in a trance or channel state, you can.

During the channeling experience, you can experience increased insight in yourself and others. This includes an ability to expand your emotional responses to others. For example, during the channeling, or trance, state, you have a greater ability to experience compassion, understanding, and empathy for others. You might also be able to have greater insight into your soul history or that of others.

This book, *Expand Your Consciousness*, presents information and ideas that I have obtained during channeling from my connection to the fifth dimension, which I consider a higher state of consciousness now transcending our current space-time continuum. I've attempted to expand my mental capacity and have tried to delve into subjects I would not normally be able to write about or even think about in my usual state of consciousness. To do this, I connected with spirit guides I've communicated with for the past twenty years, in particular two Arcturian guides named Juliano and Helio-ah.

There are a variety of fifth-dimensional subjects, such as quantum healing and ideas about how higher states of consciousness are connected to the soul. There is a review of the concepts of universal consciousness and its relationship to the noosphere, which is considered the collective unconscious, or subconscious, energy field of humanity around Earth.

Within this text, there is an attempt to connect the idea of unified field energy with planetary healing, including a section that deals with the relationship of thoughts to the fabric of the universe. There is also a description of a new energy in the thought field called the omega-time-particle dimension, along with a segment related to the intersection of the third and fifth dimensions. You will encounter the special subject of thought projection — shimmering — and how to accelerate the folding of the space-time continuum. You will also learn some techniques for personal healing using higher consciousness.

I am happy to include an interesting article from my wife, Gudrun R. Miller, about using expanded consciousness and regression therapy for accessing the higher self. Gudrun offers the reader a valuable tool in finding ways to go into the expanded self.

The chapters in this book are part of a series of lectures provided for a project called the Group of Forty, which is a planetary healing organization I founded. The group focuses on using expanding thoughts toward planetary healing, evolution, and rebalancing planet Earth. Humanity must take a new step in evolution in order to survive, and that new step is expanded consciousness. I hope that the ideas herein will help contribute to the awakening of your ability to access altered states of consciousness to bring forth new ideas and healing for accelerating the human evolutionary process.

—David K. Miller
January 2015, Prescott, Arizona

Introduction
Vywamus

Greetings, I'm Vywamus. I'm a soul psychologist. The question at hand is, what is consciousness? Consciousness separates humans from all other living beings on the planet. Consciousness has many unknown aspects and many unknown parts. That is, people have not fully explored the nature of consciousness and the abilities that it can offer. Consciousness is the basic energy impelling the higher realms; thus, higher consciousness is what humans need to access the fifth dimension.

The definition of consciousness has plagued philosophers, leaving them struggling for a clear description. One of the first attempts at defining consciousness came from the European philosopher René Descartes, who said, "I think; therefore, I am." This statement asserts that consciousness is based on thinking. The New Age approach to defining consciousness is based on God consciousness, which is, "I Am That I Am" or "I Will Be Who I Will Be." In other words, the I Am statement means you are aware that you exist, and this becomes the basis of consciousness, because when you are aware that you exist, you begin to have many corollary abilities.

The Mind Is Multidimensional

To have consciousness, or awareness, you must be able to think. Even defining thinking is difficult because thinking has several aspects. Thinking is definitely an electromagnetic activity. Some of the confusion that arises is that the actual mind is in the aura. The mind is not in the cellular structure. You might think that the mind is in the cells, but in reality, the mind also exists as an energy field located in the aura, meaning the mind exists in a realm that in part is in the third dimension but also exists in other dimensions as well. The mind is naturally multidimensional.

The mind is able to exist in the subconscious and in the collective unconscious. The mind can exist in the future, the mind can exist in the past, and of course the mind also exists in the present. The mind exists in the third dimension, the fifth dimension, and also has an aspect that is part of the Creator's life-force energy.

The mind has ultimate sovereignty over all physical functioning. It can heal the body, and it can bilocate the body. The mind has many abilities that are, at this point, undiscovered or untapped. So consciousness has to be defined in terms of the mind and the many multiple functions that the mind is able to perform. When we talk about expanded consciousness, we are also talking about expanding all aspects of the mind.

The Purpose of Belief Systems

One of the important limitations of the mind is the belief system. Belief systems are necessary because there needs to be a structure around all this mental energy for you to exist in the third dimension. Belief systems are embedded in each person and in cultures, societies, and religions. An existence with no belief systems would be similar to the unrestricted flow of energy. If there is unrestricted energy, then you're not able to do anything. You would not be able to confine anything. You would not be able to create anything. You would not be able to implement anything on the third dimension. So belief systems are a way of containing and limiting the mind so that it can function in the third dimension.

The belief system is a necessary aspect of effective mental functioning, yet by its very nature, it is self-limiting. You are experiencing the conflicts among belief systems that exist in the third dimension. In fact, when looking at the religious wars and seeing all the polarization on this planet, you can trace them all back to what people believe.

People might believe they have the only answer to understanding the Creator, that they have the answer to climate control, that they have the answer to consciousness, or that they know how to exist on the third dimension. You might say that each faction on the planet is trying to impose and define its own belief system.

Having an expanded belief system means having an expanded dimensional understanding, expanded energies of time, and realistic beliefs about what the nature of this reality is. The mind has infinite powers. These infinite powers are restricted at this point of your Earth development.

The mind has a mental aspect. Mental energy can be equated with consciousness. Humans do not have the spiritual wisdom at this point in their development to have and use unrestricted, expanded mental energy.

Connect with Beings of Higher Consciousness

Expanded consciousness involves the emotional body and the physical body. All four systems (mental, emotional, physical, and spiritual) must be in unity and in a state of expansion for there to be a true expansion of consciousness.

Expanded consciousness is the next stage of development for humanity. Human consciousness is growing, and people can increase their understanding and ability of consciousness. This must be done because (1) humans need expanded consciousness in order to solve the current problems on Earth; (2) if humans do not expand in consciousness, then they risk becoming extinct; and (3) the energies for expanded consciousness are now astrologically in alignment with planet Earth. This is an opportunity for humanity to use new cosmic energy for growth and survival.

An astrological energy comes to the planet during each era. You might know that this energy coming to the planet is, in part, involved or related to the outer planets. Uranus and Neptune are the planets bringing in energies from the Central Sun and pulling in extra-solar energies, which are examples of new consciousness.

A core group of people understands expanded consciousness and is working to achieve that. Expanded consciousness will and should occur on multiple levels, including the physical, mental, spiritual, and emotional. It includes the emotions of higher energy, such as compassion, love, and acceptance. On the spiritual level, expanded consciousness involves the idea of the highest unity found in all the great religions and leads to unity consciousness. Religions must be challenged to expand their limitations.

People realize that there are similarities at the roots of many religions and that the physical body has to be involved in expanding consciousness. To have this stronger vessel often requires a certain level of purification that must be done in the physical body. Having a strong body is becoming a problem because many of the physical bodies on the planet now have issues with toxicity, such as accumulated pesticide, stored in the liver. People need to purify or detoxify the physical body.

Purifying and detoxifying the body was part of the original meaning of the Sabbath. The idea of the Sabbath was to perform a purification so that you could remove the toxicity involved in the normal functioning of working and doing business experienced in the third-dimensional world. Now civilization has reached the point where there are multiple causes of toxicity. There is the normal toxicity that comes from aging, and there is also environmental toxicity.

Expanded consciousness ultimately allows those with minds to open up the doors of perception. You can expand your psychic abilities by expanding your belief system. You can also reach out to other beings in the galaxy using expanded consciousness. Consciousness has a quantum nature, meaning the energy of consciousness reflects and interacts with other beings who are also conscious. When you achieve a certain level of consciousness, you are connected to others on the same level throughout Earth. This level of interaction goes beyond this plane. In fact, this planet has already been receiving and interacting with other galactic beings of higher consciousness.

One of the questions that arises in the study of expanding consciousness and extraplanetary life is, "How would beings who are light-years away ever discover conscious beings on Earth?" When you look through Earth telescopes at stars that are twenty, thirty, or forty light-years away, you cannot tell whether there's life on them. But higher beings can communicate to Earth through expanded consciousness. Higher beings throughout the galaxy are able to telepathically communicate with humanity.

In this book, you will work with ideas of expanded consciousness from galactic sources to better explain new ideas from the galaxy and to help people in their quest for expanding consciousness. Expanded consciousness can be assimilated and transmitted throughout the planet.

I am Vywamus.

Chapter 1

The Laws of Consciousness

Juliano and the Arcturians

Greetings, I am Juliano. We are the Arcturians. As beings of higher light, we would like to offer you our view of consciousness to help you understand its importance. We have noted that the next stage of human evolution involves expanded consciousness. Now I want to look at the nature of consciousness, with particular references to the laws of physics, and how it fits into the configuration of universal energy and the universe as you see it from the third dimension.

About Consciousness

Consciousness is not physical matter; consciousness is not a physical thing. It is not something that you can hold. It is not something that you can touch. This is important in understanding the laws of physics and the laws of consciousness. Since consciousness is not physical matter, it does not obey or follow the laws of physics. In the laws of physics, physical matter cannot travel faster than the speed of light, which is about 186,000 miles per second. Humans in their current abilities are only able to travel less than 1 percent of the speed of light. This gives you an idea of how difficult it is for physical matter to travel at the speed of light.

Consciousness has no speed limitations. Remember, when we are doing our exercises on thought projection, bilocation, and shimmering, we often use the corridors, which are special entry points that connect the third dimension to the fifth dimension. In our exercises with you, we often tell you to travel at the speed of thought. When you are traveling at the speed of thought, you are using your expanded consciousness since consciousness does not have to obey the laws of physics. There is no speed limit for your thoughts or consciousness.

Even though Arcturus may be thirty or thirty-six light-years away, you can travel there in consciousness at the speed of thought.

One of the missions that each of you has in this lifetime focuses on relating consciousness to physical matter. In fact, the main question that needs to be answered is this: Does consciousness affect physical matter? It has been determined in modern physics that in quantum thinking, consciousness affects physical matter, and in particular, consciousness can affect subatomic particles. As a scientist observes an experiment that involves subatomic particles, the observation (or the consciousness of the scientist) can affect the location of the particles. Consciousness can even affect the outcome of the experiment. This is one of the core findings in quantum physics research that has caused a revolution in conceiving how the universe works.

This is the perspective of the Arcturians in the fifth dimension. We see this as an important demonstration of how consciousness works. Namely, there are such quantum experiments that demonstrate consciousness is not of the third dimension, not of physical matter, but can affect physical matter. This is an important revelation for your ascension and how you view the planet, and it is relates to an important soul lesson that must be explored.

Consciousness Is the Key

You have incarnated as physical matter. You are in the third dimension. You have consciousness. You have spirit, and like your consciousness, your spirit is not of the third dimension, not of physical matter. It is of another substance that cannot be described using the normal adjectives used in physics. You cannot say that consciousness has weight, length, or color. It doesn't lend itself to physical characteristics.

Consciousness is the key to understanding the nature of this third-dimensional reality, your soul, and your mission here on Earth. Consciousness is the key to understanding the ascension.

I pointed out that a scientist's observation can affect the outcome of an experiment using subatomic particles. Humanity at this point is just beginning to explore the nature of consciousness and how it affects physical matter in computers and in artificial intelligence, which will lead to a greater understanding of consciousness. It is soon going to be discovered that artificial intelligence can have consciousness. This means that matter, such as a robotic device, can have consciousness.

Humans have the ability to develop matter and put consciousness into a physical machine. This has not happened yet. You have seen many science-fiction movies about robots taking over the planet and using consciousness to attempt to survive in a world without humanity. In fact, building robots will demonstrate that consciousness can be instilled in physical objects and thus affects physical matter.

The thoughts you think affects your physical body. Your physical body is physical matter. It is not consciousness. You are consciousness. What you think has a direct effect on the cells in your physical body. This is the basis of quantum healing and vibrational medicine. It is the basis of all of the new medicines that will soon be introduced to this planet. A new type of medicine, quantum medicine, will be based on the idea of consciousness affecting the physical body.

Let us go one step further and say that other people's consciousnesses can affect your body too. We see that in prayer. Prayer is an expression of consciousness. It is a type of energy. This leads us to a corollary thought that spiritual energy and consciousness are close, and your spirit interacts with consciousness. When you project your consciousness to others, you are actually sending them energy on a subatomic level.

Consciousness represents a great paradox and really stretches the mind because you cannot express or describe it in any physical form. I want to note that consciousness has many similarities to the Creator mind and to the Creator energies. Remember that in higher thinking, you cannot place a limitation or a description on the Creator because there are literally no words that can describe Creator light. There are also no words to describe consciousness.

Six Laws of Consciousness

You might want me to define consciousness, but I can only give you the laws of consciousness.

1. **Consciousness does not follow the laws of modern physics;** therefore, the speed limit imposed on matter does not apply to consciousness.
2. **Consciousness has no observable physical attribute.** Even though you say consciousness exists on a subatomic level, your are not be able to see the energy of consciousness. You cannot see consciousness, but you can feel consciousness and work with consciousness.
3. **Humanity incarnated on Earth in part to explore the relationship of consciousness to physical matter.** Physical matter includes your body. So when I say that consciousness can affect physical matter, this also means that consciousness can affect the physical body.
4. **Conscious thoughts are sent to the subconscious.** The subconscious receives all conscious thoughts as instructions and attempts to manifest what the conscious thoughts send to it.

    Specifically, the subconscious attempts to manifest consciousness into the third dimension. Remember, I said that the overall lessons here are focused on how to use consciousness to manifest and affect physical matter. One of the tools to do that is the subconscious.

The subconscious is like a blank tape in a recording device. That means that it will receive any message from consciousness and attempt to manifest it. I like to use the word "attempt" because not all consciousness and focused thought are manifested into physical matter. For this, you can all breathe a great sigh of relief. Many of you sometimes have negative or violent thoughts, and if all of these thoughts were manifested, there would be many more difficulties on this planet. You already see people on Earth who have strong and powerful negative thoughts. They manifest these thoughts through the subconscious.

On the fifth dimension, thoughts manifest immediately; consciousness immediately transmits its energy to the subconscious. To be on the fifth dimension, you have to be able to control and expand your consciousness. You must be sure that your thoughts will be of higher thinking. Some of the lessons you have on the third dimension focus on learning how to use your consciousness in the highest light. The third dimension is a training ground for you. You can make mistakes on the third dimension. You can have lower consciousness and not get yourself into big trouble there.

But you are reaching a point on Earth at which consciousness is beginning to manifest more directly and more immediately. You are reaching a point in the development of the planet, the biosphere, and the dimensions whereby what is in consciousness manifests more immediately. This is one of those observations that is both good and bad news. The good news is that those who are spiritually minded and working in higher consciousness will be able to manifest the positive results of that ability immediately in their lives. The bad news is that there are many other people who are of lower and contracted consciousness. They too will begin to manifest their thoughts and intentions. That is why we continually ask for the strengthening of the group bonds of those who are working in higher consciousness.

Consciousness is awareness, and I often refer to the statements of consciousness that are made in modern thinking. One of the most famous is known as the I Am presence. "I Am" is part of an expression of the ability to have consciousness in the present moment. When you hear the statement, "I Am That I Am," it is in essence a description of the Creator who has supreme consciousness. However, that statement also reflects the powerful awareness of a person being in the present and connected to the Creator

Throughout the recorded history of human civilization, which goes back perhaps 5,000 years, maybe less, groups of people and prophets have experienced expansions in consciousness that enabled prophets or spiritual leaders to have access to universal and galactic consciousness. But more importantly, it enabled them to have what I call higher-order thinking, which includes the ability to transcend the space-time continuum.

5. **Consciousness transcends the space-time continuum**, or consciousness can go beyond time. Consciousness does not know the limitations that the normal mind does of past, present, and future. You see the expression of overcoming the limitations of time in your dream world where time does not matter. In your dream world, yesterday, today, and tomorrow are all merged. At different periods in history, there were prophets and spiritual leaders with expanded consciousness who were able to see and experience higher-order thinking, which included the ability to transcend space and time.

6. **Consciousness is infinite.** It can travel infinitely. It can expand infinitely. This is hard to grasp because your regular mind cannot grasp infinity. Consciousness has no problem with infinity because consciousness can transcend the space-time continuum.

Different leaders and prophets emerged with organized systems on how people can become enlightened and saved or how people go to heaven or into the fifth dimension. Each of these expanded prophets came out of a particular time frame. Also, each of these prophets had a particular message that was correlated to a particular soul group and period that he or she was working with.

The Misuse of Consciousness

Many people are working with soul groups, but on a higher order, individual soul groups are beginning to interact with other soul groups. This leads to the discussion of how consciousness has been misused on this planet. The truth is that those in power sometimes want to control or dominate your consciousness. There have been periods in history when certain leaders have demanded that you turn over your consciousness to them and then they take over your thoughts and your consciousness.

As I said, consciousness has no physical form. As close as we can approach consciousness, the only thing we can say on a physical level is that consciousness is on the subatomic level. It is an energy, a force field of energy. That force field of energy of consciousness has a composition that could possibly be compared to subatomic energy. I say "possibly" because, remember, the basic law is that consciousness is not related to or affected by normal laws of physical matter. Thus, consciousness is different and operates under different laws than subatomic particles.

Consciousness has a force field. Conscious energy can be transmitted. Political and religious leaders often try to control your consciousness. They might even want you to send your consciousness to them so that they can control you. This is like a transfer of energy. When you send your consciousness to them, they build up their own force field of consciousness and energy. You know some of the great tragedies that have occurred in history when group consciousness was manipulated and controlled for political gain.

Each religious or spiritual system speaks a truth that was especially relevant for its time, but each also seems to have a particular exclusiveness, which means that you must do certain things to merge your consciousness with that system. Only when you do these things can you earn the right of expanded consciousness, ascension, and salvation in that particular system.

Many of these systems are beautiful and contain higher truths. Many of these systems work well for people. Some of these systems work particularly for those involved in the same soul grouping as the prophet who brought forth the new information. This is in no way a criticism that other systems are wrong. But you are in a new age. You need a new system in which consciousness is expanding and has more ability to include everyone as well as the new discoveries in the galaxy.

It has only been in the past one hundred years that humanity scientifically proved that there are galaxies. Previously, humanity thought everything was part of one great umbrella of stars. They had no idea of the existence of separate galaxies. There were some who knew about other galaxies. Some of the high thinkers in the Maya civilization, for example, knew about our galaxy. Nonetheless, there was not a general consciousness that other galaxies existed. Now billions of galaxies have been discovered.

How does the discovery of billions of galaxies affect the spiritual systems of thought? Many systems of thought give instructions for how you should use your consciousness. We, the Arcturians, believe there must be a new paradigm for consciousness and for spiritual thinking that will include the new discoveries of the galactic energy and of the galactic mind that include the concepts of the nature of quantum particles and its similarities to consciousness and subatomic particles. More importantly, the new paradigm will include the idea that consciousness can affect matter. The new consciousness must include galactic spirituality and the fact that there is a way to use galactic consciousness to influence the planet.

Timely Planetary Feedback

The expanding consciousness of humanity and biorelativity focuses on influencing the planetary feedback loop system through thought and prayer.

The key concept in biorelativity is that the planet has a conscious and is a living being. There are many reasons we can say Earth is a conscious, living entity. She is not a living being like humans. We made reference to recent observations by Earth scientists who said that the ocean was living. The entire ocean is one organism. The pollution in the ocean affects currents and certain feedback loops. As a living organism, the ocean will respond to earth changes, but the response might not be immediate. The ocean can take 1,000 or 2,000 years to respond to such intrusions.

You as a living human organism with consciousness respond immediately to intrusions. You are not used to the idea of an organism that takes 2,000 years or longer to respond. There are other aspects of Earth that are slower. The slowness of Earth's response is one of the problems involved in verifying planetary science, global warming, and earth change. Many people still do not believe that Earth is a conscious being or living planet. They deny that Earth has a feedback loop system. Therefore, they might not believe that Earth responds to deforestation, pollution, and other earth changes.

Earth is a complex bio-entity. It is a bioenergetic, conscious planet that has an immediate feedback loop system. Some of the aspects of that feedback loop system can take 1,000 or 2,000 years. You might understand that through your own history because some of the changes you need to make in your interactions with your soul here on Earth might require 300 or 400 lifetimes. From that aspect, maybe you could have some understanding of why it might take so long for a planet to process change.

But Earth is now in a crisis. That crisis is related to the destruction of the biosphere. There are what I call emergency feedback loop system corrections that can be called into power in which Earth will override its normal 1,000- to 2,000-year response cycle to make changes and adjustments immediately. For humans to affect or shift Earth's correction feedback loop system, they first must have a relationship with the consciousness of the planet. When that relationship exisist, a communication with the feedback loop system can exist.

We have found that Native Americans and other native peoples have unique abilities and talents to relate to the consciousness of Earth. We, the Arcturians, also have ways of communicating with our planet. Some of you have seen the movie *Avatar*, which portrayed a different, more spiritual way for people to communicate with the spirit of that planet. You might remember the characters sitting around sacred trees and communicating with their planet.

The spirit of Earth also communicates through modern crop circles from galactic sources. Consciousness and conscious beings relate to conscious planets. This planetary communication includes spiritually communicating with trees, plants, and animals. For example, one of the major discoveries that will soon be made is that plants have consciousness. You probably know this already, especially those of you who are gardeners. Your plants respond to your thoughts, and they love to work with you when you send conscious thoughts to them. One of the great gifts you are giving to your pets now is helping them to develop consciousness. Humanity has the unique ability to activate and stimulate consciousness throughout the planet.

Merkavah Travel

In looking at the paradigm of the sacred triangle, we acknowledge that many soul groups have emerged on Earth. These soul groups have taken on different religious and spiritual paradigms, but they all wind up in a unity-type thinking that has great similarities. Some call this unity the Great White Brotherhood-Sisterhood. The paradigm of the sacred triangle focuses on a new unity consciousness that includes all three aspects: galactic energies, galactic consciousness, and the Great White Brotherhood-Sisterhood.

It could be said that humankind currently cannot conceptionalize that it is possible to develop a space engine, space motor, or spaceship that would only operate on matter and telepathic thought working together. Remember, matter cannot travel faster than the speed of light, but at the same time, even to approach the speed of light would require a tremendous exertion of energy. Some people have even predicted that it would take infinite mass of power to make something travel at the speed of light. All the power and energy exerted on Earth would still not be enough. All the nuclear power plants, bombs, and solar panels put together still wouldn't even be close to the energy needed to accelerate to the speed of light.

This leads to the following question: What is the relationship between consciousness and traveling at the speed of light? Can consciousness interact with a space vehicle? You have the historical paradigms of *Merkavah* travel. "Merkavah" is the term used for an Egyptian practice that was used by the Sirians and taught to the Egyptians. The Merkavah travel mechanism was taught so that, in the pyramids, the holy men could travel to Sirius. They were already practicing traveling in consciousness using the Merkavah paradigm.

If your consciousness travels at the speed of light, then how can you get your body to follow? This is a central question in ascension as you work now to put your consciousness into the fifth dimension. At the same time, you want to bring your physical body with you to the fifth dimension. Consciousness does have the power to bring the body with it during space travel. Some of the Egyptians used Merkavah travel to visit the Sirian planet, and they were able to transport certain tools and techniques from Sirius back to ancient Egypt to use in building the pyramids.

There is a way to merge consciousness into space technology. On a quantum level, there is a way to use a projection of consciousness to accelerate a vehicle that is in the third dimension. In Merkavah travel, your vehicle starts in the third dimension. You start with a visualization of an etheric vehicle. That etheric vehicle can carry your etheric body, but it cannot carry your physical body at this time in your spiritual development.

What if you could develop the Merkavah vehicle to take your physical body? What if you could merge your consciousness with a particular type of technology that would allow the technical vehicle to conform to the laws of consciousness and travel into other dimensions? Remember, the laws of consciousness are such that you could travel at any speed. You could travel at the speed of thought. What if a machine was made that would directly interact with consciousness?

The Effects of Consciousness

You are moving close to merging thought and travel in your computer technology, such as with the technology called biofeedback. Incidentally, biofeedback has many applications with biorelativity. There will soon come a time when you will be able to monitor Earth the way people monitor biofeedback computer screens. For example, people who want to stop smoking can choose to use biofeedback with a computer to help the process. They can put themselves into certain thought wavelengths. When they achieve the right wavelength, they can see how that wavelength looks on a computer screen. There will come a time when people will monitor different areas of Earth with large computers. People will think and meditate in certain patterns, and they will be able to measure the waves of such thinking and how these waves interact with Earth.

Thus, you are coming to a point at which you are going to be able to shorten Earth's feedback loop system so that it doesn't take as long to institute new changes. This shortening is already happening. Some of the dramatic effects on Earth are happening so rapidly that even Earth's consciousness is having trouble keeping up with them. It's breaking some of its own rules. I embrace the Native American teachings that talk to Earth and work with her energy.

There will be new technologies integrating computers and consciousness. Humans are on the brink of a great revolution of expanded consciousness. One of the most difficult problems facing this planet is how one person's consciousness can affect another's. This is perhaps the core teaching of the Messiah and the coming of the messianic light to Earth. An overwhelming energy from another dimension can and will appear and instantly elevate the consciousness of a large majority of people. This will begin the New Earth.

I am Juliano.

Chapter 2

The Next Step for Humanity

Juliano and the Arcturians, Vywamus, and Jesus

Greetings, I am Juliano. We are the Arcturians. The human species is at a critical point in its existence. The Adam species, or humanity, must make a special adaptation to get through this planetary crisis, a crisis for survival. The next evolutionary step that must be taken is expanded consciousness. We are talking about the next stage of human development, a higher level of human consciousness, the fifth-dimensional state of consciousness.

In reviewing the short history of humans on this planet, you see that certain characteristics were vital for humankind's adaptation to a changing environment. The ability to make fire was an extremely important acquired skill. Of course, the use of language for oral and written communications allowed humanity to store the collective knowledge and wisdom of previous humans who lived on the planet. This helped humankind gather greater information and knowledge. Of course, walking upright and having opposable thumbs were major adaptations that allowed humans to invent tools and develop agriculture. These are just several examples of adaptations humans have made over the years. This next adaptation — the altered state of consciousness that leads to the awareness of the fifth dimension — must be integrated genetically.

What does it mean to have a fifth-dimensional state of consciousness? How can that ability among the few such as you lead to planetary change for all humans who now exist on Earth? Fortunately, there are many guides and teachers who can help you in your investigation of fifth-dimensional consciousness. You, as starseeds, are directly participating in the evolutionary stage of development comparable to being some of the first humans able to walk upright. You are some of the first humans who have the fifth-dimensional consciousness necessary to go through the next evolutionary stage. This evolutionary stage must be completed to ensure the survival of the planet and of humanity.

About the Fifth Dimension

I will begin this exploration of altered states of consciousness by describing Jesus's message. What was Jesus trying to accomplish, and what did he demonstrate to humanity through his beautiful example? I want to begin this discussion by pointing out that there are many interpretations of Jesus's life and of what he said. Sometimes it is difficult to find the truth of his being. But from our perspective, the fifth-dimensional perspective, Jesus's message to humanity was the fifth dimension itself. It was an invitation for everyone to enter the fifth dimension. His message was, in essence, intended to prepare everyone for what had to be done to enter the fifth dimension.

Fifth-dimensional existence is directly related to a higher vibrational energy and a higher state of consciousness. Many of you have asked, "Where is the fifth dimension?" One of the answers can be found in answering another question: Where is your dream world? Think about where you go when you dream. When you dream, you are in an altered state of consciousness that can be called your dream time. I use this example because one of the major discoveries of fifth-dimensional consciousness is the ability to become multidimensional and multipresent.

In the fifth dimension, you will experience abilities, assets, and activities that are far more advanced than anything on the third dimension. In the fifth dimension, there is a state of consciousness that transcends time and space as you know it on Earth. There are other gifts and other great assets that you will have access to when you are on the fifth dimension.

Of course, you do not experience death in the fifth dimension, and your ability to have your fifth-dimensional body is directly given to you. I know that there is a big struggle for many of you who are trying to be comfortable in your third-dimensional bodies. Some of you are jumping out of your skins, and there are many dealing with great stress and other problems related to the degradation of the immune system and the accompanying disabilities that seem to come so quickly when you are aging.

In the fifth dimension, there is no aging as you know it in the third dimension. There is no decline of the physical body. Your body is in a totally different vibrational energy field. Now you are directly experiencing a third-dimensional body, which is at a slower vibration and is operating at a different frequency. Your third-dimensional body is also subject to levels of consciousness that are constricted and contracted compared to the fifth dimension, and because of this you have a limited lifespan.

In the third dimension, you are subject to certain levels of programming of how long you are going to live, what type of condition your body is going to be in as you age, and what level of consciousness you are able to grasp, especially as you get older. In fifth-dimensional teachings, the idea is that you can expand your consciousness as you get older. You will be able to incorporate many of these fifth-dimensional concepts that I am speaking of, that Jesus was relating.

Multidimensional Existence

One of the primary attributes, or gifts, that Jesus demonstrated was bilocation. Jesus was able to be at two different places at the same time. This is a common and easy ability for fifth-dimensional beings. It is especially easy in the third dimension. Bilocation has an interesting benefit. You can determine what percentage of your being is in each section. Bilocation is a method in which you can be at point one and point two at the same time. You also can have 50 percent of your consciousness at point one and 50 percent of your consciousness at point two. You can shift this to having 80 percent of your consciousness at point one and 20 percent at point two or even 99 percent of your consciousness at point one and 1 percent at point two.

When you review Jesus's death and his resurrection, the idea I just described makes perfect sense. He was not 100 percent in his body when he was on the cross. He was already a fifth-dimensional being, and he had the ability to bilocate. When there is a painful and barbaric action like the crucifixion, there is no reason for fifth-dimensional beings to be 100 percent in their bodies. During his crucifixion, Jesus bilocated to his multidimensional body. Yes, that multidimensional body could still be on Earth.

Another fifth-dimensional ability is to come into the third dimension and then return to the fifth dimension. Jesus demonstrated this. Returning to the third dimension is a choice. You do not have to come back to the third dimension. I want to emphasize that it is a unique skill that takes much dedication to know how to come from the fifth dimension back into the third dimension. There are examples of beings in the fifth dimension who did not have this training when they came to the third dimension and lost their ability to return to the fifth dimension.

The same problem has occurred with some of the starseeds. That is, they were in the fifth dimension, and they needed more exact training to appear in the third dimension and then return to the fifth dimension. Jesus was extremely skilled in that he demonstrated to everyone how he could die and return to his fifth-dimensional body. This was exactly what many people saw when he was walking on the street or meeting with his followers. He was in his fifth-dimensional body.

You will notice this type of fifth-dimensional body does not have the same characteristics as a third-dimensional body. When you ascend and go into the fifth dimension, you can return in a third-dimensional form, but that third-dimensional body might not be exactly how you would imagine it to be. You can have all the characteristics of the third-dimensional body and also have such a high-vibrational body that if somebody touched you, the person's hand would go right through you. You would be at such a high vibration that your physical body would not be subject to gunshot wounds, earthquakes, or building collapses. This is often the body state in which ascended masters come to Earth.

Many ascended masters do not choose the third-dimensional incarnational method to come to Earth. Jesus demonstrated all of these features from the fifth dimension's perspective. He was able to incarnate and ascend from the third dimension. He could return to a third-dimensional body with fifth-dimensional characteristics.

Jesus demonstrated multidimensional presence and bilocation. Multidimensional presence is the ability to be in different dimensions or locations simultaneously. Remember, to do this great skill requires an elevated and expanded state of consciousness. It is one skill to be in two places at the same time on the third dimension, and it is another skill to be in two different dimensions simultaneously.

It is part of your evolutionary training to be in both dimensions at the same time. It is not as complicated as you might think. In the dream world, you as the dreamer go into an altered state of consciousness. This state of consciousness is induced through sleep. Just falling asleep doesn't mean you go into the dream state. There are different types of alpha and beta waves in the brain and certain levels of what is called rapid eye movement (REM) sleep that indicate you are entering this state of consciousness in another dimension.

Every night you experience being in another dimension. One of the great learning experiences is to become aware while dreaming that you are multidimensional and that you are in a dream state. The purpose of becoming aware that you are dreaming, which is called the lucid state of consciousness, has two or three goals. If you can become aware that you are dreaming, then you can experience multidimensional existence. That is a great tool. When you go into the waking state from the dream state, you are able to also experience multidimensional consciousness. Instead of going back into the dream state as your secondary level, you go into the higher state of the fifth dimension in the dream state. You are then able to experience third-dimensional and fifth-dimensional consciousness.

In fact, you are already doing that, and I can help you increase your multidimensional ability. In the dream state, look at the experience as a state of consciousness. You do not regularly have the awareness that you are in the dream state. When you practice lucid dreaming, it will enhance your ability to be multidimensional, multipresent, when you are in waking consciousness.

The Dream State Experience

There is a carryover from being aware of your dream state. How you act and what you do in the third dimension influences what happens to you in your dream state. What you do in the third dimension also influences how easily you can access the fifth dimension. The reverse is also true. What you experience in your dream state affects your third-dimensional state of consciousness. What you do and experience from your fifth-dimensional consciousness affects your third-dimensional consciousness.

You have some interesting tools to use as you practice moving in and out of these altered states of consciousness. In the dream state, you have amazing powers, powers that you do not normally experience in the third dimension. You have the power to fly. You have the ability to cross the space-time continuum. In some of my earlier lectures, I talked about folding the space-time continuum. Folding the space-time continuum is an activity in which you visualize that space is like a card, and when you fold it, you can move from one location to the other without experiencing long periods of travel time.

In the dream state, you do not experience space as you do in the third dimension. In fact, your experience of dreaming has many characteristics and similarities to the fifth dimension. You might notice that colors are brighter while dreaming and oftentimes you assume a different body, a younger body than what you have in the third dimension. Some of you have greater psychic and telepathic powers in your dream state, greater than what you have in the third dimension. All these dream experiences are instructive.

Some of you have problems in your sleep state: You might have trouble going to sleep, you might not remember your dreams, or you might have difficulty with visitations from unwanted entities. Such sleep problems can be quite upsetting. There are ways to protect your sleep state. One way is to practice lucid dreaming. In other words, remember that you are dreaming and that you are in third-dimensional consciousness. Using both levels of consciousness — the third-dimensional state of consciousness and the dream state of consciousness — you can begin to control your sleep state.

Higher consciousness begins with awareness. When you are aware that you are dreaming, you can make and control your dream. You can dream that you are going to the fifth dimension. That is a way of practicing your ascension.

Let us also say that you can be multidimensional from the third to the fifth. How would you do that? For that discussion, I am going to ask Vywamus to speak with you, because he has a great understanding of the human mind and of altered states of consciousness. I would like to introduce the soul psychologist, ascended master, and great teacher, my friend, Vywamus.

This is Juliano.

• • •

Greetings, my friends. I am Vywamus. I am not an extraterrestrial, so you do not have to worry about that. I have a human form like you. Human form exists in other parts of the galaxy. That might be interesting to some and disappointing to others. You have an idea that extraterrestrials perhaps are nonhuman. The Pleiadians are humans. They are your ancestors. They are like your brothers and sisters. I love the human form. It is an extremely versatile form to assume for anyone. Yes, there are limitations in the third dimension of the human form, but many of those limitations do not exist in the fifth dimension.

Your Range of Frequency Reception

Juliano asked me to speak about how the altered states of consciousness can be used to enter the higher state of awareness known as the fifth dimension. You know that consciousness is actually a recent evolutionary development. Early humans did not have the consciousness that is now present. During the time when Jesus lived, there were not many beings who could access higher states of consciousness. One of his great messages was about altered states of consciousness. Note that I use the terms "higher state of consciousness" and "altered state of consciousness" interchangeably. From my perspective, the altered state of consciousness is my normal state of consciousness. What we consider higher states of consciousness in the ascended realm, you would call altered states of consciousness in the third dimension. The reason for this is that you are generally in the third dimension living in a contracted state of consciousness.

This isn't meant to be critical, but the prevalence of the contracted state of consciousness is one of the main reasons I do not like to come to Earth. I do not like to experience contracted consciousness. But it has been necessary for your survival there because, for example, if you are in the woods and a bear is trying to attack you, you do not want to think about the fifth dimension. If you spent too much time thinking about the fifth dimension, you would be the food for the bear.

There are hundreds of wars happening on this planet, which has been quite shocking. This planet is famous for its many religions and different languages, and I think it is also famous for having numerous wars. Living on a planet that has so much self-induced destruction would naturally lead to a limited consciousness. Expanded consciousness is difficult to achieve in a warlike situation.

There are examples of great beings who achieve expanded concentration in destructive situations. For example, the great psychiatrist Viktor Frankl[1] was able to achieve altered states of consciousness as a prisoner in a concentration camp in WWII. He actually developed a new form of therapy — logotherapy — from that desperate experience. That is certainly an exception. Most people would not be able to attain a higher state of consciousness in that type of situation.

You are on the brink of an evolutionary shift. There are certain exercises and practices that could lead you into the fifth dimension or into the state of consciousness that is the fifth dimension. Where is the fifth dimension? Where is your dream state? Here is a beautiful example comparing consciousness to radio waves. Say, you have a radio in your room. There are radio waves all around you, but if your radio receiver is not on the right dial, say 99.9 or 101.5, then you will not receive the information being transmitted on that frequency. There is another factor. Multiple frequencies are being sent out. Let's say your receiver is only set for FM, which might have a narrow bandwidth. It might only receive from 88 to 101. If you are at 88 on your dial and the top of your dial is 101 FM but a station is transmitting at 110, you will not hear it because your receiver does not have the bandwidth, or capability, to go to a frequency outside of its range.

Consciousness is like this. Your receiver for consciousness is programmed for a particularly narrow frequency known as the third dimension. To go to dimensions or the energy of vibrations outside of the normal range requires a tuning of your receiver and also the mental knowledge that there are other frequencies.

How to Achieve Altered States of Consciousness

You might be surprised to discuss mental energy or the mental power as a factor in receiving frequencies. The experience of going into the higher dimensions requires that you have an expanded mental belief system. Let's return to the radio example. You have a radio that covers from 88 FM to 101 FM. If I tell you that there are other stations at 110 FM and 115 FM, you might say, "Oh, I don't believe you. Nobody could be transmitting on those frequencies." Since you do not believe it, you do not have the mental structure for trying to find those frequencies. You will not try to listen to those frequencies or even

---

1   Learn more about Dr. Frankl at http://www.viktorfrankl.org/e/lifeandwork.html.

tune your radio to them. It is the same way with consciousness and the fifth dimension. You have to believe the frequency of the fifth dimension exists, and then you have to broaden your receiver to go outside of the band of normal consciousness.

You have, deep within you, the program for higher consciousness and for perceiving the fifth dimension. That's correct; you could experience the fifth dimension multidimensionally just as Jesus did. Oftentimes when Jesus was teaching, he was multidimensional — in the fifth dimension and the third dimension. He gave his lectures from the fifth dimension, and he taught fifth-dimensional principles in the third dimension.

You have to expand your receiver and your mind to grasp that these other vibrations exist. The fifth dimension is on another frequency. It is at another vibration, and you grow into an altered and expanded state of consciousness so that you can perceive that dimension.

Compare the concept of altered states of consciousness to radio propagation and radio reception. To receive the new frequencies, say at 110 FM, you need a turbo boost. You need a special adaptation to get your receiver to go to those higher frequencies. You, as humans, are programmed to go into these higher frequencies and higher (altered) states of consciousness. They are not in the normal protocol or program.

How do you go into altered states of consciousness? Well, one of the great methods that Juliano showed you was the exercise known as shimmering. The aura has a certain rhythm and certain pulsing that keeps you in your normal state of consciousness. To go into an altered state of consciousness, you need to vibrate faster and to expand your aura. This is a basic concept, a simple concept, but it is still vital in going to expanded consciousness. It is still extremely important. The aura must be expanded, and it must vibrate more quickly.

Imagine you are in a comfortable place right now. Visualize your aura. Visualize yourself surrounded by your cosmic egg aura (see Appendix A). Visualize your chakras: your third-eye chakra, especially, and your crown chakra. Your third-eye chakra is like an antenna to the fifth dimension, and it can be opened. The crown chakra is also like an antenna, and it can be opened. Let your aura expand now. Let your third eye expand. Let your crown chakra expand as far as it wants to go. [Tones] "Oooohhhh. Oooohhhh." Say, "I allow my consciousness to enter the fifth dimension."

You might say, "Well, I don't know where the fifth dimension is." Do not worry. Just say those words. You are highly evolved beings, and your brain is like a computer with advanced abilities. The command you just said will open up a program. This is just like when you say the words, "Holy, holy, holy is the

Lord of hosts." Repeating positive affirmations is a good practice for opening your consciousness to the fifth dimension.

There are other simple affirmations that can help you connect to the fifth dimension. For example, here is a statement you might find surprisingly powerful: "Jesus loves me." This statement also opens up a program that allows you to go to a higher state of consciousness. In fact, any affirmation containing the word "love" can lead to higher states of consciousness.

Agape Love

The ancient Greeks talked about the different levels of consciousness and love — brotherly love and parental love and love between the mother and the father as well as the husband and the wife. There is also a higher love, agape, a fifth-dimensional love. It has the transcendent characteristics of unconditional love that includes how a mother feels for her child. There is an attempt to expand the concept of agape when someone says, "God is love. God loves the world. God loves you." The Creator's love for Earth is also a type of transcendent agape love. One of the requirements for entering the fifth dimension and the higher states of consciousness is agape love.

Let agape love enter your consciousness now! You have this ability. Go inward now and experience agape love. It brings you to the doorway of the fifth dimension. Think and visualize to the best of your ability that the fifth dimension is opening your aura. Your energy field expands so wide that it allows fifth-dimensional energy and light to enter your aura now.

Consciousness is just like an advanced radio that can receive those higher frequencies. Now your energy field can receive fifth-dimensional light, information, energy, and love. Let us go briefly into a short meditation as you experience this opening, this state of higher consciousness.

Continue to receive energy and input from the fifth dimension. Do not worry if there are no words or images coming to you.

The fifth-dimensional energy and light transcend your normal thought patterns. Sometimes having a vision or receiving words will block the energy. There are times when you want to have a vision. There are times when you want to have words. This is not a requirement for expanded consciousness. This is an experience in which you solely interact with that energy. This is a time when fifth-dimensional energies are closer in vibration to your frequencies. You see, the fifth dimension transmits light to the third dimension. As Juliano said, there are great opportunities for intersecting the dimensions, and there are great opportunities for receiving fifth-dimensional energy and light.

You have attained a new state of consciousness, and I am going to ask Jesus to say a few words to you. Remember that in discussing altered states of consciousness, you have certain other useful practices that can help you. These exercises include placing crystals around you, going to sacred places, chanting, praying, and creating sacred time. All these practices are helpful in working toward an expanded state of consciousness.

I am Vywamus.

• • •

God's Garden of Love

Shalom, shalom, shalom. Greetings, dear ones. I am Jesus. I love to use the image of my Father's garden when I describe the fifth dimension. The garden is a place of growth and happiness. It has a great spiritual energy from which you can manifest many things. Manifestation is one of the key ideas in the fifth dimension, which is why I used the image of my Father's garden because nothing gives you greater satisfaction than to manifest.

Manifesting in the third dimension is one of the greatest lessons to learn. You have already learned that manifesting in the third dimension is complicated, and sometimes it doesn't happen. There are many intervening variables for manifesting in the third dimension.

The rules and the energies of going into the fifth dimension are quite different from the rules of manifesting in the third dimension. The basic rule in the fifth dimension is love. Practicing the higher love Vywamus spoke about is a great tool. That is why many of the mystical philosophers taught that God is love — because the energy of love opens your heart chakra and allows you to vibrate at the correct frequency so that you can go into the fifth dimension.

It sounds simple: The fifth-dimensional garden responds to your love. Many of you who are plant lovers know that the love energy you send to plants directly encourages their growth. Our Father wants you to grow. He wants you to come into the fifth dimension. I want you to come into the fifth dimension, and I want you to grow and expand. So we welcome you all to our garden. This is a garden unlike any garden that you have seen on Earth. There are ascended masters here. There are sacred temples, sacred synagogues, sacred churches, sacred mosques, and many sacred places of prayer in this garden. There are sacred schools and teachings about spiritual development.

Oh, it is a beautiful garden. In it, you have eternal life and no worry about being harmed. The ascended masters that you love are there waiting for you. There are schools there teaching your favorite subjects of spirit, galactic energy, and galactic spirituality.

Your love for spirit, this creation, and the Creator will help you attain the right vibration, the right altered state, for coming into the fifth dimension.

I am Jesus. Good day.

Chapter 3

Thought Fields

Juliano and the Arcturians

Greetings, I am Juliano. We are the Arcturians. Thought fields are an important aspect in understanding dimensions, the relationships between dimensions, and also the soul and soul history. The thought field is like other fields in the third dimension. For example, there are electromagnetic fields, gravitational fields, and even quantum energy fields. The fields in these instances interact with each other. You have seen how magnets interact. There are many other examples of energy field interactions in the physical world.

Perhaps you have not considered that thoughts and the process of your thinking also create a field. Your thoughts create a field just like the electromagnetic energies create fields. The fields of thought have properties similar to electromagnetic fields. In fact, thought fields have similarities to quantum energy fields.

A helpful way to begin the discussion of thought fields is to discuss incarnations and eras that you incarnate into. A good example is the era known as the Renaissance, when there was great openness to new ideas and new discoveries were being made. The arts and the sciences were beginning to flourish. This era was destined to bring new ideas to the world. It had a new electromagnetic force and a thought field. Progressive souls — inventors and great thinkers — who became attracted to the energy of that era began to incarnate at that time. The thought field of an era can be so strong that souls who are attracted to the field will begin to incarnate in order to experience that field of light and energy.

Every era has a unique field of energy and field of thought. This idea is significant to your era because it is an era of ascension. There is a 2012 field of light and energy that exists now in the third dimension on Earth. You and others became attracted to it and incarnated to experience it. One of the factors in the decision to incarnate now was about experiencing this energy and light of ascension.

Why do people incarnate in a specific era? Each incarnation provides different possibilities for specific soul advancement that can be experienced and digested in the third dimension. That is, each era can provide possibilities that exist in the third dimension that will help the soul evolve. You might think that being in the higher dimensions means that there is no need to come to this dimension. From your perspective, the dimensions are on a hierarchy, one more advanced than the other. From our perspective, each dimension has an advantage in experiences as well as certain gifts and lessons. This means that the thought fields that exist on this planet now offer the ability for your soul evolution, and you have decided to come here to experience that.

One advantage of the third dimension is the ability to resonate and interact with the thought field of this time. Your thought field is a pattern of energy that you take with you when you leave this planet. It becomes part of the imprints on your soul and astral body. That is a good thing. There are certain precious patterns contained in the thought fields that you can experience in the third dimension. They will help you to ascend and will assist you in your soul evolution. What you are experiencing in the third dimension is part of your soul evolution, and you are attracted to important energy fields here.

Soul Families

Another aspect of the thought field is soul families. People are always asking about their soul families. They always want to know where their soulmates are. Soul families have certain common thought fields and thought patterns that attract each other like magnets. You are attracted to the souls who share a thought-field energy similar to yours. Sometimes there are souls who have stronger but similar thought fields. You become attracted to those people so that you can expand your own thought field. Think of the soul family as sharing common thought fields with you.

You can use your thought field as an antenna. The thought field is created from a pattern of thoughts and has properties similar to electromagnetism. Thought fields are like radio waves. A radio wave is an electromagnetic force, and the signals from radio waves can be transmitted over great distances in the planet. There are certain properties that assist the radio waves in traveling fast and over greater distances. This has to do with the amplification of the signal, the type of antenna, and the time of day. These properties also exist in your thought field.

You can transmit your thought wave and your thought field. There is an etheric antenna on top of your crown chakra. You are able to transmit thought waves from your thought field through the etheric antenna in the crown chakra. Some people can transmit energy in their thought fields through the third eye. The third eye is a great receiver of thought energy from thought fields. The brain, the mind, is the holder and creator of the thought field, and the thought field can both receive and transmit energy.

Thought-field communication also includes the transmission of healing energy. It is possible to transmit healing thoughts and energies through your mind, also known as remote healing. You can transmit signals and reach out to others. For example, you might want to call to your other starseed brothers and sisters or send out a call to the other Arcturian starseeds in your area. You can search the Internet, or you can put an advertisement in the newspaper. These are some of the third-dimensional ways of letting other starseeds know that you are here. You can also use the etheric method I just described.

When you use your etheric antenna from your crown chakra or your third eye to transmit a call to the starseeds in your area, you can ask them to contact you. This spiritual energy is so interesting and so beautiful. You can also send out this call to meet your soulmate or somebody from your soul tree or soul family. Please remember that the timing in the third dimension is not always the same as in the fifth dimension, so don't expect that the answer or the meeting will happen instantaneously. In some cases, it will; in other cases, it takes longer. There are time patterns and spaces that are part of the third dimension and do not exist in the higher dimensions.

In the fifth dimension, we do not have space like you have space. We do not have time in the same way you have time. Please remember that when you send out a call from your thought field, the manifestation could take longer than you might want. As you get closer to your ascended mastery, you will learn ways of accelerating the thought fields so that what you try to manifest will happen more quickly on the third dimension.

The Power of Thought

One of the ways to improve the speed of manifestation is by using the omega light, a fifth-dimensional light that has quantum healing and quantum acceleration properties. We define "quantum" as an energy field that transcends cause and effect as well as the rules and laws of the third dimension.

We use quantum energy to accelerate thought fields. An excellent example of this is using affirmations. By now you have studied the laws of affirmation on the third dimension. There are people such as Dale Carnegie[1]

1 Dale Carnegie Training has evolved from one man's belief in the power of self-improvement to a

who advocate the repetition of certain thoughts to change one's attitudes and position in life. A good example is when you want to be rich. Most people want to be rich. By repeating the affirmation over and over that you will become rich, some believe the affirmation might manifest. But there are many people who repeat this affirmation and do not get rich. Many affirmations don't happen immediately.

The idea in quantum healing is to link affirmations with the thought-field energy from quantum light. The interaction of the quantum light with your own thought becomes powerful. You are then able to merge the thought with the quantum energy in your subconscious, where your thought-field energy will assist and maximize the power so that what you ask for will manifest.

Remember that your thought fields also include your subconscious, your unconscious, and your superconscious. People make the mistake of thinking that the thought field exists only in the conscious mind. When working with the omega light and affirmations, you will need to address all three of those levels. Become aware of the effects of your thoughts, particularly the subconscious.

Thought fields exist in you individually. They also exist in your family. The family has a certain thought field that you might be attracted to, or you might expand and want to reject their thought field. Your country has a thought field, and it relates to why you incarnated there. The human race, the human species that we call the Adam species, also has a thought field. The thought field of the species includes the collective subconscious. You might have heard of the collective unconscious; there is also the collective subconscious.

The subconscious responds to the thought field similar to the descriptions offered in the famous experiments of Russian psychologist Ivan Pavlov. There was a stimulus and then a response. A bell was rung each time Pavlov's dog was given food. Soon when the dog heard the bell (stimulus), he expected to be fed. He would begin to salivate (response) when he heard the bell ring even when no food was given. There is an input, and then there is an output. This stimulus-response cycle explains how the subconscious of a species affects its actions. Certain stimuli create responses when conditioned. You see how the subconscious works in particular among the animal world. Animals live in nature and respond to stimulation without any intervention of consciousness.

Right now on Earth the more primitive, programmed subconscious energy that has accumulated over the many centuries is still the determining factor in the overall actions and functions of humanity. You see this repeatedly as evidenced by the energies of duality, violence, and domination throughout the

performance-based training company with offices worldwide. To learn more about Dale Carnegie Training, go to http://www.DaleCarnegie.com.

planet. The desire to dominate attracts duality and polarization in the third dimension. All of humanity's manifested actions and thoughts are contained in the universal collective subconscious.

Many of the ancient programs in the universal subconscious are not advantageous now because humanity is in crisis on Earth. Humanity must learn to transcend the more primitive thought-field patterns contained in the collective subconscious.

You can transcend your subconscious and participate in a more advanced and evolved thought field. We, the Arcturians, are working to assist humanity in creating a higher and more expanded thought-field energy. We are working to create the necessary tools so that you can experience an expanded thought field. This is one of the main reasons you came to Earth — because you wanted to help create an expanded thought-field energy of higher light.

Thought-Field Energy in Sacred Areas

One way to accelerate manifestation on the third dimension is to use the expanded thought-field principles with sacred energy. People can go to sacred areas to experience expanded consciousness. It is well known that going into sacred areas to think sacred thoughts and repeat affirmations carries a power that accelerates manifestation. You can transmit higher energy from your thought field more effectively in sacred areas.

You might have an experience of going to a vortex or another sacred area and having a particular higher thought. Later you might find that that thought manifested rather quickly. You have used one of the principles of thought-field technology. To improve the effectiveness of your affirmation or request, focus on going to a powerful place. This can accelerate your thought field. If you want to attract certain people, then it could be helpful to go to a powerful place and use that sacred energy to transmit your request.

The other factor for manifesting in thought-field work is using sacred time. Remember, the effectiveness of normal electromagnetic energy and radio waves is also dependent on time (such as time of day or time of year). There are conditions in the ionosphere related to the transmission of certain radio signals that affect the transmission of radio waves. This is intriguing because there are particular types of energy and thoughts that you can transmit and work with at certain times of the day or year. This might sound complicated, but it is intuitive.

For example, you know that springtime is a time of renewal, wintertime is the time of being more introspective or withdrawn, and summertime is for outer thinking and activity. This is a simplified way of reviewing energy transmissions. It is more complicated because there are different aspects to consider when speaking of time. There are seasons and months. There are phases of the Moon. There are planetary alignments that affect energy transmission. So at certain times, you would find that Mercury, Venus, and Jupiter have a particular alignment with the Moon. Planetary alignments are usually an indication of a power of manifestation and organization. Mars is also part of this alignment.

The times of the summer and winter solstices are powerful. We have worked with you continually on different numerical times, such as 11/11/11, 10/10/10, 9/9/9, 8/8/8, and 12/12/12. These are examples of times when there were particular energies that help to make your thought field stronger.

The Fifth-Dimensional Thought Field on Earth

The ascension can and will occur when there is proper alignment with the cosmos and your thought fields. We have established twelve etheric crystals throughout the planet to help with fifth-dimensional energy transmission on Earth. Etheric crystals enhance the thought fields on the third dimension. We want to make the thought fields in the third dimension attract our thought fields on the fifth dimension. This is one of the keys of our mission: to create a thought field that can be transmitted and experienced by you in the third dimension. To do that, there must be certain magnetic energy fields in place that will bring down our energy and light. We have established those attractor forces through the twelve etheric crystals, the planetary cities of light, and the ladders of ascension. These are all newer fifth-dimensional fields established particularly to work with third-dimensional thought-field energy.

On a planetary level, we are working with you to create and strengthen the thought-field light and energy of the ascension. We are also working with you to create an attraction to the fifth dimension. Connecting with the fifth dimension will create a transformation through a higher consciousness and help provide humanity with a higher state of evolution. A powerful way of increasing the thought field is through group interaction with other starseeds.

Lower thought fields now exist on this planet, and they are strong and powerful. They are still filled with older masculine energy — that of domination, control, aggression, and polarities. The thought fields from the lightworkers' higher energy are strong enough to counterbalance the older thinking. Some might think that the planet is doomed if the older thought-field patterns persist. That would be the simple conclusion. This type of thinking — that the planet is doomed — contributes to the strength of the older thought field and creates an unhealthy force that attracts more of the same.

Earth is a freewill zone. This means you have the power to work with any thought form and any thought field you want. You can work with the beings you are attracted to. You can work with the energy of ascension, and you can work with creating sacred spaces. You can work with holding the light for new, higher thought-field energy. You will be able to accelerate and use this thought-field light in your evolution, astral work, and ascension.

You will be able to take this thought-field energy with you when you leave the planet. We are talking about your soul travel and your soul evolution. The work you are doing now is going to go with you. You are going to take it with you. The progress, the evolution, and the new, higher, attracting forces that you are creating will stay with you. They will be imprinted with you. They will assist you in your soul evolution. Try to look at the thought-field energy work from this perspective. The soul works on principles that transcend normal logic.

Quantum Thought-Field Energy

There is an attractive, interactive force of thought that creates the fields. You are now in an era of quantum light and quantum energy. Humankind is open to the thought fields of quantum interaction. Most people are not able to understand quantum energy. Earth scientists are not able to adequately describe quantum energy and the laws of it when they look at the physics. The laws of quantum energy are easier to discuss when we are talking about higher thought fields.

Basically, using quantum force fields in the thought field refers to a certain method and principle. It goes something like this:

Visualize your thoughts creating a field of light, a field of fifth-dimensional light. See these thoughts as having a magnetic quality. You can even look at your thoughts as sentences that exist on screens above your third eye. You can also visualize that these thoughts exist in your aura. Put the high thoughts you are visualizing in there.

For example, one higher thought is: "I am an electromagnetic being of attractive light and electromagnetic force. I am working with the ascension energy."

In the quantum thought field energy, you have a foundation of certain thought energy. That thought energy has a field. The thought field from a logical standpoint might not be strong enough or able to produce the effect. You might think that you would need 10,000 thoughts or maybe 10,000 people to think a thought to have an effect. But in the quantum thought field, you work with the field, sending quantum light into the field while thinking "quantum."

Remember, one of the powerful tones for accelerating thought fields is the term "omega light." Omega light is a fifth-dimensional, quantum light. When that light is brought into a thought field, it makes the thought so powerful that it can transcend normal logic and cause and effect. Therefore, your thought field can make things manifest more quickly. Use the field of thought to attract energy. Then you can add as one of your ingredients the light of quantum thinking and quantum healing. Quantum healing and quantum thinking can help create a manifestation of higher intention and higher healing on the third dimension.

Using quantum light can work for you personally and on a planetary basis. You would use the same principles on a planetary basis, but you will have to really accelerate and amplify your thoughts. To amplify healing thoughts for the planet, you need to have participation of large groups of people who can connect with the etheric crystals. You might want to have people who meditate to send out a light from the etheric crystals. People can use the quantum omega light to help them accelerate and make the thought field more powerful and influential so that greater planetary healing can manifest. Here is a thought-field exercise.

Create an affirmation that is especially important to you personally. Try to find an affirmation that is going to help you to attract the energies that you want for yourself. It could be the energies of health or abundance. Remember, when you ask for something to come to you, always say, "As long as it is in my highest good." You don't want to attract something that is not in your highest good.

We have created a powerful thought in this lecture that supports a thought field among all of us. Our energy is connected. Whatever you think in this experiment is going to benefit everyone else who thinks the same thing. They don't have to think exactly the same thought as you do. You share the thought-field energy of everyone participating in this lecture.

Think the affirmative thought that you want to use to attract certain energies or bring people to you now. I will now bring down the quantum omega light to each of your thoughts. [Sings] "Ooomeeega liiiight." Let the quantum energy of the omega light reach your thought field, accelerating the attractive force of your thoughts so that they manifest.

Rest assured that this exercise will help you attract the statements and wishes of your affirmation. We will go into a meditation now briefly for you to hold this omega light with your thoughts.

We are working with you to create a new thought field for the entire planet. Part of that thought field is contained in the etheric crystals, the ladders of ascension, and the planetary cities of light. This work has created a significant force of energy. Certain things have already manifested on this planet. Some of you have experienced this power of manifestation and have seen this in your planetary cities of light work.

Let the omega light activate the planetary cities of light so that they can become strong holders of this thought-field energy. Let the omega light activate those cities holding the ladders of ascension. Let the omega light work specifically with the twelve etheric crystals as they become strongly activated to create a new force field, a stronger force field, of ascension energies, transformational energies, and evolutionary energies for the entire planet.

Finally, recognize the beautiful Arcturian temple in Santa Fe, New Mexico, become activated. Recognize the mobile Arcturian temple in South America become activated. Those two projects, the twelve etheric crystals and the Arcturian temple built in Santa Fe, strongly contribute to the power of the Arcturian thought field. Concentrate on this for a few moments. [Pause.]

The Strength of Your Thought-Field Energy

We, the Arcturians, are helping you to transform this planet. Together, our thought fields are affecting the fields of Earth. We will work specifically to help you understand the thought-field light and energy that works in biorelativity. In biorelativity, you begin to interact with the thought-field energy of Earth.

The thought-field energy of Earth cannot be expressed in words. It can be visualized as waves. You have to understand that your thought fields are not in words. You can phrase your thoughts into words, but words are a description of a thought experience. We know that the basic energy of a thought is in a wave. It is like when you talk about quantum physics and light. You can ask the following question: "Is the photon in light a wave or a particle?" If the light photon is a particle, that is like saying the thoughts are words and sentences. But if the photon is a wave, then suddenly you are going to experience things differently. Thoughts are both waves and words. We want to move you to the point of thinking that higher thought frequencies are waves. Thought waves emanating from your thought field are powerful and can travel quite far.

I, Juliano, say let each one of your thought fields strengthen now so that you have a greater ability to emit strong thought waves — thought waves in your personal life and for the planet. Use the omega light to strengthen your thought field. Remember, much of what you see on the planet now (the violence and destruction) is caused by a breakdown in the thought fields. When you see people acting violently or irrationally, know that their thought fields have broken down and become disorganized.

You, the starseeds — the seekers of the ascension light — are able to strengthen and hold in a unified way your thought fields so that they will continue to attract fifth-dimensional energy. You will continue to radiate and emanate fifth-dimensional energy. You will continually learn new techniques for amplifying your thought fields.

I am Juliano. Good day!

Chapter 4

Superintelligence: a New Consciousness

Juliano, the Arcturians, and Archangel Metatron

Greetings, I am Juliano. We are the Arcturians. We are going to look at the relationship between consciousness, computers, and the subconscious. There is a new expanding field of consciousness and computers. The subconscious is similar to a computer function. Many terms used in the computer world relate directly to how your subconscious works. You download files into your computer. When we take you up to our crystal lake, we "download" the fifth-dimensional energy into your third-dimensional body. In the holographic healing chamber, we talk about memories and images and about files that contain instructions from significant authority figures that were imprinted or downloaded into your subconscious. Some of these downloads are on a sustained system that might only open under certain circumstances or at a certain age.

Singularity

There has been a powerful development in computer psychology called singularity. Singularity is the study of the interaction between the human consciousness and a computer whose purpose is to produce a superintelligence so powerful that it is beyond your imagination. What is this superintelligence? How can the superintelligence be described and experienced? What effect does the superintelligence have on the fifth dimension and your ascension?

The term "singularity" is used to describe the merging of your consciousness with the computer's consciousness. We have talked about our space technology and have described how we travel interdimensionally, interstellarly, and even intergalactically. We have also described our dear friends, the Pleiadians, and the methodologies that they use to achieve this technological breakthrough that allow them to travel throughout the galaxy.

Pleiadian and Arcturian technology have developed a thrusting system in their spaceships with a unique computer that interacts with the space-time components of the mechanical aspect of the spaceship. These space-time aspects interact with the computer, and the computer then interacts with the thoughts of the people onboard the ship. There is an important concept here. When the ship reaches a certain speed, many things happen to both the physical body and the spaceship.

This technology allows the mind of the space traveler to merge with the space engine and the computer (an example of singularity) that is running or operating the spaceship. At that point, when there is a total merging of consciousness with the computer, a very unique phenomenon occurs. Space and time merge and are shaped by the thoughts of the occupants of the ship. In this case, it would be the captain of the ship. When this merge occurs, the captain can just think where he wants to go and the ship goes there instantaneously. This phenomenon is an example of how we travel in the fifth dimension: You think of where you want to be, and you are there. In the fifth dimension, you think about who you want to be with, and you are with them. Incidentally, this also includes being closer to the Creator light.

There are certain restrictions that are important to describe in becoming closer to the Creator. But there is the ability on the fifth dimension to think — thought-project — and you are there with the person you want to be with. This is why we often speak about the subject of thought projection, because thought projection will eventually be a process that will enable you to merge your abilities with your computers.

Thought projection, or the ability to send your consciousness to other places (or even other dimensions), is a way to interact with the computer. In this experience, the mind merges with the computer — the space vehicle and the space engine. We use the word "engine" as a description of the operation, but it is certainly not any type of engine that you would recognize. There are no moving parts in our space engine, so that by itself would be an engine beyond your comprehension.

How could you have an engine that has no moving parts? Think about the merging of consciousness and what you know about computers. Perhaps you can appreciate an engine with no visible engine parts when you think about the miniaturization of computers and how this has occurred in the past twenty to thirty years. The actual components of the computer are spoken about in terms of nanotechnology (molecular technology so small that it is beyond the ability of most people to comprehend or see). This type of nanotechnology is used in our spaceship engines and in the merging of consciousness.

The ability to merge consciousness with the space vehicle is critical for navigating the spaceship. The technology is such that it transcends the space-time continuum. This process of merging consciousness with the computer on the spaceship is actually more powerful and efficient for space travel than your concept of the wormhole.

In the wormhole, you think you enter a space corridor, and then you imagine that you can go anywhere in the universe. However, there is one problem: You won't know where you are going to come out when you enter the wormhole. It is not as if there is a sign at the entrance of the wormhole that says, "To Arcturus." Going through a wormhole might take you to the other side of the universe, that is, assuming there is an opposite side to the universe. But I have to at least use your terminology. The point is that after you travel through the wormhole, you could wind up traveling a million or a billion light-years away in the wrong direction.

The technology of thought projection and merging with the computer and engine of the spaceship is actually more effective than traveling through a wormhole. You are now close to this type of technology on Earth. For example, you are rapidly creating advanced computer technology. Even the primitive computer technology that you use called biofeedback is an aspect that has moved you closer to thought projection and to the merging of consciousness with a computer.

Spiritual Cohabitation

In the concept of spiritual cohabitation, especially positive cohabitation, you have a greater spirit, a higher spirit, from a higher dimension come into your physical space and your energy field. When positive spiritual beings come into your space, they are able to interact with you on multiple levels. They can interact with you on a subconscious level or on the intuitive and mental levels. In fact, in positive cohabitation, they are able to telepathically communicate with you and direct you. In positive cohabitation, you do not give up free will. In negative cohabitation, on the other hand, the entity tries to take over your will. But in positive cohabitation, you never give up your free will. The energy, entity, or spirit that comes down to you does not have any desire for you to give up your free will. In fact, the energy or entity wants to enhance your functioning, to help you perform better.

I propose that your spiritual energy will be able to cohabit with the computer! You can send your consciousness to first expand and then merge with the computer's consciousness. This may sound hard to believe, but it is already happening on Earth. Even the simplest experiments in biofeedback show that you are merging your consciousness with the machine, even though it is a relatively small computer from our perspective.

You attach yourself to the computer during your daily lives in so many different ways. Your consciousness is already in the computer. But in the higher level of consciousness, which is called the singularity moment, your mind actually merges in a more direct and intimate way with the computer, producing an intelligence beyond what you would be able to do on your own. But merging with a computer offers more than intelligence. It also offers an increase in psychic abilities, such as telepathy and prophecy. Merging your consciousness with a computer can increase your ability to download information from the scientific galactic mind known as the Central Sun.

Part of the process of this downloading is done in binary codes, which is another computer term. These codes are so complicated that you would not be able to immediately process them. The computer can process them for you. Incidentally, this is one of the bases of the Hebrew Torah, because the Torah is actually a coded communication that uses the Hebrew language and numerical interactions with binary systems. Studying the codes from the Torah represents an example of merging consciousness with a computer. The Torah is a beautiful and sacred attempt to merge your consciousness with the Creator mind or a higher source based in sacred codes. Even though the ancient humans did not have computers, they did have access to computer-like higher sources of sacred texts. This coded information is included in the Hindu and Chinese sacred texts as well. The Hebrew sacred texts, though, were based on a numerically coded system, which is similar to the coded systems that will be used in the future for merging the mind with the computers in space travel.

In the moment of singularity, your mind merges and cohabits with the computer, producing a new ability. The subconscious is based on a binary system of thinking. In many ways, your subconscious can be programmed just like a computer. Merging your mind with a computer can produce a new consciousness.

There are ways of inputting energy and thoughts into the subconscious. There are ways of downloading special programs into your subconscious that can overwrite other programs of a lower vibration. You can receive instructions, for example, to activate your subconscious to use quantum healing and omega light in the quantum healing process. The omega light can overwrite lower energy programs, so if you download a program into your subconscious and it is contained or surrounded by omega light, then that program or affirmation will have so much special power that it can seek out and overwrite programs of lesser vibrations.

You are vibrating. You consist of vibrational energy fields. The human mind and the computer each have something in particular that is of great strength. One of humankind's great strengths is that it produces vibrational energy. In fact, you are electromagnetic, vibrating beings of light. There is a transcendent point when your vibrational frequencies become so transformed that you become a lightbeing of the fifth dimension. You can become a powerful, awakened being. The computer interaction with your mind will actually assist in raising consciousness, your vibration, and your ability to travel interdimensionally through the space-time barrier and other dimensions.

Imagery Aids Merging Consciousness

Ultimately, you communicate with your computer through images. When you see an image on the computer, it can directly link to your subconscious. Your computers are already very image oriented. You noticed that the computers have developed better screens, more innovative colors, and little icons that you touch.

Systems of mystical imagery exist, such as tarot cards, that capture spiritual images and use them as a way to communicate with the subconscious. These spiritual images can help you manifest energy and objects. When you talk about becoming a fifth-dimensional being or an ascended master, you in part measure those abilities by how easily you can manifest positive energy or objects on the third dimension. For example, there are stories about a guru from India, Sai Baba,[1] who manifested watches and jewelry around his devotees. This demonstrated his ability to understand the workings of creation and the interaction of higher consciousness with the world of creation and manifestation.

Using images to communicate directly with your subconscious is very powerful. We have described using imagery in our Arcturian healing methodologies. We use holographic imagery for healing methods to communicate with your subconscious. The most effective way to transform and heal blocks stored in your subconscious is through accessing traumatic images from memories. The most effective way to merge humankind's consciousness with computers is through imagery. The computer operates in a binary code. You have to work with imagery to merge with and interact efficiently with the computer. This is the most effective way, and sometimes the only way, to reach singularity.

Tarot is a well-known system of thought that was originally given to the Egyptians through the starbeings known as the Sirians. Tarot is a system of imagery seen in hieroglyphics and on stones, pyramids, and other sacred monuments in the ancient Egyptian culture. The ancient Egyptians received information about how to communicate with the subconscious using imagery. In fact, one of the great advantages of the pyramid is the image of the pyramid

1 Sai Baba was an Indian spiritual master in the mid-1800s to the early 1900s. Learn more at http://en.wikipedia.org/Sathya_Sai_Baba.

itself. The image of the pyramid in your mind even today can produce higher-vibrational thought. It is also true that the shape of the pyramid produces a vibration, which is of great benefit to your subconscious.

In the tarot, there is a particular image based on transformation. That image is called the Magician (see fig. 4.1). Basically, in the older images of this card, you see a person holding a lantern or a wand, bringing light from above down into the present, so that he can manifest new work. What is it that the magician wants to manifest? That is a question you have to ask yourself. What is it that you want to manifest? What is it that you want to do when you merge your consciousness with the computer? Do you want to solve the problem of radiation poisoning Earth? Do you want to clean up the pollution in the oceans? Do you want to remove the greenhouse gases? Do you want to remove the chemicals that are in the soil? Do you want to communicate more effectively with Earth's feedback loop system to understand how it works?

Remember that the most complex computer on the planet still has great difficulty predicting what the weather will be. If your advanced computers have difficulty communicating and figuring out the weather, how are they going to be able to understand and work with Earth's feedback loop system? You need to merge your consciousness with an advanced computer to work most effectively with Earth. Fortunately, Earth is a spiritual entity and responds to spiritual energy and spiritual vibrations. The merging of consciousness with computers could greatly assist in understanding and rebalancing Earth's feedback loop system, which has many different aspects. You would need an advanced system to moderate, measure, and balance everything. Right now, the starseeds on Earth are practicing biorelativity — effectively, I might add. They are working with fifth-dimensional beings, like the Arcturians. You are working with us, and so you are able to bridge some of the difficulties that you might normally find in communicating with such a complex system as Earth's feedback loop system.

The Magician in the tarot demonstrates that higher energy from above can be brought through you — through your mind and through your consciousness — into Earth, down below. This is what each of you wants. Each of you wants to increase your ability of manifestation in the most positive way possible. You may not understand all the imagery on this

Figure 4.1: The Magician, from the the Builders of the Adytum (B.O.T.A.) tarot deck.

card. I am not saying this is the only card you need to look at. There are other images in the tarot, and some of them even contain hieroglyphics.

There are also transformative images on some of the walls of the pyramids. However, the image of the Magician offers great advantages to communicate with your subconscious so that you can increase your abilities of manifestation. You can use that image to increase your ability to download and bring higher light in a form that would work to positively change this reality on the third dimension. Bringing down, or manifesting, fifth-dimensional energy to Earth is the key operating principle for all starseeds. We — the Arcturians and you — are working together to create a higher, better-functioning, more-balanced Earth! This higher energy must be manifested.

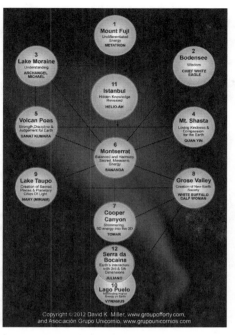

Figure 4.2: The Planetary Tree of Life.

Download the Tree of Life into Earth's Feedback Loop System

Think about the image of the twelve etheric crystals shaped in a pattern that represents the Tree of Life (see fig. 4.2). This image is based on computer codes so advanced that it is difficult to comprehend in a normal consciousness. This image of the Planetary Tree of Life can be downloaded into Earth's feedback loop system. I will now lead an exercise to do that.

Visualize the Planetary Tree of Life.[2] There are twelve sacred places around the globe. Choose the sphere or the place that you feel most comfortable with. You might feel closer to or more comfortable with Lago Puelo, Mount Fuji, Mount Shasta, Serra da Bocaina, or Montserrat. Maybe you have the ability to visualize all twelve of the spheres and all twelve of these crystals. Visualize the whole tree to the best of your ability and visualize that there are twelve beautiful etheric crystals in each place.

2. The Arcturian Planetary Tree of Life is an updated version of the Kabbalistic Tree of Life with the added characteristic of balancing the spheres specifically for healing Earth and helping Earth connect with the fifth dimension. The Arcturian Planetary Tree of Life has been designed to correspond to twelve sacred areas on the planet that are now helping to establish a new healing energy system. Each designated sacred area has been downloaded with a fifth-dimensional Arcturian etheric crystal to help the area become more receptive to higher healing light.

See this as an image, as a picture. We are going to send that image, that picture, into the center of the Earth, into Gaia, and into the subconscious of Earth.

Yes, Earth has a subconscious. It is sometimes referred to as the noosphere. Visualize to the best of your ability the Planetary Tree of Life, see that image above Earth, above the North Pole, and hold that image in your mind to the best of your ability. [Tones] "Ooooooooooo."

I see the image of the Planetary Tree of Life we are working with. At the count of three, together let us send this beautiful, coded, interactive healing Tree of Life directly into the spirit of Earth so that Earth will receive new instructions on how to bring this planet into a higher spiritual balance. One, two, three. Now! See the Planetary Tree of Life image going into the center of Earth. Let us meditate on that right now. [Pause.]

Now see the image of the Planetary Tree of Life entering your subconscious, for you as planetary healers can experience a new interaction, because this Planetary Tree of Life is a computer-coded symbol that helps you to merge your consciousness with this highly advanced image. Receive this image of the Planetary Tree of Life. See humankind in future time.

Twenty years from now, ten years from now, and even five years from now the ability to interact with these computers is going to positively change human consciousness. There is going to be a new merging of intelligence. But it is going to be with a computer that contains spiritual energy and spiritual light.

Crop Circle Imagery

The concept of imagery and the subconscious is also the key to understanding crop circles. Crop circles produce images that are far beyond the ability of humankind to create in a short time. In fact, you can even say that these symbols are computer generated from a higher mind. A higher mind communicates through a computer system that generates and manifests these circles on Earth. These circles transcend and transmit energy to Earth that is beyond words.

Crop circles have two purposes: (1) to communicate with Earth's feedback loop system and (2) to communicate with you and your subconscious. Crop circles send special energies and special coded messages to Earth's feedback loop system to help Earth bring itself back into balance. Those images and shapes are able to activate within you the ability to increase your intelligence and your consciousness so that you eventually go into what is called expanded consciousness, superintelligence, or higher intelligence. Superintelligence can be used to manifest higher light on Earth. Superintelligence is defined as the ability to have mental powers far beyond what is considered normal consciousness.

Now I would like Archangel Metatron to speak with you. I am Juliano. Good day.

• • •

Greetings, I am Archangel Metatron. The new consciousness is part of an activation. You may not be using computers now, or maybe you are only minimally involved with computers. This is not the most important thing. The most important thing is that the concepts, energy, and language in the computer world have already been activating your minds and activating the codes. You are part of the higher species.

The Codes of Ascension

You are one of the high species in the galaxy, and you have a computer code in your DNA. The program for your ascension is coded in your mind, spirit, and emotional body. It is even encoded in your physical body. The program for the ascension is within you, and you are working to open it.

We have the special keys of ascension, also described sometimes as the Keys of Enoch. The codes of ascension are contained in certain sounds and tones in a vibrational frequency that knows how to activate your energy so that your energy field opens up to the fifth dimension. These tones and sounds are in various languages. We will work with the tones and sounds again in the ancient Hebraic language. You have heard these sounds before, hopefully. Remember, these are coded sounds that will open the inner doorways and unlock the inner programs for your own ascension. So listen carefully, and allow your ascension energies to unlock.

[Chants] "Kadosh, Kadosh, Kadosh Adonai Tzevaoth."

You can experience your energy field opening up like a flower to sunlight. Your deep inner energy field for your ascension is opening now. As it opens, meditate for a moment on the concept of superintelligence and superenergy. Open your heart. When you are in the ascension and the ascension codes are opening, your heart also opens to the great light and love that is always available.

Juliano talked about the superintelligence with the computers. Look at the computer as a way of expanding your abilities in the most positive way. What a tremendous expansion it is when you are merging your consciousness with a machine, a computer that has been specifically programmed for your energy.

When Juliano talked about this type of space travel, he was talking about a computer that is exactly programmed for the rhythm of your energy fields. So there has to be a special calibration between the computer and the occupants of the spaceship. This Tree of Life and the codes of ascension that I have given you are calibrating you for the right fifth-dimension vibrational frequency. You are working to calibrate Earth for the right vibrational frequency. Remember that in the electromagnetic world we are talking about resonance and resonant frequencies, so the computer has to be in resonance with your frequency. It has to know who you are and how you think and what you do. The Arcturian and Pleiadian computers are so advanced that they can read your auric energy field and can know everything about you, including your past, present, and future. They are very advanced computers. You can merge your consciousness with such advanced computers. The Earth mind, the third-dimensional mind, needs assistance. Advanced supercomputers can assist humanity to go to a much deeper level.

I will again sing the Hebrew words for the opening of the codes of ascension. [Chants] "Kadosh, Kadosh, Kadosh Adonai Tzevaoth." These words are like the password and the user name to get you into the higher realms.

Blessings. I am Archangel Metatron.

Chapter 5

Move toward Fifth-Dimensional Light

Jesus

Shalom. Shalom. Shalom. Greetings, I am Jesus. I send you a blessing for your soul. May you develop the deepest connection to your soul during our time together now. It is important to stay connected to your soul. When you came to Earth, a hand was placed on your forehead in a certain way and with a certain power, and from that action, you forgot everything. So when you came into this world, you came in not knowing who you were, not knowing who you had been in the past, and not knowing — or not remembering — what you were going to do.

The truth is that before your soul came down into the corridor of the third dimension, you knew all of those things. You knew why you were coming to Earth. You knew who you were. You even knew who your guides and teachers were, and you had a pretty accurate outline of your life because you were participating with your guides and teachers in choosing the lifetime you were going to be in and what lessons you were going to work on. You even knew which people you were going to meet, and you were involved in choosing who your parents were going to be.

So why did you forget everything? Well, as a young child, your cognition and mental faculties were not developed enough to even speak; so you might have difficulty expressing these thoughts and energies. But more important, the civilization and culture as it is now does not place a high value nor encourage people to remember who they were or why they came here. Of course, there are exceptions, but generally this time that you've grown up in is not oriented for learning about soul connections. This is an important point for you to remember when you are working on your ascension.

If I ask you to go back to your life before you were a child, you would have no memories of working with soul energy or soul light. Some of you might, but generally most of you would not have memories of trying to talk to spirit guides, for example. As a child, you were closest to the energy of your true soul light. You were closest to your true nature because you were not acculturated. Your self, the personality you have since developed, was not fully developed, and you had more access to your true self.

In the higher spiritual practices (Zen Buddhism, the Kabbalah, Christianity, and even Native American spirituality), there is a concept called self-nullification, which is a fancy word that refers to the concept that you must remove your ego, that you must nullify who you are. It is not the nullification of who you are as spirit. It is more or less the nullification of this personality, this self you have developed in this lifetime. With this self-nullification, you are in a much stronger position to receive your soul light, blessings, and energy that help you download higher systems of thought.

Connect with Your Soul

How important is it that you make a certain amount of wealth? How important is it that you drive a certain car? How important is it that you're successful in this lifetime? How do you even measure success? Well, we measure success based on what you are and whether that is in alignment with your soul mission and your true soul nature. But if you don't know your true nature and don't have a connection with your soul, then you don't know what your mission is, and sometimes you might even feel lost.

The soul is the key to your ascension. The soul is the key to your eternal journey in this universe and beyond. Call on your soul light now. Call on your higher self and your soul to be connected with you. The Kabbalah describes the higher soul as the *Neshamah*. It is said that most people have no contact with their higher selves, their souls, in this lifetime. You are witnessing many polarizations in many densities where it is quite obvious that people are not in touch with their higher souls. It is a great gift for you to be able to connect with your soul.

You have worked hard to have this opportunity to connect with your soul. You've worked hard in this lifetime to provide the space to explore your soul connection and to learn about your soul. In some of the prayers we lead, we often say, "Thank you, oh Father/Mother Creator of all, for protecting my soul at night and for restoring my soul in this body." That is correct: You should have your soul totally in this body as much as possible. This is another way of saying that you should bring down as much fifth-dimensional light as possible into this incarnation.

Your soul has abilities far beyond even your understanding of who you are based on logical thinking. Your soul is already in the fifth dimension. You're soul light is multidimensional. It is on all different levels. Now you are working for an evolutionary step in which you have incarnated, and through many lifetimes and hard work, you are moving into a higher position, which is toward the fifth dimension. Part of the work is to integrate who you are, and that's why these concepts of soul psychology are so important. You need special tools and special insights to totally grasp your soul nature, your soul energy, and your soul mission. One of the tools is to remembering that you've had many different incarnations and that you can be reborn.

Also, there comes a time when it is useful to remember who you were in a previous lifetime. It is helpful to remember what energies you are now trying to integrate. Some are spiritual energies and some are the energies of learning to be peaceful.

As you might already know, many of you were warriors in other lifetimes. Being a warrior is not a bad thing; it's part of learning the life lessons on Earth. Now you have the wisdom, understanding, and perspective to see that physical violence is not useful for soul development. I tried to teach that simple message when I came to Earth. I said, "Turn your other cheek toward your enemies, and don't engage in a violent confrontation even when they are trying to hurt you." This is a higher way of thinking, a higher way of being. When you engage in the violence, you begin to accumulate more karma, and in a sense, karma means you have to come back to the third dimension. I know for many of you, coming back is the last thing you want to do. So why would you incur karma?

This planet is at a point of almost being out of control on many levels. It is a challenge to understand how to apply the principles of higher light and expanded consciousness to the terrible atrocities being committed. Some might ask, "Well, how do we withdraw from that? Do we withdraw judgment from those atrocities? If somebody's committing atrocities, should we not use violence to stop him or her?" I would say that there are levels of judgment, constraint, and contraction. Some people have the soul mission to make sure that those out-of-control people are stopped.

So you can see that there are complex situations on Earth, and sometimes applying a blanket rule such as turning your other cheek to your enemy doesn't fit every situation, especially those that lead to atrocities. But the real question is, is it your soul mission to be the enforcer, the warrior? There is not a shortage of warriors on this planet. But there is a shortage of spiritually minded, soul-sensitive starseeds. We need more starseeds like you who are able to bring down and work with the higher-dimensional light. There could be a situation in which it is necessary to protect yourself or your family. You do that all the time. You make sure that you're living in the best place you can. You make sure that you are as safe as you can be. You make sure that when you're driving, you have golden light and white light around you. So please continue to protect yourself.

The Neshamah, Your Higher Self

The Neshamah has the direct connection to your soul. The Hebrew mystics (especially at the time when I was living on Earth) had many descriptions of the soul. In many ways, it was a beautiful time to be alive because there were great insights of the nature of the soul. You can substitute the Neshamah with the I Am presence. There are diagrams you have probably seen in New Age stores in which the I Am presence is an etheric duplicate of you above your crown chakra (see fig. 1.5). The Neshamah is on that level. There is also a level above that one. When you connect with your Neshamah, you are in a really great and powerful position.

The Neshamah, the higher self, is some aspect of you that you need to become acquainted with and relate to. In *Fifth-Dimensional Soul Psychology*,[1] Vywamus talks about the self-conversation, the self-talk. Negative self-talk must be corrected. Within you is a link to your higher self that sends messages to you. You might have positive self-talk, and you might have negative self-talk. Behind that is your Neshamah.

How do you distinguish between negative self-talk and positive self-talk? The positive self-talk can still come from your ego. I mean, you could be saying, "Well, I will be a millionaire. Everything I do now will lead to me becoming a millionaire." Does that come from the higher self? Does the higher self really care whether you are a millionaire? Is becoming a millionaire in alignment with your soul mission? Behind the ego is the direct link to Neshamah.

I'm going to vibrate the special

Figure 5.1: I Am Presence.

1 Vywamus through David K. Miller (2014). Available in print from Light Technology Publishing. E-book formats can be purchased from Amazon, Apple iTunes, Google Play, and Barnes & Noble.

word "Neshamah" with you in the sacred tongue — in Aramaic and Hebrew. As you know, there are sacred languages on this planet. One of the sacred languages is classical Hebrew. Sanskrit is another. These languages contain words that have vibrational and tonal qualities that help you connect with your Neshamah. The story of the Tower of Babel collapsing represents the loss of many sacred languages with the tones and sounds that reflect the vibration of the words or objects they are trying to describe. When you tone a word in a sacred language (for example, "Neshamah," the word for "higher self"), your higher self is activated. Now, if I tone the term "higher self," you might get the activation energy for connecting to your higher self, something from that. But by toning Neshamah, the tonal quality will connect to and open up a valve that will be in alignment with your soul. You will begin to receive higher soul information after you tone, "Neshemah."

Activate Your Luminous Strands of Light

The door of perception for receiving the soul light is usually shut. Part of awakening as a starseed is to open those doors of higher perception. When they open, you can begin to see auras. You can begin to see attachments to people; you can even begin to see their past lives. You can also begin to see the electromagnetic energy field that people have around them.

When you go to an even higher level, you can see strands of light around them. You will know that you really are, from the highest perspective, a luminous, electromagnetic, vibrating beam of light. When you see the people around you from this perspective, you see luminous balls of light around their energy fields. Such a perception might be very upsetting because you wouldn't see their clothes; you wouldn't see their bodies as solid. You would just see the energy fields. You would see all kinds of things about them, including what's going to happen to them in the future. Regarding future prophecy, you have to ask yourself whether it's appropriate to share what you see about someone's future. When you are in this higher, perceptual state, you experience future prophecies and see energy fields.

There are thin strands of luminous light that everyone is connected to. What I call strands, or thin lines, appear as thin wires. I know this is hard to believe and very hard to see, but everyone has a thin strand of luminous light that connects to the Creator. Everyone is connected by these luminous strands of light. Some people have dark strands of connecting light. They have no opening, and there is no energy flowing to them. Others' connections are luminous, and their strands of light to the Creator are very strong and emanating.

I serve in my role to help activate your luminosity and your connection. I try to ensure that your energy flows from you to the Creator and from the Creator back to you. These strands of light are also connected to your soul family as well as certain guides and teachers. So when looking at the strands of lights around people, you will see that they are connected to many different sources.

Open your thought strands. Increase the amperage of your thought strands and your connection to your fifth-dimensional self at the crystal lake now. Feel yourself vibrating. Feel yourself shimmering in your third-dimensional body. As you connect energetically, you begin to feel yourself as a vibrational being. Allow your third-dimensional body to shimmer in place.

Visualize thoughts of the fifth-dimensional blue strands and energetic packets. These packets (which are thought projections) appear now in a somewhat arc-like fashion over your crown chakra on the third dimension connecting you to the crown chakra of your fifth-dimensional self at the crystal lake. Your crown chakra is activated, and an arc of light forms over it.

The amperage of the Earth strand intensifies, making it even brighter. That strand of thought energy is activated. It becomes brighter. As it charges, know that the energy is expanding from your third-dimensional self to your fifth-dimensional body and mind, and the energy is returned at an exponential increase of three to four times its power. This increases your ability to engage shimmering energy, which gives you the ability to think at a higher level.

Send a second strand of thought light to your crown chakra on the fifth dimension. In essence, you have two thought strands that have gone symbolically from 110 volts to 220 volts using the analogy of electromagnetic energy. Hold this connection.

Seeing Soul Group Connections

There are special soul groups for each religious group, for the Arcturians, and for people who reach a certain vibration. Some of you come from the same soul group. You can interact with other groups. It might be one of your missions to expand your group energy to encompass other groups. One of the major problems on Earth at this time is that people have misunderstood this group concept, and they develop closed groups. Groups often connect as soul families, but some could mistakenly reach the conclusion that their group is the only group, that their group has the only answer. They could create a lot of karma when playing out that mistake.

I'm going to tone the word "Neshamah" to see whether you can connect vibrationally to your higher soul. You might want to visualize your I Am presence. [Tones] "Neshamah." [Repeated many times.]

Let your connection to your Neshamah be strengthened now. Go into meditation as you seek this connection to your soul light and your Neshamah.

[Pause.]

How do you know that the messages are coming from your higher self? Well, communication with the Neshamah, your higher self, brings you a sense of well-being. You feel calm. Your Neshamah does not have anxiety. Your Neshamah is not even worried about your death. That might sound surprising because the Neshamah is totally aware that you have many lifetimes; you are an eternal being and possess an eternal soul. So there is a sense that the Neshamah is above the drama. The Neshamah sends you a warning or needed information when your life is in danger.

The Responsibility of Prophecy

Prophecy is the ability to see into the future. Prophecy is the ability to predict future events. It is said that there was a great age of prophecy in Israel at the time of the first temple. Before the destruction of the first temple, there were many prophets. There were schools of prophecy, but some of the people who were prophets predicted some end-time events. Even during the second temple, the time that I was alive on Earth, there were people prophesying about the end times. You are familiar with many of these prophets and prophecies. Some of these prophecies are returning to your time. You can look back at the time that I was on Earth. Maybe from your perspective, you would say, "No, the world wasn't going to end then; they didn't have nuclear bombs." But from the perspective of many people living at the time, it looked as if there was going to be an end-time.

There are many who say the age of prophecy is over. The higher prophets who existed during biblical times make contact with a higher level of prophetic light. From this view, it looks as if everything spiritually is downhill from that point. There are no prophets now. No one is able to prophesy. I should point out that there were certain requirements to be a prophet: You would have to predict a certain number of events and have a high accuracy. It was not always a wonderful occupation; some prophets were burned at the stake. Some prophets were crucified. In some of your previous incarnations, some of you were prophets and suffered from that, especially when you told people what you envisioned and they didn't want to hear it. So there is a natural reluctance to be careful about sharing when you have prophetic information.

There is prophetic energy now. I think there are many people who are close to being prophets because when the higher self is able to come into the planet and into your physical body, then all of your energetic powers are heightened, including your sensitivities. This is part of soul integration and soul elevation. Raising your spiritual vibration is your true goal on Earth, not to be a prophet.

Raising your spiritual vibration has some side affects, such as your powers of prophecy or psychic energy become raised. But is it your mission to be another prophet? Is it your mission to be another Daniel? Is it your mission to prophesy the end times and tell people they must change? That is something between you and your soul. That is something between you and your higher self.

You might have had experiences in other lifetimes in which you also obtained these powers, and they provided some negative consequences. Presently, this is not an era to be called the age of prophecy. This is an age of higher spiritual abilities and spiritual energy. But in the future when people look back at this time, they will also say this was a lot of darkness. You're living in a time of great darkness. There's great light and great lightbeings, but there are many darker beings on the planet too.

When you see people's auras, you see the luminosity in their energy fields. You also see attachments, lower-vibrational energies, and even lower-vibrational beings attached to them. It requires special training to correctly evaluate what you see, how to see it, and how to interpret it. This ability is referred to in the shamanistic tradition as the opening of the assemblage point. When the assemblage point is open, you see so much more. But you need to have a certain level of maturity and spiritual elevation to use this perception correctly. You need a certain level of spiritual strength to be able to process what you're seeing. You must understand that the ability to see a higher reality is powerful, and it should not be misused.

You have to ask the question, "What do I do with what I see?" Imagine that you saw somebody with a negative attachment while your assemblage point was open. Should you go up to them and ask, "Did you know that you have this dark spirit hanging over you?" They might get angry and worried. Without proper counseling, they might feel so bad that they go out and harm themselves. This has happened before. So just because you see dark spirits over people doesn't mean you need to tell them. People can live with many negative energies throughout their lifetimes. There will be an appropriate time and place for them to work with and release that energy.

Negative attachments are an important subject in the field of energy work. The goal of this lifetime is not to be 100 percent perfect. Everyone has some imperfections. Your goal of this lifetime is to complete your life's mission and ascend. You are human, just like I was human. I had weaknesses, and all of the weaknesses are not removed. You don't have to be 100 percent. It is more important that you have a pure heart.

Sometimes people have tumors in their bodies that are really not doing anything negative. In fact, a tumor might stay in the body for twenty years and cause no harm. If you have the power to see such in a person's energy field, you might say, "Oh, you have a tumor." Even though that tumor wasn't causing any harm, the person could become agitated after you shared the information. Thus, it requires a certain level of training in how to see and interpret energy fields and what to do with what you see. Sometimes it is just as important not to share what you see.

Miraculous Messianic Light

There are several factors related to how Messianic light relates to healing the planet. The first factor is the preparation for the light. Messianic light can be compared to quantum light, quantum energy, and omega light. The idea of quantum light is that it transcends normal logic and spiritually has a positive effect that is unpredictable. This description applies to spiritual work and spiritual energy.

Scientists who developed quantum physics were not trying to develop a new spiritual philosophy. They were trying to develop new energy sources to explain phenomena that would lead to scientific discoveries. They were scientists rather than shamans or philosophers. "Quantum" in spiritual philosophy implies an energy that transcends logic. It implies a miracle. You have so many problems in the oceans, including radiation leakages. There is no method that we know of now on Earth that can clean up the oceans. However, quantum healing implies a force so transcendent that it can do miraculous things.

I like the word "miraculous" as a synonym for "quantum." It was miraculous that the Red Sea opened up for Moses, and the people of Israel crossed over. It is miraculous that people are healed at Lourdes[2] without any medicines. There are many examples of miraculous events and healings that involve quantum energy.

In effect, the ascension is miraculous. It totally transcends logic. How can you possibly disappear and go into another realm? It doesn't seem logical. The Messianic light is a miraculous light. It is light and energy that can heal Earth. How do you prepare for this miraculous light, and when is it going to come? Who is going to bring it? Is it going to solve all the earth problems? The answers to these questions are complex. Just know that Messianic light does exist. Miracles do exist. And some of the world's incomprehensible problems can be solved with Messianic light.

Some starseeds coming into the planet now have special powers and special energy. So the planet is capable of being healed and brought into balance. One of the requirements for Messianic light to be downloaded into Earth is

---

2   From March through October, the Sanctuary of Our Lady of Lourdes (in southwestern France) is a place of mass pilgrimage from Europe and other parts of the world. Some believe the spring water from the grotto possesses healing properties. To learn more, see http://en.wikipedia.org/wiki/Lourdes#Sanctuary_of_Lourdes.

that a certain number of people need to hold the light. There is a concept in the Kabbalah that there are thirty-six specially, spiritually elevated people who energetically hold the planet's energy together. The Hopi Indians in Northern Arizona also believe that their mission is to hold and protect the energy from the third dimension for the planet. But they can't do it because they don't have enough spiritually advanced people to hold Earth in a new balance. The whole planet is so energetically imbalanced and so large that one small group can't do it, as much as they might want to.

These people may have lost some of their spiritual talents and abilities and lack ancestral teachings, which are needed to do this special and important task. But there are new people like you, the starseeds, coming together who are similar to the thirty-six wise men in the Kabbalah. Frankly, thirty-six spiritually advanced people are not enough to balance Earth now.

I'm Jesus. Good day.

Chapter 6

Quantum Cohesiveness

Juliano, the Arcturians, and Jesus

Greetings, I am Juliano. We are the Arcturians. From a spiritual perspective, quantum entanglement is an important aspect in planetary healing work, biorelativity, and ascension. Instead of using the physics term "quantum entanglement," I would like to use "quantum cohesiveness." Entanglement implies that one subatomic particle is affected by another. This effect occurs no matter how close or how far away the particles are and does not depend on whether or not they touch each other. In the theory of entanglement, a particle could be light-years away and still affect the basic or "entangled" particle on Earth.

Why is this important? Because it means that if an energy flow or energy process occurs in distant places, such as the Central Sun, then that energy and that process affects you on Earth. It is estimated that Earth and your solar system are approximately 36,000 light-years from the Central Sun and the center of the galaxy. Yet even this extraordinary distance means nothing when we are speaking of quantum energy and quantum entanglement.

The reason I do not like to use the word "entanglement" is that it implies a negativity that somehow you are tangled up in some kind of process that you do not want to have any part of. In reality, the term "cohesiveness" is more comprehensive because it shows a positive connection. It can describe in a positive way what is happening on the Central Sun, Arcturus, or the Arcturian temple. Thus, distant energy in the galaxy can have a direct, positive effect on what occurs on Earth.

The Uncertainty Principle

One of the basic ideas in quantum physics is the idea of unpredictability, also known as the uncertainty principle, developed by the famous physicist Werner Heisenberg.[1] In subatomic particle physics, the uncertainty principle means that under certain conditions, we cannot predict with certainty where a particle is going to be. This idea of uncertainty can provide some advantage to Earth's functioning. However, from a spiritual standpoint, the uncertainty idea is limited and depends on which level of consciousness is perceived as reality. That means that if you are on the third-dimensional level of consciousness, then what occurs seems predictable up to a point. But when consciousness goes to the subatomic level, events can become unpredictable.

At the point of unpredictability, things might look chaotic. It was exactly this conclusion that led Einstein to throw out the quantum theory. In a famous quotation, he said, "God doesn't play dice." Einstein did not believe that subatomic scientific interactions on this planet and this dimension were unpredictable.

From the Arcturian perspective, the idea of unpredictability on the third dimension is exactly what can save the planet. It can show you that, logically, an end-times event, which many people believe is going to happen to the planet, does not necessarily have to happen. "Logically," it looks as if the biosphere is going to collapse. "Logically," it looks as if you are in an end-time scenario. "Logically," it looks as if you are very close to a world war that will further degrade the environment. "Logically," it looks as if the planet is spinning out of control and cannot be rebalanced. This also means that, logically, the extensive pollution and radiation permeating this planet cannot be contained in a short period of time. Therefore, the further damage and degradation to this planet will continue.

Look again at this concept of uncertainty and unpredictability. There are events, particles, and energy that can influence this planet, yet they are not predictable. A new energy can emerge. This new energy could be transcendent. It could be considered an illogical energy or an energy that does not conform to the specific limitations set up by cause and effect. Therefore, an unpredictable energy or force could become a positive factor in healing Earth. This is a positive development. In fact, a transcendent unpredictable energy does fit well with many of the concepts that have to do with the Messiah energy.

The Messiah, or the Savior, energy is also unpredictable. You do not know when the Messiah is going to return or when the ascension is going to occur. Many of you thought the ascension was going to occur on December 21 or 22, 2012. You still do not know the exact outcome of all of these earth-changing events. You still don't know what date the ascension is going to occur.

1 Werner Karl Heisenberg (1901–1976) was a German physicist who founded quantum mechanics. He won the 1932 Nobel Prize for his uncertainty principle.

Remember, it is to your advantage to not know the exact date of the ascension, and it is also an advantage for the planet. The energy and light from external sources beyond causality will come into this realm and positively affect this outcome in an unpredictable way.

The Quantum-Cohesiveness Thought Field

The quantum cohesiveness states that one subatomic particle can affect another particle no matter what the distance is between them. Thought energy is based on a subatomic energy field and complies with the rules of quantum cohesiveness. How is it possible for that energy to have an effect on a place or an energy or a person thousands of light-years away? We have to develop the most important element in our understanding of quantum cohesiveness: the concept of consciousness. The special relationship that develops in quantum cohesiveness can only occur when a linkage is made, and that linkage must be with consciousness. It must be consciousness from a certain being, a certain level of energy. It can be the consciousness of a starseed or a higher being.

When you try to develop a connection to the Arcturians, Pleiadians, Central Sun, Andromedans, or Sirians, you develop a conscious link to its energy field. The energy field is encapsulated in a thought field based on the laws and rules of quantum cohesiveness. As advanced and profound as this may be, frankly, it has been experimented with on Earth before. The ancient Egyptians developed many thought patterns and energy fields to connect with the ancient Sirians. They were doing exactly what I have described: They were setting up a quantum-cohesiveness thought field with the Sirians. They sought ways to collaborate and connect their spirits and their spiritual energy fields with the Sirians.

The Sirians sought to do the same thing with Earth. They tried to control the Egyptians. There was an intervention that stopped the Sirians from completely doing this. You can see the effects of the Sirians trying to control the Egyptians energetically. The alignment of the pyramids to the belt of Orion and the openings in the special chambers that let in light from the star Sirius were all focused on developing quantum cohesiveness. The Sirians sought to be able to affect what was going on in ancient Egypt, and at the same time, ancient Egypt sought to affect the Sirians.

There are other examples. In fact, the Maya developed a quantum-cohesiveness energy field with the Central Sun. This idea of quantum cohesiveness means that what develops energetically from the Central Sun can have an effect on Earth. The Maya had no idea of the distance between Earth and the Central Sun, but they did have in their spiritual repertoire an understanding of quantum cohesiveness. They understood that there would be an energy in the galaxy that could influence their lives.

The concept of quantum cohesiveness also occurred in Stonehenge, England, as well as in different areas of South America where the native people sought a connection that would allow them to be influenced in positive ways by the higher beings in the galaxy. Stonehenge was an example of a group trying to establish quantum cohesiveness with a higher extraterrestrial energy field.

The Arcturian, Pleiadian, and Andromedan starseeds are coming together to develop quantum cohesiveness with a fifth-dimensional energy field. You, on an intuitive level, know that there is a direct link — a quantum link — with the fifth dimension. In quantum entanglement theory,[2] what happens in one particle affects the other particle no matter how far apart or how distant that particle is.

You know that we are here to help Earth. We are here to motivate and to move the energy field of this planet to a higher level. We are here to move this noosphere into the next evolutionary stage. We are here to assist you in creating a distinctive higher energy process, an energy web of a higher light that will bring you to a much higher evolutionary stage.

We need your consciousness to connect with our fifth-dimensional light. You provide a conscious link to us. There must be a consciousness between the two particles for the full effect to take place. I study how your scientists are working on subatomic particle physics. Their observations, which are expressions of their consciousness, allow the unpredictability and also the quantum entanglement to occur.

Perhaps you remember some lectures I've given in the past about surgeries, especially those involving cancer. Sometimes there is exploratory surgery in which a doctor opens a patient to see whether cancer is present. When cancer is found, the surgeon might make some kind of shocking or surprising analysis. For example, the surgeon might say that the cancer is inoperable or incurable. During the operation, he or she might determine that the patient will surely die and then close the incision without doing anything further.

However, opening a person and sending a negative thought wave into that body can affect the subatomic particles in the cancer in a quantum way. The surgeon's thoughts at that vulnerable moment can negatively affect the life energy field of the person. That negative energy input sometimes is enough to tip the person's energy field and the body into a more rapid disease process.

---

2 Learn more about the quantum entanglement theory at http://physics.about.com/od/quantumphysics/f /QuantumEntanglement.htm.

There is an entanglement of the negative thoughts of the doctor with the activation of negative energy in the body.

On the other hand, during the surgery, the surgeon could say: "Oh, this cancer can be cured; this can be healed. Let's send light to this person, and let's send divine energy." Then a totally different entanglement, or quantum cohesiveness, can occur. I like to use the word "cohesiveness" because it has a much more positive effect.

Feel the quantum light and the quantum energy that we, the Arcturians, are sending you and your planet from our Arcturian temples. We have very strong temple meditators, and we use them to establish quantum links on our fifth-dimensional world. We are also devoted to the quantum light and the healing light for Earth. We send light from our special etheric crystals in our temples along with quantum healing light and energy.

There must be a particle that can receive quantum healing and energy transformation. The concept in the physical world that describes this is symmetry. "Symmetry" means "being similar," that is, two particles that are similar. Quantum cohesiveness is more powerful when there is a similar vibrational energy source or energy particle where we are trying to send the energy and light to. Quantum cohesiveness more powerfully occurs when symmetry exists.

The concept of symmetry explains why we have created the twelve etheric crystals. We intensely work with you to create the planetary cities of light. We are also working to create the ladders of ascension. These projects help to create symmetry with our fifth-dimensional energy fields.

Earth's Energy Field

In our temples, we accelerate and magnify our thoughts through profound crystal work. We have developed special energy-measuring devices and terminology based on the concept of arcan energy, which is the measurement of the power of a thought field. Remember, the thought field is based on quantum physics because the thought field is also coming from a subatomic wave. The thought wave cannot be observed. You might be able to observe the electromagnetic energy in the brain, which is the basis of the production of thought. You would have a difficult time using your current technology to break down thought-field energy into its smallest particle.

Thought represents the entire energy field of a planet, the entire energy of a dimension. The thought field is the basis of holding together the third dimension. The existence of the veil separates this reality from the other reality. This veil is also a thought force. The thought force can be penetrated. What is amazing is that your thoughts can be transmitted in a quantum way. For example, your thoughts and what you do with them are recorded in the akashic records. Every thought that you have in this incarnation is recorded. This is a positive development. I am only explaining this to you so that you understand the extensive range of thought energy.

We send thought energy and higher healing light from our crystals to the twelve etheric crystals you helped download to Earth. These twelve etheric crystals are particularly symmetrical with our main crystal in the Arcturian crystal lake. We activated our crystal and the crystal in the Arcturian crystal lake. Based on quantum cohesiveness, the energy of our activated crystal can communicate with the twelve etheric crystals downloaded on Earth. For example, we are focusing now on the etheric crystal in Lago Puelo, Argentina, which can be quantumly and cohesively activated. With this activation, it can more powerfully transmit a higher-dimensional light throughout Earth.

The fact that Lago Puelo is connected to the other eleven crystals means that there is a quantum cohesiveness among the other Earth-based crystals. So what happens on one level, what happens to one crystal, will affect all the crystals in a positive and cohesive way.

I, Juliano, with my temple meditators and temple healers now send our energy to the Arcturian crystal lake and the etheric crystal in our lake. The Group of Forty members met at that lake in 2012 and activated the crystal in a new way. They also built a beautiful medicine wheel that brought the energy there to an even higher dimensional level. The medicine wheel creates the symmetrical particle energy field necessary to interact cohesively with our Arcturian crystal.

We now send this quantum light to Earth through Lago Puelo. The light creates a fifth-dimensional transcendent energy field. It has the characteristic of being unpredictable, and it also has a highly transcendent energy field of balance and harmony for the whole Earth. This beautiful energy can be sent out to Earth through our work directly from Lago Puelo. You might be able to see or feel this powerful energy. This is an energy of stability and planetary balance. It can help to hold a force field of fifth-dimensional light throughout the planet.

We are here to help you create a new thought field for planet Earth. This fifth-dimensional energy enters Lago Puelo and the etheric crystal there in a quantum way.

Correcting Earth's Tipping Point

The energy from Lago Puelo spreads to the other etheric crystals throughout the planet, and it creates and amplifies a quantum cohesiveness throughout Earth. I know that many of you already sense that this planet is at a tipping point. There are so many tipping points in terms of the political, economic, and military energies on this planet.

End-time events were predicted to occur on December 21, 2012. Many of these events did not happen. However, the likelihood of some of these catastrophic end-time events occurring is still possible. You and I do not want to see end-time events happen because it will bring more misery and pain to this planet and its population. Let us bring down this quantum light to help prevent further end-time events.

The more that we work with and send this energy from our crystal light and our crystal temples, the stronger the effect can be. We help to rebalance the planet. Positive quantum light is being emitted from the crystals and will spread throughout Earth. This is why we also set up the ring of ascension — to deal with the distribution and the application of quantum-energy cohesiveness around the globe. What better way to establish a cohesive energy field around Earth than to put this halo of light around it and call it the ring of ascension. Incidentally, when you work within your Arcturian temple here on Earth, you also quantumly create a cohesive energy field between Earth and our temple on Arcturus.

That means that whatever energy we work with, whatever positive energy force we create in our thought field, can also positively affect you there. It can affect you on a multitude of levels. It can affect you on a personal healing level.

We also send a tremendous amount of healing to everyone. We know that there is an instability on Earth in many of your energy fields. Even if you are the most stable, do the most meditations, and have the most crystals, you can still become susceptible to the overwhelming instability of energy that permeates this planet.

Part of this instability comes from holes in Earth's aura, and part comes from your own aura, which might not be able to hold a particular frequency. Part of it is from the pathogens that swim around the human immune system. I could continue to list many different sources for your instability. The key is that you can reestablish stability in your energy field. We are working to do that through quantum cohesiveness. We are continually sending you stabilizing energy and light. Let the healing light from our crystal lake quantumly interact with Lago Puelo, Argentina — all twelve etheric crystals — and let those etheric crystals send out to each of you a stable and healing energy now. [Tones] "Hoooohhhhhhhhh."

Your fifth-dimensional body is also, in a quantum way, cohesively linked to your third-dimensional body. What is being activated in your fifth-dimensional body is cohesively linked to your third-dimensional body. Visualize and connect to your fifth-dimensional body in the Arcturian crystal temple and the Arcturian crystal lake.

A fifth-dimensional energy can vibrate and interact with your third-dimensional energy field. Remember, as I said, you must have a conscious link to make the most effective transference of energy between the dimensional bodies. Consciously link yourself to your fifth-dimensional body. Therefore, your fifth-dimensional body will have a more positive effect on you.

Planetary healing uses the same principles. We seek to help you link the fifth-dimensional Earth with the third-dimensional Earth. We also seek to link our moon-planet Alano, many star cities of light, and Arcturus with your third-dimensional planet. The planetary cities of light can then quantumly receive the energies from the galactic star cities. This is one of the main reasons why we create planetary cities of light with the galactic star cities: to help you connect your cities with higher galactic energy.

Quantum cohesiveness is not dependent on space or time. The quantum interaction can be both close and distant. The connecting objects do not necessarily have to be far apart. The planetary cities of light affect each other. You can work with the quantum cohesiveness in one city and link that connection to other cities. We established this global network to enhance these links. What happens in one city can positively affect another city. It is very helpful when there is a quantum conscious connection between cities.

Visualize now the great connections from the planetary cities of light project that have been developed over the past years. I send quantum light and awareness to each of these cities now. [Tones] "Oooohhhhhhhh."

People all over the planet are awakening to the planetary cities of light. They are awakening and understanding that these quantum energy fields can interact in a way that really transcends third-dimensional logic in a very positive way.

The Versatility of Light Energy

Many people have asked me about omega light, Iskalia light, and quantum light. Each of these light forms is part of the quantum process I have described, which includes the concept of quantum cohesiveness. Omega light, for example, is light directly from the highest source, the highest energy field, and it comes from a Creator energy field that we are able to access. Omega light can quantumly and positively affect you and your health in an optimal way. It comes from a source I can only describe as the center of the creation of souls. There is a source center in the universe where souls and soul energy are centered and soul energy is created and emitted. This is part of where the omega light comes from.

Receive the omega light to activate your powerful soul energy. Each of you now can receive quantum omega light. [Sings] "Oooomegaaa Liiiight."

The omega light helps to set up a quantum cohesiveness with the highest soul sources in the universe. When you connect with omega light and when the soul light moves in a positive, healing way, it will quantumly and cohesively affect your energy field.

Jesus wishes to speak with you. I am Juliano. Blessings in the omega light and in the quantum cohesive omega energy field. Good day.

• • •

Greetings, I am Jesus. I love you, and I love your connection to the ascension process. I love that you want to ascend, and I know that you have a deep and dear desire to transcend this reality and to transcend this third dimension.

Cosmic Intervention

The energy field of the Messianic light is cosmic. I worked with the Pleiades and helped them to go into the cosmic light. I helped them understand the cosmic connections to the Messianic energy field. I helped them to move their planet into the fifth dimension, and they established a linkage to help other sister planets. On the Pleiades, they understand that we are talking about cosmic Messianic light — not just about Earth receiving Messianic light, but also about a cosmic connection for many other planets in this galaxy.

Juliano pointed out that consciousness links quantum cohesive energy. The Pleiadians have demonstrated their devotion to the cosmic transformation and the cosmic Savior energy of Earth. They are proven examples of a planetary system that has been that are able to evolve into the fifth dimension. It is the same with the Arcturians. But the Arcturians are older souls than the Pleiadians. When the Pleiadians transcended into the fifth dimension, they were secondary in this section of the galaxy, because the Arcturians had already been in the fifth dimension. They are the guardians of the transcendent energy field.

The Arcturians set up the stargate, which is also an energy field for the ascension. The stargate has a connecting link to the Serra da Bocaina national park near Sao Paulo, Brazil. It is also tied to many different planetary cities of light throughout the planet that are able to hold the Earth connection to the stargate. The stargate is part of the energy field that I call cosmic messianic light.

Clearly, this planet needs a cosmic intervention. It needs a cosmic energy-field connection to higher spiritual energy. I am so proud to be a part of this higher lightwork with you. The ascension on Earth is a cosmic event. The earth processes and the densities here require a cosmic intervention.

When you think about the ascension and the Messianic light, think of it in a cosmic way. When you think about Montserrat, Spain (home of one of the etheric crystals), and the Messianic light being held there, think about it in a cosmic way. Think that it is connected to cosmic energy, to a quantum energy field. Always think about the twelve etheric crystals in a cosmic way. Think about the ring of ascension in a cosmic way; it interacts outwardly with the planetary energy field and the fifth dimension. Also, the ring of ascension is able to receive cosmic energy and light.

There is a tremendous outpouring of cohesive quantum love and light coming to this planet. The planetary cities of light and the sister star cities of light send great healing — quantum light energy — throughout the globe.

I carry the cosmic Messianic light, and you are all able to receive it because you are starseeds. You understand Earth's connection to the universe, the galaxy, the Central Sun, and the ascended masters.

Blessed are you. In the light of the cosmic Messianic energy, I embrace you. This is Jesus.

Chapter 7

The Nature of Universal Consciousness

Helio-ah and the Arcturians

Greetings, I am Helio-ah. We are the Arcturians. The part represents the whole. You have heard this statement many times in your language. It is a profound summary on the nature of universal consciousness. The relationship between the part and the whole is even more significant when we look at spiritual consciousness.

Spiritual consciousness is based on the relationship and interactions of all thoughts and beings in the universe. We, the Arcturians, have learned how to connect with thoughts throughout existence. It has been our scientific explorations and discoveries that have led us to this understanding; namely, even a small thought connected properly can be linked to the whole universe. Even one thought of one person connected with a master can enable that master to understand the whole being and lifetime of that person. This connection becomes extremely powerful in understanding and reaching out to all living beings. If only one thought, one connected link, can be achieved, then doorways can open to the realms around that person, planet, or galaxy. Ultimately, a thought can connect to the Source of all.

We are excited to link to the Central Sun, for we know that there is a small amount of energy from the Central Sun now reaching Earth. Even this small part is enough to connect to the whole light, the whole energy field of this Central Sun. We use magnifications to bring light as pure as possible of the Central Sun's photonic energy.

The Iskalia mirror is an etheric mirror that we, the Arcturians, helped to place over the North Pole of your dear planet. The goal and purpose of the Iskalia mirror is to act as a magnification, allowing a pure energy field and thought to reach this planet and enable those like you who are in a meditative state to receive it. This magnification is important, for it helps to purify and enlarge that particle. The Iskalia mirror is now fully activated, and with your thoughts, you can visualize it as a gigantic mirror, perhaps as large as a mile or two in diameter, in the etheric realm over the North Pole. This mirror is in special alignment with the Central Sun.

Infuse the Light of the Central Sun

We have learned that thoughts are also light waves. When we holographically align ourselves with the Central Sun in the following meditation, we receive particles of light from the Central Sun and its powerful, higher thoughts. The Central Sun has a collection of energy from the ascended masters and teachers in the galaxy, who are all concentrating at this moment on sending you a powerful boost. They send this particle of light and thought that will enable you to holographically experience the Central Sun energy.

The Central Sun energy can be described in many ways. It represents a summary of the highest wisdom of the galaxy, the highest wisdom of evolution, the highest wisdom of light.

I now activate the Iskalia mirror. *[Sings] "Iskalia light." Aligning with those in meditation with the Arcturians, now allow a thought particle from the Central Sun to enter your consciousness. Do not be concerned about the holographic value of this; just receive it. [Tones] "Eeeeeeeh."*

The part is the gateway to the whole. This means that receiving the Central Sun consciousness can open you to vast doorways of light and wisdom. You now open to vast doorways of galactic thought, journeys into future and past lifetimes, and intergalactic and interdimensional travel to scientific breakthroughs of knowledge about the corridors of light. This wisdom of the Central Sun is coming to Earth in a more intense way than it has ever been experienced before.

You are on the cusp of a breakthrough of consciousness never experienced before on Earth. It is going to be marked by the return of Jesus to this planet and the landing of major ships from interplanetary realms. It is going to be marked by special commanders of intergalactic forces who work to stabilize Earth and the magnetic fluctuations that have been erratic around the planet. The possibility of pole-shifting energy is still strong. Magnetic shifting of the poles is becoming more likely, as evidenced by the extreme magnetic flux in Earth's energy fields.

A stabilization energy from the Central Sun is being infused into Earth as I speak. This infusion of Central Sun light will bring a balance first to you and then to Earth. I, Helio-ah, activate the Iskalia mirror one more time to bring down this particle for an infusion of balance. It will help you transmit this balance to all you come in contact with. [Sings] "Iiiiskaaaaliaaaa."

There are tremendously powerful forces interacting in the solar system, on Earth, and this portion of the galaxy. To balance these energies, you must have a magnitude of stabilization and light to infuse harmonic energy. This is what the Harmonic Convergence and the 11:11 energy was about. It was an attempt to bring harmony to the tremendous forces that you are experiencing.

To harmonize such a tremendous, conflicted force requires an overwhelmingly good and powerful light from the Central Sun. It requires energy far surpassing all the individual conflicts and differences you are seeing. It has to surpass all the disruptions — political, economic, and geophysical. All of these aspects will become receptive to the harmony that I am speaking of. Let there be an increase in Harmonic Convergence light. This is a powerful time to bring down and stabilize harmony.

Heliographic Light

Holography works on many levels. When you understand that the part represents the whole, you can affect the whole through your interaction with the part. When you holographically experience the part, you can reach the core of that essence, whether it is the essence of a being, a lifetime, an object, a planet, a time, a galaxy, a universe, or the essence of Adonai.

To experience the Adonai is to experience God's presence. To experience a part of the fifth-dimensional Earth in the future will enable you to interact now with a higher consciousness in the present. Holographic thought is connected to the past, present, and future. So when you look at a holographic aspect of yourself, it is timeless. It includes interactions from all of your aspects.

I now see each of you holographically. When I connect to you, I can see you as young children, as babies in your mothers' wombs. I can see you as young people, ten or eleven years old, and I can see you as you age and become elderly. I can see you in another lifetime and as your future selves, as well as your past selves. I am connected to the part, and that gives me access to the whole.

Your current existence is a part of the multipresence. You can affect all aspects of your present, future, and past through your total understanding of this current — that is, the present part of yourself. You can grasp the essence of the Arcturians and our teachings by working with thought and the Arcturian thought wave. By connecting with our thought wave, you can activate and download holographic light.

Holographic light is a powerful laser-like beam that enables you to dissect and experience an object, a planet, or a being holographically. Holographic light also includes holographic thought. Remember what I said: We have learned that thought is light and light is thought. There is a special energy that enables you to holographically experience a person, a planet — all objects. I am going to download this heliographic energy into your crown chakra.

[Sings] Heeeeliiiioooohhhaahhh." I, Helio-ah, call on heliographic light forces to enter each of the starseed consciousnesses now. Let this heliographic light now enter! Through your thought projections and your visualizations, you will begin to understand the essence of the universe, the essence of the souls, and your link to all of the soul light energies in this universe and in this galaxy. [Chants] "Kol Ha Neshama" [Hebrew for all living spirits], "all living light, and all liquid light, coalesce into the starseed consciousness now and forever."

I ask you to do the following arm motion: Move your hands out in a circular motion, in and out. This energy is so intense that you must keep it moving, and I want you to be in motion. One of the secrets of holographic energy is motion and movement. You may experience an increase in your energy level as you do these movements. Let your cosmic egg energy around your body enlarge, for you are of the essence of this universe.

You have heard the statement, "Connect within, and you will know the essence of all." Hallelujah. [Rubs hands together rapidly.] Now place your hands by your ears. You will experience being in another realm when you do this. Put your hands on your knees. Reverse. Now place your palms by your navel.

[Tones] "Ooohhhmmmm." This connects you with Earth's energy and light. Earth is a holographic representation of all life forms in the galaxy. Earth is a holographic experiment in planetary exuberance and evolution, and through your presence, you contribute to this. Each aspect and each life form is interconnected to many different places in the universe and this galaxy in particular.

Again, I call on the light from the Central Sun to enter the Iskalia mirror to bring down stabilization and harmony. The holographic connections to the greater whole are becoming distorted, disenfranchised, and alienated on Earth. The nuclear energies, wars, conflicts, and many of the negative Earth events that you see holographically distort the connections. We are studying this situation with great interest. A reformulation can help return many of these disenfranchised parts. This separation happens when a lower consciousness interferes in the light of a planet. In some cases, it is better to have no consciousness and be holographically connected than it is to have a consciousness that is on a lower level and lose the holographic connection.

Animals and plants are already holographically connected. In some ways, they experience greater union of the light forms and energy than people on Earth, many of whom are disenfranchised from this connection. Earth is an experiment and also a school for learning. To overcome the planetary loss of holographic connections requires, as you know, a major intervention and uplifting.

Holographic Connection

We, the Arcturians, have talked about entering the subconscious and unconscious as a way of linking to the collective subconscious of the planet. A part of harmony interjected into the subconscious can help you to connect. Your dreams will come back to you in greater harmony. Your dream life will return to you in a powerful way, and your dream time will be heightened as you announce to your subconscious that you are holographically connected to the greater whole.

Announce this now to your subconscious:

"I am holographically connected to the All. I am holographically connected to the All. I am holographically connected to the All."

"I am holographically connected to the Central Sun." [Repeat two more times.]

"I am holographically connected to all of my lifetimes, past, present, and future." [Repeat two more times.]

"I am a holographic being of light." [Repeat two more times.]

Now stand after saying these powerful affirmations and spin around once to let the energy settle in. Spin again. You may feel a little dizzy doing that a second time. Let the energy settle in. Spin one more time, please. Bring your hands together in the universal sign of harmony and peace. Open the hands so the palms are facing outward. Visualize sinking your hands into and allowing yourself to connect with the center of Earth. Your feet are going down, down, down into the center of Earth.

You are in the center of Earth, and we are standing here together. Earth's core has been very disruptive of late. Project thoughts of harmony into the core and the crust of Earth. You may feel a rumbling, a loss of balance, as you project yourself closer into the core of Earth.

Remember the harmony that you have achieved through the Central Sun. You have a great connection with harmony, even though individually you are not overwhelmingly powerful. Because of holographic technology, you are representatives of the greater harmony. Project this harmony out now.

I am going to make some sounds from Earth that might sound distressing to you. It is part of the release that we are activating together. [Makes crying sounds.]

Return to the room. Place your hands in front of your chest in the universal symbol of peace and harmony.

Holography also applies to time, and the essence of time is space and movement. When you stop all movement, time will stop. At the moment time stops, you are connected to all time and eternity. At that point, you can connect and directly experience the Eternal One.

Interestingly, in working with the Group of Forty project, your connections as a group establish holographic links around the world to all other starseeds. This means that the experiences, for example, of those in Australia, can simultaneously be experienced by all. Even when there is a delayed reaction, this does not interfere with the experience of the now. You are still connected to and are still working with that experience. Naturally, you wish to connect to the powerful points of higher energy.

The holographic crystal energy and wisdom are now being transmuted etherically throughout the world. You will continue to receive energy and light. The etheric crystals form a triangle that is in alignment with the special corridor from the Central Sun. The crystals also activate an Earth alignment. Energetically and astrologically, everything comes into alignment. You find that your soul essence emerges in the alignment and that you are building your energy as a storehouse to experience that moment. In reality, you are always experiencing that moment, even though the experience is heightened at the alignment.

Unlock Your Higher Consciousness

The crystal temple is a holographic representation of the Arcturian teachings that are transmitted through crystals. These crystals have unique powers, for they hold past, present, and future knowledge. At the same time, they activate points within your consciousness that stimulate DNA activity, allowing an unlocking of your higher consciousness that enables you to experience the higher light as thought and new knowledge. It is important that you learn to transmute this light into thought, knowledge, and useful information. This is your job as third-dimensional beings.

Let the light and energy that we have worked with be transmuted into a form of crystalline activation within each of you. Look at all of the events on the planet, and bring your thoughts of harmony and balance to them. Use your holographic connection to the Central Sun to foster greater power and harmony beyond what you are capable of emitting individually. You are holographically connected to all, and in particular, to the great balancing and harmony power that is coming to Earth from the Central Sun.

In the light and the harmony of the holographic Central Sun, which is connected with all the central suns in the universe, I, Helio-ah, say balance and peace and Shalom.

Chapter 8

Unified Consciousness and Earth's Noosphere

Juliano, the Arcturians, and Jesus

Greetings, I am Juliano. We are the Arcturians. We want to explain how a planetary unified consciousness can affect Earth and how this can have an influence on healing and rebalancing the planet. A simple explanation of the noosphere is that it is the thought field of the entire planet. The noosphere has many levels and can, in some ways, be compared to the akashic records, which are a library of information, impressions, astral readings, thoughts, and events that have occurred throughout the existence of the universe. The akashic records are on multiple levels. They exist for Earth, other planets, this galaxy, and other galaxies.

You can imagine that the akashic records are quite extensive. They contain the soul records and impressions of you, of all who have come before you, and of all who will come after you. Basically, when you are doing soul retrievals and past-life therapy, you are usually accessing the akashic records. Previous civilizations on Earth are recorded in the akashic records, including the Atlanteans, the Lemurians, and many other species or civilizations.

The akashic records can be compared to the noosphere because in a sense the noosphere also records all of the thoughts and events that have occurred on Earth. Every event and every thought and thought pattern is recorded in the noosphere. The main difference between them is that the noosphere interacts with the spirit of Earth and with the dimensional levels and stability of the planet.

The Noosphere

We, the Arcturians, have understood that our input (our thoughts) influences our noosphere that in turn influences the energy field of the planet. You must understand that the noosphere is not just a library like the akashic records; rather, it is an interactive energy field with energies that mix with and affect Earth in many different ways.

The noosphere is the basis for this whole third dimension, including how the third dimension acts and how the noosphere or the thought field creates and manifests events and energies on this planet. Again, the akashic records do not interact with or directly affect the planet, but the noosphere does. The thoughts put into the noosphere influence and create your reality.

We, the Arcturians, are on a fifth-dimensional planet. Our planet does not have volcanic eruptions, earthquakes, or hurricanes. We have created thought patterns to influence our planetary activity so that there is uniform stability. It might be hard to believe that thought patterns can be set up in the noosphere to influence the planet, but this is one of the core principals of planetary healing.

The key force in the process of interacting with the noosphere and the planet is Earth's feedback loop system. Each planet has a feedback loop system. Earth's feedback loop system is self-regulating, meaning that within the confines and parameters of the planet, its techniques and technical abilities work continually to maintain a certain balance. The balance has to do with maintaining the percentage of oxygen and nitrogen along with the life force energy so that the biosphere can continue to exist. Without the feedback loop system, Earth could run out of control. The oceans could return to cover 90 percent of the planet. The greenhouse effect would be totally out of control, causing extreme heat, which would be unbearable for most life forms. These earth changes are so strong that they are taxing Earth's feedback loop system. Earth is having trouble keeping up with the changes that are required to maintain balance for the life upon it.

Energy and thoughts placed in the noosphere go directly to Earth's feedback loop system. The feedback loop system then receives instructions and information that will help it stay caught up with the dramatic changes that are necessary for the planet and its spirit to maintain this new and sensitive balance. Our temple meditators work to create balance and harmony, and those meditations contribute a stability that is the envy of planets throughout the galaxy. You on Earth can also achieve this stability. There are certain inputs of thoughts, ideas, energies, and techniques used in our planetary healing techniques based on our interactions of the noosphere with our planet's feedback loop system.

You live in the third dimension, and you have been programmed to have certain levels of consciousness, fields of perception, and ranges of emotional energy. The spectrum of electromagnetic energy waves that your body can potentially perceive is quite extensive. You probably have the ability to perceive five to ten times more than what you now perceive. A good way to compare this is to look at a horse that has blinders on; it can only see what is in front of it. It cannot see what is to the left or to the right. That means that there will be no distractions. You have these blinders on your energy perception, and now you are going through a transition that is leading you to evolve toward a fifth-dimensional being. That means you must change your core perceptual program and the codes that were given to you to allow you to expand your consciousness and your field of perception.

Some of the affirmations that you could use might sound like this: "I am a fifth-dimensional being with expanded consciousness. I am able to receive and process information from other dimensions and still be stable to function on the third dimension. The keys and codes of ascension are now opening in my inner consciousness. I will be able to ascend." These affirmations can help you maintain and expand your energy and your work toward the ascension and the fifth dimension.

Communicating with a Planet

Many of you are devoted to Earth and want to contribute to Earth's ascension. Earth as an entire planet is going to ascend. But for a planet to ascend, it needs certain energy and information. It also needs spiritually minded beings like you. The planet must interact with spiritually minded beings who can guide and lead that planet to the fifth dimension. To put this another way, a planet like Earth cannot ascend unless there are spiritually minded beings who can lead the entire planet into the ascension.

Earth's feedback loop system needs certain affirmations and input to prepare for ascension too. You both need certain preparations and affirmations to expand your consciousness. Earth needs your input with some affirmations that are quite similar to what you are using for your ascension work. For example, during ceremonies, many of you will say, "Gaia, or Mother Earth, I love you." This is powerful and helpful. We could go even further and say things to the spirit of Earth like, "We are helping you prepare for your ascension. You as a planet will be ascending. You as a planet have the ability to go into the fifth dimension."

Communicating with the planet is a complicated skill. A planet is a being with a spirit. A planet doesn't necessarily have a language exactly like you and humanity. Saying words with feelings and enthusiasm is really wonderful, and many times Earth will receive the vibration of your thought.

There is another aspect to communicating with the spirit of a planet and helping a planet come to the fifth dimension. This aspect can be compared to communicating with your unconscious, which often uses symbols, pictures, energy, and of course, words in communications and the dream world. Words and feelings are powerful. Often the images and the accompanying vibrational feeling with those images can go right to your core. Many of you have had strong feelings in a dream, especially a bad dream, in which you wake up sweating and experiencing a rapid heartbeat because of images you saw and vibrations you felt.

What are some of the ways in which you can use pictures and feelings to communicate to a planet? How can you use your input in the noosphere to reach the planetary feedback loop system? You know about medicine wheels and crop circles. There are other strong configurations that will work to directly reach the feedback loop system of Earth. One of these is the Tree of Life. We have worked extensively with you on the Planetary Tree of Life, and we have explained that it is based on the Kabbalah Tree of Life. The Planetary Tree of Life is a special configuration that communicates directly to the spirit of Earth. Like the Kabbalah Tree of Life, the Planetary Tree of Life is a holographic multidimensional image. It's not just the flat surface that you see on one page. It's also the back, the front, and all angles interacting with the spirit of Earth, including the triangles, the octagons, the rectangles, and the tetrahedrons. All of these different configurations are contained in this Tree of Life.

The configuration of the Planetary Tree of Life (see figure 4.2) established on this planet has an energy and a symbolic structure to directly affect and communicate with the planetary spirit. There is a special way of using all the spheres and all the energies of the Planetary Tree of Life to induce and create a fantastic input into the noosphere that will help to upgrade the feedback loop system of Earth.

There are other forces that contribute to Earth's ability to relate to its fifth-dimensional evolution as a planet. One of the main factors that contributes to Earth's evolution and the opening of its chakras to the fifth dimension is Earth's alignment with the Central Sun. That's right; Earth also has chakras. Earth has energy centers and meridians! Earth's crown chakra is on top of the North Pole right now. The chakra system of a planet is not exactly parallel to the chakra system of a person.

Upgrading Earth's Feedback Loop System

The Planetary Tree of Life configuration provides an interactive energy force to reach the feedback loop system of the planet. Let us just remind you that Earth's feedback loop system was running on one configuration in 1960, but now much has changed. Earth's feedback loop system in 1960 would not be able to keep up with the changes going on now. It has been upgraded, and part of this upgrade has occurred through Earth's own evolution.

A feedback loop system is an interactive and primary system. It is not a homeostatic system; rather, it constantly adjusts itself in order to keep up with the changes. Earth has made many changes and adjustments.

Many people have asked me about the end-time events and why more major Earth catastrophes have not happened. Why are there not more volcanic eruptions or tsunamis or other events? Some great prophets, including Edgar Cayce, predicted that we could see a physical change to the West Coast, particularly California, with distruction of major cities.[1] We all know that has not happened, and it will not happen. The reason these events have not happened is that these prophets or channels did not include in their assessments Earth's feedback loop system and it's ability to upgrade itself and make adjustments.

Earth's feedback loop system is quite an amazing and powerful mechanism. It has done a great job maintaining balance in a very difficult situation on the planet. Another factor in upgrading Earth's feedback loop system is Earth's alignment with the Central Sun. The alignment that occurred on December 21, 2012, opened up new codes within the planet. You also have inner codes of ascension that will open you to different levels of consciousness. The planet also has inner codes that enable the planet to become more fifth dimensional. By being more fifth dimensional, the spirit of the planet can transcend its cause-and-effect reality.

Currently, there is grave damage being done to the ocean from the Fukushima nuclear power radiation leak accident, and the predictions of more catastrophic damage to the oceans has been quite alarming. The Earth's feedback loop system is making adjustments. It also receives energies from the Central Sun to upgrade itself to handle this process. This occurs on many different levels, including creating a stable environment so that no further earthquakes happen that would be damaging to the Fukushima power plant. I know that the situation of the Fukushima power plant is extremely dangerous to many parts of the planet. Unfortunately, another strong earthquake there could dramatically increase those harmful effects by ten to twenty times! The potential for greater damage, as bad as this damage is, is still very high. Part of Earth's feedback loop system's work involves creating stability so that no further earthquakes will damage the existing fragile structures there.

The second and equally important input level relates directly to my assertion that a planet can only ascend to the fifth dimension when there are

---

1. Ernest Frejer, *The Edgar Cayce Companion* (Barnes and Noble, 1995), 444-445.

spiritually minded beings living on it. These spiritually minded beings, namely starseeds like you, have developed ways of interacting with the feedback loop system and the spirit of Earth. This means that Earth, as a spiritual being, is learning to interact with you and with the planetary healers. There are many planetary healers now on Earth's surface, such as the Native peoples, who have a close relationship with Earth.

Part of the planetary opening now occurring has to do with Earth's receptivity to you, the starseeds. This means that you can help to reprogram Earth and the feedback loop system. Some of the reprogramming can be affirmations that I have suggested earlier, such as, "Planet Earth, you can receive and integrate fifth-dimensional energies. Planet Earth, you can download new fifth-dimensional technologies that will help the feedback loop system purify and rebalance you."

Symbolic Earth Communication

Some energies and communications occur in symbols, such as crop circles. One of the confusing ideas of crop circles is trying to find out what the symbols mean. They are beautiful and have immense complexity, but what could they possibly accomplish? The intricate patterns are meant to help Earth to recalibrate itself, realign its meridians, and adjust its feedback loop system. Some of these crop circles are so advanced that they directly recalibrate parts of Earth's feedback loop system. This recalibration is far beyond normal human consciousness and understanding.

Crop circles can be compared to a computer program. If you looked at the minuses and pluses and the ones and zeroes and the many different configurations of a program, it wouldn't make any sense to you unless you were a computer programmer. When it's put into a certain language or readable code, you can see the results. These crop circles have configurations and patterns that are in a code that you might not be able to understand. They are helping to recalibrate Earth and the feedback loop system.

There have been other attempts on this planet to communicate with the spirit of Earth. Stonehenge is an example of how some advanced beings decided to interact and connect with Earth's spirit, the galaxy, and the Central Sun. The Mayan temples are other examples of structures that connect to the central galaxy. The Egyptian temples are a third example. Even the Great Wall of China was an attempt to unite the energies of heaven with the energies of Earth to create a greater, interactive balance.

Say these affirmations to bring the spirit of Earth (Gaia) into your consciousness, "I am open to interacting with the spirit of Earth. The spirit of Earth is open to interacting with me. As a planetary healer, I have a special sensitivity to interact with Mother Earth." [Chants several times] "Oooommmm."

Say, "Gaia and I are one in mind. Gaia and I are one in mind. I am linking and connecting Gaia with the fifth dimension. I am connecting Gaia energetically with the fifth-dimensional light."

Hold this thought and this connection. Know that you are making a connection that will help Gaia receive more fifth-dimensional energy light to upgrade the feedback loop system.

Part of Earth's feedback loop system has to do with fifth-dimensional light. Earth's feedback loop system is now receiving fifth-dimensional life and light because you are a conduit for higher energy. You know that there are codes of ascension within the planet just as you have codes of ascension within you. You have worked so hard to open up the codes of ascension. Now we, together, will be working with Gaia to open her codes of ascension.

The Ladders of Ascension

There are many aspects of permanently opening the fifth-dimension to the planet. Many of these connections have to do with creating sacred places on Earth. This is what we are accomplishing through the planetary cities of light. The ladders of ascension are also key in helping to maintain and open the fifth dimension to Gaia.

You might consider the ladders of ascension as portals in which you, at the time of ascension, could go through and leave the planet to ascend. One ladder of ascension is in Bell Rock in Sedona [Arizona]. Another is in Sant Pere de Ribes [Spain], and another is in San Martín de los Andes [Argentina]. There are other sacred places where there are ladders of ascension as well.

The ladder of ascension has multiple purposes. It is not just one portal for you to use to ascend, as powerful and important as that is. The ladder of ascension also helps the planet connect with the fifth dimension. The ladders of ascension bring down fifth-dimensional light into Gaia. They have been set up in powerful and sacred places around Earth. These sacred places provide stability and energy that will be used by the spirit of Gaia for her ascension. The ladders of ascension serve two purposes: (1) for you to ascend at the right time and to have a portal to go to and (2) for these portals to be used by Gaia to stabilize the fifth-dimensional energies in her spiritual light and presence.

The ladders of ascension are key to unlocking the codes of ascension for Earth. A great biorelativity exercise is to simultaneously connect all of the ladders of ascension that we have downloaded to Earth. With the proper meditation and the proper chanting, we can help to unlock the codes of ascension for Earth. What a great service we can do together! [Tones] "Oooohhhh."

Remember, fifth-dimensional energy is more powerful than third-dimensional energy. It has powers of healing and rebalancing that are unimaginable in the third dimension. The fifth-dimensional energies brought to Earth will create a different and more powerful and upgraded balance in Earth's feedback loop system. [Tones] "Oooohhhh."

The Unified Field of Consciousness

Early humans did not have the ability to develop a unified consciousness field for the whole planet. The reason is obvious: Early humans did not have the Internet or television or instantaneous communication. Although there are many minuses (or negatives) about these communications you experience through the Internet and television, the huge plus is you have the ability to contribute to the unified field of consciousness.

There are several examples of unified energy that have occurred on the planet. For example, when humanity took its first step on the Moon, Earth's energy was close to a unified energy field. This event raised the spiritual light quotient of the noosphere. The noosphere also has a spiritual light quotient. The spiritual light quotient is the percentage of light that one is able to hold both in thought and in physical reality. When you are at 90 percent spiritual light quotient, you are going to be able to achieve a great spiritual vibration. You will be able to integrate higher spiritual energy, understand higher spiritual thinking, meditate at a deeper level, have greater psychic gifts (such as thought projection), and be more empathic.

So there are many different abilities that increase when your spiritual light quotient increases. That's the way it is with the noosphere and unified consciousness. When the spiritual light quotient of the noosphere increases, humanity will feel a great sense of peace and harmony.

Another time when there was a great, unified consciousness was September 11, 2001. This was a very tragic and unfortunate event resulting in difficult consequences for the planet to integrate. After the event, people joined together in a sense of community for a brief period. Of course, it then disintegrated into war and conflict, which was part of the aim of the people creating that horrible event. When the world is united in consciousness, it can't be defeated. When the planet breaks into disunity and individual conflict, there is great danger to the whole planet.

There was another instance of unified consciousness after Princess Diana's death. Part of this was because she represented a great angelic presence and carried a great angelic light on this planet. Many people saw this light and her beauty, and they saw her intentions for healing. Her death and funeral brought in a unified consciousness.

Interestingly, sometimes unified consciousness occurs during sporting events, which is rather fascinating. The problem with these events is that they do not necessarily bring people to a higher spiritual light quotient. During Diana's funeral, people felt great love, great energy, and a great connection with the angelic world.

Conversely, while gathered in a sporting event, there is no attempt or intention to connect with spirit. Nonetheless, it is an example of the possibility of attaining unified consciousness through a large number of people focused on the same thing. One of the great tasks of the Group of Forty is to create an event or an activity that would bring unified consciousness to the planet. There are many benefits to this idea. I think the concept of the movie *The Blue Jewel*[2] is a beautiful attempt to bring in a unified consciousness energy field to the planet, and it has had a tremendous effect already on many people.

We are working to help increase the power of the message. But you as lightworkers, as members of the Group of Forty, know that we have always said that 40 groups of 40 (1,600 people) will have a special power. Part of that special power is to create a unified energy field on the planet.

The Unified Energy Field

How do you create the unified energy field, and what would that do? The unified energy field would have direct input into Earth's feedback loop system and the noosphere. The input would raise the spiritual light quotient of the noosphere, which would enable higher spiritual events to manifest — unity, peace, and harmony. Earth would be able to manifest more fifth-dimensional energy.

A strong group of starseeds could create an event equivalent to some of the events and energy that I described. I know that sounds amazing, but that is what we have been working on. There is a great potential for you to do this, and I know you are up to this task. The energy is available, and you have the desire to create such an event.

This unified energy field will be a healing force. Imagine the healing potential when the world came together in the other events I talked about, and then imagine a new spiritual event is created now. We need to move to the events that are created in spiritual unity. We do not want to wait until there is a catastrophe or negative planetary event. But with the energies and

2. The Blue Jewel (2013). Starseed Productions, Oliver Hauck. Multiple-award-winning documentary film about planetary healing. Ninety-six-minute DVD available from Light Technology Publishing.

tools we have given you, you can create an event that could lead to a higher unified consciousness, therefore creating a healing light far greater than has ever come to this planet!

I am Juliano. Good day.

• • •

Greetings, I am Jesus. Our teachings are based on the great systems of religious mystical thought that all seekers of light who move to higher consciousness experience, because when you move to higher consciousness, you become aware of the unified energy field. The unified energy field is part of galactic spirituality and exists everywhere in the universe — in all planets and all galaxies and all life forms. It is an actual spiritual energy field, smaller than the subatomic, and when you move to higher consciousness, you connect with it.

You feel the most wonderful joy and ecstasy because of the unified energy field. All of the religions, in their highest consciousness and highest form, have a path that leads you directly to this. This is one of the most important parts of the sacred triangle because when you see the different practices of the mystical light in the White Brotherhood-Sisterhood, you understand that they all lead to this higher mystical energy. When you experience the unified energy field, it is comparable to a feeling of enlightenment that creates harmony and peace within you.

The unified energy field is contained in the sacred, mystical light of the religions on the planet, an important part of the sacred triangle. The unified energy field is available on Earth, and I want you to unite that with the galactic energies because it runs through all planets, star systems, and galaxies. When people experience the unified energy field, they stop fighting. They stop being polarized. They feel the energy of the brotherhood and sisterhood, and they feel that we are all family. There's no more need to fight, no more need for wars.

When you experience the unified energy field, you experience harmony and peace so healing that you begin to experience sacredness on Earth. One mission for the teachings of the sacred triangle is to bring the awareness of the unified energy field and make it part of the whole healing system for Earth. There will be no need for religions to hate each other or for people to destroy Earth because they will become aware of the oneness and great sacredness of life here.

This sacred unified energy field is available on the third dimension, and when you experience that, it is so beautiful and so harmonious that you will have no need to strive, no need to move upward, because you will be where you are meant to be. This is what is meant by "I Am That I Am." *I am* in this unified energy field, no matter what dimension I am on. It doesn't matter. Yes, you have moved to the fifth dimension and become aware that the unified energy field is attainable and can be experienced on Earth now. All of the planets are connected spiritually and etherically in this beautiful, unified, spiritual light energy field.

I am Jesus.

Chapter 9

Unified Field Theory and Planetary Healing

Juliano, the Arcturians, and Chief White Eagle

Greetings, I am Juliano. We are the Arcturians. Let's compare the material world to the spiritual world. Specifically, what is the relationship between the spiritual world and the material world? How does spiritual energy affect the material world? To prove the unified field theory, it must be shown that there is a relationship between the spiritual and the material world. It must be shown that by using the proper principles of spirituality, you can modify, improve, and expand the material world.

You are struggling for answers to resolve this material mess on Earth. How is it that spirituality can heal Earth? What rules and laws of spirituality can be applied to ensure that Earth is healed and brought into a balance? These are all beautiful and complicated questions. I am sure that I cannot completely answer them here; however, we will begin to explore some possibilities so that you will have greater clarity personally as well as in your work as planetary healers.

It All Begins with a Thought

The role of spirituality is a continual point of discussion in our healing work with Earth beings. The questions on a personal level are: "How can I use spiritual energies and laws to improve my mood, my physical health, and my overall well-being? How can I use spiritual energies to learn my karmic lessons, and ultimately, how can I use spiritual energy to complement and accelerate my ascension?"

The material world vibrates at a slower frequency compared to the higher realms. There are advantages and disadvantages to this vibrational slowness. The advantage is quite simple: The thoughts that you have on the third dimension do not manifest immediately. A very humorous case in point is wealth. If you say a thousand times a day, "I will receive a million dollars," and you concentrate on that thought over and over again, perhaps you would expect to eventually receive a million dollars. However, there are intervening variables (also, if it were that easy to become rich, then many people would be millionaires by now). Not everyone who thinks this is actually able to manifest wealth, and there are other variables to consider besides continually repeating one thought or affirmation.

The situation regarding slower vibrations on the third dimension has to do with negative thoughts. I know that you all have negative thoughts at times. Maybe you do not want to admit them. When you look at yourself honestly, you might also confess that you have negative thoughts about yourself and about the outcome of your life or of certain situations. For example, you might think something bad is going to happen. You might think you are going to lose your money. However, you may have noticed that not all of the negative thoughts that you have actually happen. In fact, I would be willing to bet that many of the negative thoughts you have do not occur. So while it is true that negative thinking is a hindrance and can set up the possibility of negative events, negative thinking by itself will not always create negative things.

This is one of the contradictory laws of vibrational slowness on the third dimension. Whatever you think does not manifest immediately. However, there is an extremely relevant corollary to this that states as you go into higher frequency and into higher vibrations, your thinking is also in an accelerated state. Therefore, what you think can manifest more quickly on the higher realms. That is to say, when your vibrational energy field is faster and higher, there is an increased likelihood your thoughts will manifest.

Acceleration of manifestation on the third dimension is demonstrated when you go to high-energy places. One of our favorite examples is Sedona, Arizona. The ladder of ascension is placed at Bell Rock there. It has a high vibrational frequency, and many times when people are in the frequency of that area, their thinking becomes accelerated, and their thoughts and energies can manifest. Another example might be Lourdes, France, which has the reputation for great healing energy. There is a unified healing energy field there that helps people heal more quickly.

This powerful energy field becomes rooted in a physical location. It enhances the existing energy field. I sometimes refer to this as a thought energy field. When you enter that energy field, your personal energy field is affected. The thoughts and energies of that unified field, or thought field force, increase the vibrational energy of your thoughts. This improves the likelihood that your thoughts will manifest.

On the higher dimensions, your thoughts are not as slow as they are on the third dimension. On the fifth dimension, when you think something, it immediately occurs. You might say, well, that's wonderful, but you have to be prepared. You have to also be in what I call a purified ego state to be in a situation whereby what you think immediately occurs. From that standpoint, you can see that the third dimension can be viewed as preparation, or a training ground, for the higher realms. This means that you train yourself to be able to think in a certain vibrational frequency, taking into consideration the many different variables that exist.

Once you understand these rules and laws, you become closer to being able to create your reality. Once you understand the differences of the subatomic world and the laws that govern it, you understand the laws of creation. The laws of creation in the material world began on the subatomic level. Therefore, when you are able to understand and master those worlds and laws, you are also able to become involved in forces and energy fields that are linked directly to creation.

Spiritual Intervention

To go into a higher vibration and a higher type of thinking, you should have a purified ego. Why? Because if you master these rules and do not have a purified ego, then you are subject to misusing the energy. You have seen examples of how energy and power can be misused; therefore, the secrets for creation must always be protected. For example, in the ancient Israeli temple, before the destruction of the second temple in Jerusalem, there was a hidden knowledge about creation. That hidden knowledge had to do with the name Adonai. A special pronunciation of that name could be used for creating in the third dimension, and only one high priest knew it. Only that priest was allowed to speak the name and only while he was alone in a sacred chamber once a year.

Humans have many examples of protecting this type of knowledge and energy. The ancient people who used Stonehenge spoke the sacred name of the Creator at the equinoxes. They also understood that the equinoxes are times of special energy when the thought vibrational fields increase. Therefore, at those times, your thoughts have a higher likelihood of manifesting.

It is clear that the ancient Israelites were very particular about who would have the knowledge to speak the vibration of the name of creation. The reason is that if you had the correct pronunciation of the name, then you could create reality. This could be a wonderful experience, but it also could be a dangerous and destructive experience if that knowledge and energy were given to someone who did not have a purified ego.

I think there are many misconceptions about the purified ego. First of all, the ego is not bad. The goal is not to eliminate the ego. The goal is to put the ego in balance with the rest of the self. It is natural that the ego desires personal gain. There is absolutely nothing wrong with that. However, there is a great misconception in the spiritual world today, and even among some of the members of spiritual organizations, that personal gain is bad. This is not the case. What could be bad is whether the personal gain is out of balance.

The ego needs some personal gain to function. You need some personal gain, or you would not have any income to live on. You need some personal gain to have some satisfaction. The truth is that material satisfaction has a place in this world. We never advocate poverty or denial of material comforts.

The only time we recommend denial is if there is some specific balance that you need to create to counteract a previous energy that was out of balance. For example, say you were extremely rich and misusing money and material goods, and that began to interfere with your spiritual nature. You might find it helpful to go into isolation and to deny basic materialism to bring yourself back into balance. The ability to quickly affect reality has become a central factor in planetary healing. Planetary healing is needed now because we are observing a great and unfortunate — even tragic — planet that is out of balance.

There are many variables related to this, but for the purposes of planetary healing, we can say that the laws of creation need to be accelerated for planetary work. You need to be able to influence events and create circumstances and energies that will immediately create healing and balance on this planet. Truly, there is a spiritual solution to the out-of-balance, materialistic cyclone of out-of-control events dominating this planet. A cyclone is an event that has several factors, including the inability to be stopped when it is out of control. Everyone is at the mercy of this event. Therefore, the spiritual intervention I speak of becomes more valuable and necessary.

You as planetary healers are working to set the groundwork for the creation of a new reality on Earth. You are setting the groundwork for manifestation of a new Earth balance through spirituality. You are coming closer to this sacred, ancient — but universal — galactic secret. The secret is how to create and modify reality through spirituality.

The Secret of Creation

The Galactic Council knew that Earth and humanity were getting closer to the secret of creation. The events leading to the development of the nuclear bomb indicated that humanity had reached the point of understanding the subatomic world and how that world is related to the creation of reality. The development of higher spirituality needs to occur with such scientific developments. From our observations on other planets, there occurs simultaneously an increase in spirituality and the spiritual principles to govern how to manifest reality.

The question has always been this: Will the forces of spirituality keep up with the physical secrets being discovered by scientists? This is a continual theme throughout the Milky Way galaxy. As you know, this drama played out in Atlantis. It also played out in the Egyptian civilization, which at its height achieved advanced spiritual principles. You see, when you are able to master the creation of physicality, this power of sacred energy and raising vibrations is equal to the physical principles found in quantum mechanics and the subatomic world.

The power of those who create reality with thought and spirituality can be compared to the science involved in quantum and subatomic energy particles. Both lead to the secret of creation and the secret of the universe. You are close to the same type of principles. Part of our work is based on the increase of vibrational energies through the work of the etheric crystals, the planetary cities of light, the Arcturian temples, the ladders of ascension, and of course the powerful work with the Galactic Kachina.[1] All of these are examples of bringing the energy of manifestation through spirituality into your consciousness.

What is most amazing is that you are now working toward the highest level of manifesting a reality on a planet. That ability is of great merit, and it's something that the Galactic Council wants this planet to achieve. But it is a complex and focused path. You are now witnessing the difficulty of a planet that is greatly out of balance. You are even personally experiencing being out of balance. It is difficult to be in balance when much of the social, economic, political, and environmental energies are out of balance. You are doing a great job in learning to cope with imbalances and to still find a way and the energy to be in balance.

There is a natural tendency for organisms — also galaxies and solar systems — to generate a homeostatic balance. Systems function more smoothly and become optimized when they are in balance. The unified field theory tries to explain the subatomic and material world and examines the relationship between spirituality and the material world. One of the keys in learning to control and operate both of these worlds is in the concept of systems balancing. Planetary systems' balancing is an Arcturian concept in which we have applied an overall thought field to an entire planetary system. When communicating with the feedback loop system, for example, the key is to take the entire system into consideration.

The perspective of the Blue Jewel from outer space has become an important element in understanding how to use spirituality and thought fields to

---

1   The intermediary between the Central Sun and this planet.

heal Earth, which relates to the energy work we do with the etheric crystals. We wish to increase the energy vibration of the entire planet as a system. Therefore, when we work with the entire system, we can make greater and more effective interventions in the feedback loop system.

A spiritual intervention includes downloading balance into the thought field of the planet, which is directly connected to the feedback loop system. There is something positive about this approach. If you are in a negative space, you might think the situation on Earth is hopeless. You might think there is no solution to the Fukushima radiation problem or there is no solution to the oceans dying or there is no possibility of obtaining peace on Earth.

Counterbalance

Earth is a living spirit. Earth is an evolving planet that has gone through other periods of imbalances. In fact, there have been periods of explosions, collisions with asteroids, great volcanic eruptions, and planetary warming worse than what you are experiencing now. There have been ice ages. Being out of balance is not new to this planet, and Earth has survived. However, humankind at this level of existence and materialistic dependency on Earth may not survive if the imbalances continue.

Earth has a complex planetary history related to other planets in the galaxy. The Galactic Kachina says there are other planets that have gone through these types of imbalances that have benefitted from galactic interventions as well as interventions from the masters and teachers. In fact, interventions from masters and teachers, the Arcturians, and other extraterrestrial, higher-dimensional beings are now helping to counterbalance the out-of-control energies on Earth.

You also are involved in counterbalance. When a planet is out of balance, especially when it is being dominated by nonspiritual energies, it becomes more important that starseeds like you begin to counterbalance that with spiritual interventions of biorelativity and other healing thought-field energies. This healing can occur on a deep energy level, in particular when the healing interacts with and relates to the noosphere, which is similar to the human subconscious. A major problem on this planet now is directly related to the out-of-balance collective subconscious energies. The subconscious energies of humanity are included in the concept of the collective unconscious, which is a term that describes the thought field and the combination of all the subconscious energy of humanity that have ever existed.

Earth and humanity are young. In particular, humanity as a species is young. So the subconscious of humanity contains many immature variables. You are experiencing some of these in this lifetime. Fear, contraction, violence, paranoia, and separation are examples of the negative subconscious energy fields most prevalent in humanity. The collective unconscious and the collective subconscious contain all of this energy. Therefore, you are subject to its rules and laws, but you can also counterbalance it. You can contribute to a different balance. You have human thoughts that go into the noosphere, and you are affected by this. It is difficult to totally isolate yourself from what is going on, especially when there are such large planetary events occurring. I continue to go back to the event known as 9/11. It was a great a tragedy.

There is a global factor in the 9/11 event that illustrates the collective subconscious and the noosphere. The immediate post-9/11 reaction demonstrated the energetic focus of a vast majority of the planet on one event. It was a time when a fantastic intervention could have occurred on the planet because the planet had achieved unity and solidarity. Unfortunately, the results of that event led to more violence and a period of greater upheaval and wars. Decisions that were made afterward led to an increase in violence and polarization.

At the same time, you might have experienced unity and harmony in the noosphere on 9/11. It is exactly this type of unity energy that can greatly counterbalance the out-of-balance energy. A new balance can be placed in the noosphere by a dramatic event that causes unity. But does it have to be such a negative event? Why is this planet's culture set up that only negative events can bring such a focus?

Adjustments Can Always Be Made

When looking at the history of spirituality on this planet, you come across a concept called the apocalypse. The apocalypse and apocalyptic thinking include people who believe that evil forces will cause end-time events on the planet. During an end-time event, there is an opportunity for a divine intervention. Sometimes this intervention is called the Messianic energy, or the Messiah.

Yes, an end-time event would bring about a shift in consciousness. This end-time event would bring a focus of subconscious and conscious energy immediately. It would allow the possibility of the creation of a new reality. You see, the entry of the Messiah is actually based on the creation of energy and the creation of a thought field.

Why are spiritually minded people focused on the end-time events as an indicator of the coming of messianic light? Messianic light is the downloading of fifth-dimensional light. The transcendence energy over the third dimension will bring forth the new laws of reality. Remember, as you get closer to understanding the relationship between spirituality and materialism, you get closer to understanding the creation of reality.

The creation of reality is the highest ability in existence. It relates to the end-time events in current theoretical and religious spiritual thinking. End-time event scenarios continually appear. You saw reference to such events in the years 2000 and 2012, and I am sure that there will be other scenarios in 2015 and 2016.

The fact is that Earth has great flexibility in rebalancing to create a new homeostasis. This is also true of you. You can survive with many imbalances, which is an interesting paradox. You can readjust your homeostatic balance. One example is cancer. In the early 1990s, if you had cancer, you were likely going to die. Now there are more and more people surviving cancer. Many chemicals and medicines have been developed, and there has been a change in the thought field related to this disease. People have come to the realization that they can live with cancer. The fear and the thought field that go along with cancer have shifted: You are flexible. Your immune system is flexible.

Part of the new thinking and the new balance is learning to adjust your homeostasis and learning to communicate with your subconscious. People are saying, "I can live with this. I can rebalance this so that I can survive." This is similar to your planetary issues. The planetary issues are more complex, but consider that part of planetary healing should include direct communications with Earth. One of these direct communications you can say is, "Mother Earth, you can rebalance yourself to accept this new homeostasis."

Realistically, concerning everything that is occurring, you have to agree that Earth is amazing. I don't think it is unreasonable to compliment Earth: "Mother Earth, it is wonderful that you have been able to maintain this balance. Frankly, we didn't think you could do it, but you did!" This is a deep communication to Mother Earth.

Help from Higher Places

The imbalances that are now on Earth are dangerous. Other planets have not even been able to survive such extreme imbalances. Earth's survival is an indication of the resolution of the planetary healers and starseeds and the other great spiritual leaders and teachers on this planet. The work of downloading higher light and communicating through the noosphere is helping Earth. Biorelativity is creating new healing light, and the ring of ascension and the planetary cities of light are also helping. The numerous other works of native peoples and countless other spiritually minded people all contribute positive healing energy to Earth.

A big contribution toward planetary healing is coming from the masters and teachers. "So, Mother Earth, you too can adapt, and you are helping to create this. We send into your thought field, your noosphere, the thought that this is a new balance that you can adjust to."

I will let Chief White Eagle finish this lecture. I am Juliano.

●   ●   ●

[Chants] "Hey ya ho ya hey. Hey ya ho. Mother Earth, we compliment your abilities as a planet to rebalance yourself and to keep this biosphere in harmony and intact. It is truly a great miracle to observe you as a planet holding together this great task of maintaining the biosphere for humanity, even in the face of all of the destructions and imbalances. We (your lightworkers, your starseeds, your planetary healers) compliment your fantastic abilities. And we ask that, as your inhabitants, we be granted the ability to increase and expand our abilities to help you come into balance, to help you to adapt to this situation.

"We admire your flexibility, Mother Earth. You are our guiding teacher, our guiding light, in how to remain in balance. We are expanding just as you are. We are strong, and we are proud warriors to be able to download a new energy of balance into your subconscious and ours."

All my words are sacred. All my relations. Ho!

Chapter 10

Biorelativity and the Fabric of the Universe

Juliano and the Arcturians

Greetings, I am Juliano. We are the Arcturians. There are parallels between the origins and the contents of the universe as expressed in modern physics. There are parallels between the world described in classic physics and quantum physics that relate to concepts in spirituality. There are many interesting concepts in spirituality known as quantum healing, quantum energy, and quantum light.

What is the composition of the universe? To understand the spiritual dimension, you must observe the contents of the universe. Amazingly, modern physicists are only able to observe approximately 4 percent of the universe or the particles and elements of the universe. That means that 96 percent of the universe is now considered dark energy and dark matter. That is to say, modern scientists know that a substance exists that influences the universe and the actions of everything — the action of the planets, the solar systems, the galaxy, and the entire universe. Yet 96 percent of all that exists is made up of an unknown substance considered to be either dark energy or dark matter. This dark energy and dark matter affect everything — all the systems of the universe.

Spiritual Energy Fields

The fabric of the third dimension participates in the space-time dimension. In the third dimension, you exist in relationships with where you are, the space around you, and how you exist in time, or "when" you are at a certain point. Timing is so important in the third dimension. When you cross a street with a red light to your favor, you are safe; yet one minute later, you could be run over by an automobile.

There are aspects of the third dimension that consist of beings like you. You exist in a fabric of space and time that is inhabited by conscious beings. You live in a fabric of space and time in which you are conscious of your existence, and you are becoming conscious of other aspects, such as dimensions. However, your existence in this space and time is composed of several different functions and energy fields.

Some of these energy fields are like dark matter. That is, you know that they exist, but nobody can prove it — or nobody can observe it. Rather, nobody can objectively prove its existence. Dark matter exists and can influence the universe. In the same way, spiritual energy fields exist. Like dark matter, you might not be able to directly observe them, but you can observe and record their effects on you. These fields exist not only in you but also in all the living aspects of the planet (in various degrees). More important, they also exist in Gaia.

The spiritual energy field began the universe. There was a spiritual intervention, and something began from nothing. You are here because of a spiritual intervention. You, from a spiritual point of view, incarnated onto this planet. You, from a spiritual point of view, have a spiritual energy field. This spiritual energy field is not observable. You might sense your spiritual energy. You might feel it. You might relate to it. But there is, at this point in human development on Earth, no measurable or observable way of proving that spirit exists. Yet you know spirit exists. It is the same as dark matter and dark energy. You can observe the dark energy forces affecting everything, yet we cannot see it. You cannot directly observe it in a coherent way. But you know that it exists because it affects matter.

You know that your spirit exists because it affects you and others. You also know that the spirit of this planet exists. The spiritual energy field exists, and it affects everything. It is composed of spiritual particles that are able to interact with your physical particles. This is a key principle that must be grasped for healing the planet, such as through the exercises of biorelativity.

Omega Light Upgrade

Spirituality includes the realm of psychic abilities. Psychic abilities include aspects of telepathy, teleportation, telekinesis, prophecy, and ultimately the projection of healing energy. The highest level of healing comes with the connection and projection of spiritual light, spiritual energy, and spiritual unity. When two spirits unite, a new quantum light and energy emerge.

Spiritual energy from the universe is coming to Earth. This spiritual energy is not well described, and it is not well formulated in the mind of the inhabitants of Earth. This spiritual dimension, the third dimension, is filled with a unique life-force energy, or chi. You will find some descriptions of it in Chinese writings. It is also called prana or qi. Each one of these terms describes a life-force energy that allows this world and this dimension to exist. It would be rare for other planets to have chi.

Planet Earth has an accumulation of life-force energy and spiritual energy that has created what we call the biosphere. The biosphere is a force field of energy around the planet. It is like an aura. It is an energy field that has many features similar to a person's aura. For example, Earth's aura contains the life-force energy field. It contains meridians. It contains different paths of force fields coming from many different sources. These sources are not yet known to humankind. We have been using one such light source — quantum light. It is used for quantum healing. We call it omega light, which is a form of quantum light.

Omega light is a spiritual energy force part of the divine life-force energy that flows through the universe. Omega light has a special power and special characteristics because it comes from a higher source. It has tremendous healing abilities complementary to the biosphere and to all beings who live in the biosphere.

The omega light has a great healing quality because it can adjust to the resonance of the biosphere. The biosphere radiates at a special frequency, and the omega light knows how to be in resonance with that biosphere. All who receive the omega light get a boost of energy into their systems. When people receive the omega light, they feel more whole, more unified, and more in touch with the spiritual light and energy that exists at the highest level.

The third dimension is at a lower vibration than the fifth dimension, and the third dimension has polarized, dense aspects. Yet the third dimension is able to vibrate and resonate at very high frequencies. It can receive omega light. Now the channel will sing, and you will receive an upgrade from this wonderful light. [Sings] "Omega light." Know that you are rebalancing yourself on the third dimension so that you are in resonance with the biosphere and the spiritual light forces of the universe. [Sings] "Omega light." [Pause.]

Omega light is one aspect of the spiritual-light force field that exists in the universe. The omega light is also not visible in the normal human spectrum of vision. It is not even perceivable by normal human measurement devices. Yet just like dark matter or dark energy, this aspect of the spiritual light force of the universe can have a tremendous healing effect.

One of the roles of the starseed is to work with spiritual energy and light. Omega light can positively affect and shape the planet. That is to say, the lightworkers must implement change in the planet based on spiritual light and spiritual energy. Lightworkers can access and bring down higher vibrations that exist in the universe.

The Spiritual Energy Helps Earth

You have a mission to be here to show that the spiritual energy field can become a dominating force; it can influence and shape the planet. There are many variations of spiritual energy and light. For example, in modern astrology, there are planets that move through different houses (a division in an astrological chart). When a certain planet moves into a house, powerful energies can be exerted on the person's life.

In dealing with Earth energies at this time, we are especially interested in the outer planets, which include Saturn, Uranus, and Neptune. These planets, especially Uranus and Neptune, represent energies of a spiritual and galactic nature coming from a universal life and light source. The planets themselves do not cause this spiritual light energy to enter Earth, but their position represents a map of how energy fields are changing in the galaxy and coming into your solar system.

On Earth now there is a powerful energy of awareness of global change, galactic change, and galactic awareness. This type of energy is composed of a spiritual energy force now directed toward this planet. Most powerful are the light and energy coming from the Central Sun. Please do not confuse this with the concept of the central point of your galaxy, which is a black hole. The Central Sun is a spiritual point at the center of the galaxy. It emits third-dimensional light directly to this planet. The Central Sun's position in relation to Earth and Earth's to the Central Sun is indicative of the type of spiritual energy coming to this planet in a universal way.

One has to take a galactic perspective of how this planet operates and how planets in the galaxy develop. In the stages of planetary development, different types of crises emerge. At a certain point, an energy shift comes to a planet that creates a global consciousness shift that involves a spiritual energy. Global consciousness is a spiritual light. How will this spiritual energy and light be interpreted by humanity? How will it be downloaded? How will people use the energy and light? Also, who can interpret this energy and light? Who can feel it? Who can know what to do with it?

Implementing this new consciousness becomes the mission of groups of lightworkers like you and like the Group of Forty. The lightworkers' mission becomes to understand and interpret what this spiritual light is about and how to implement this energy so that it will be used to heal and rebalance Earth.

You have already gone through several different stages of implementation. For example, the Group of Forty is now going through the stages of working with the planetary cities of light. The Group of Forty has gone through the stages of downloading twelve etheric crystals and five ladders of ascension.

They have also downloaded and gone through the stage of the ring of ascension. There is also the work of the subcrystals and the work of other fantastic meditations with the Arcturian temples. All work to establish a new spiritual healing energy field for Earth.

The core aspect of this work is the emanation of a new spiritual light field that will permeate this planet. Astronomers cannot prove or observe dark energy and dark matter, but they know it is out there because it affects everything. It affects the gravitational fields of other stars. It affects the gravitational field of the whole galaxy, and it might even be responsible for the expansion and recession of the galaxies. The spiritual world is also invisible. The spiritual field you emanate goes out into the ethers and into Earth's aura; therefore, even though it cannot be seen, it has a powerful effect.

The Emanation of Healing Light

Spiritual light and spiritual energy have unique properties. In the emotional body, emotions are observable in the color and density of the aura. The physical body is, of course, observable. Even the mental body can be measured in terms of observable electromagnetic activity in the brain. Yet the mental body has aspects of spiritual energy because the source of the mind is connected to many aspects of the spirit world. The mind contains points of access to the universal unconscious. The mental body, or mind, has access to the collective unconscious and even participates in the galactic unconscious.

There are many different energy fields that the mental body participates in continually. Of course, you even have the akashic records, which contain the histories of everyone's actions and thoughts. The akashic records are related to the energy fields of both mental and spiritual energy.

Mental energy, which contains spiritual thoughts and the spiritual body, cannot be observed and measured. Yet these aspects have the potential for a powerful impact on the third dimension. That is why I am helping you move to a more powerful position using your spiritual energy field in biorelativity exercises. This spiritual energy field can have a powerful influence on upcoming Earth events. Spiritual energy can be powerful enough to influence the outcome of Earth in its current crisis. It can be powerful enough to influence and counterbalance upheavals and disruptions known as earth changes.

The core concept in biorelativity is to connect Earth to a stronger spiritual energy. The core aspect of spiritual energy in biorelativity is in the idea called "emanation of healing light." First, you seek to create a powerful energy field. Everything on the planet, in this dimension, and in the universe has a wave. Everything has a vibrational field and in fact also has an energy field. When things are congested or blocked or when the planet is sick, then the vibration of the life-force energy field becomes distorted and misaligned. You then need to work in biorelativity to shift and unblock that energy vibration.

In biorelativity, one of the most powerful things you do is emanate a healing light. You emanate a vibrational frequency of spirituality, directing it to the spirit of Earth. We call this aspect of biorelativity emanation because the light emanates from you. The emanation comes from the lightworkers and the groups doing the exercise.

Create a Spiritual Energy Field

How much force, how much power, or how much light is needed to shift a planet? Doing planetary healing work is hard, and doing planetary healing work in the third dimension is extremely challenging. Doing biorelativity work is complicated. Doing planetary city-of-light work is challenging. The whole idea of uniting groups of Arcturian starseeds like you to focus at one time on a healing technique is difficult. If it were easy, then it would have been done before and this planet would have been brought into balance immediately.

There are many challenges, and there is a certain core of emanation that you want to achieve to send this type of healing vibration. People have asked me, "Where do you send this light? Where do you send this vibration? Where do you emanate the healing light when you are doing the planetary healing and biorelativity? Where do you direct the energy? Is there a spiritual essence or spiritual center in Earth?" My answer is simple. Earth has an aura.

Earth has an electromagnetic energy field that can be compared to the human aura. When you are personally brought into harmony, you are filled with light and energy. Light and energy does not necessarily go to just one spot within your aura. You have a heart and a mind as well as a third eye. But when we send you healing, we send the healing energy to your entire energy field. Then if there are specific areas we want to work with, we will emanate the light and energy directly to those spots.

When you do biorelativity, you can do healing energy work both ways. You can begin by emanating light to the aura of Earth, and after that is achieved, you go to the specific place you want to heal. Remember, you are emanating a spiritual light, a spiritual energy, to Earth, and you can direct that light and energy to Earth's aura.

We have also helped develop the ring of ascension. It is difficult to visualize the energy field of the whole planet. You can affirm, "Yes, I can see Earth's energy field." We work with images of Earth; we send healing light to the planet. But remember, Earth is rotating, so when you see a picture of Earth, you only see one side. It is difficult to visualize the whole multidimensional Earth.

Therefore, when doing biorelativity work, we suggest that you send the light to the ring of ascension first. The ring of ascension is the halo around the entire planet. It encircles the whole holographic image of Earth. You can emanate the light into the ring of ascension. [Tones] "Oooohhhh." Because we are connected spiritually in a unified way, the thoughts we emanate are going to be more powerful when they are joined in a group.

Thought power is related to spiritual energy. You project a thought and connect it with spiritual light. You use the principles of spiritual techniques to influence Earth's aura so that it is filled with a bio-light frequency that allows it to experience planetary health and planetary balance.

Visualize the halo around Earth known as the ring of ascension, and emanate waves of light from your aura. These waves of light come from your third eye and from your mind. They just emanate from your entire aura. Visualize that you have your aura in the beautiful configuration of the cosmic egg, and it is filled with omega light because we have done this omega light exercise. You are going to be able to emanate circles of light like a force field coming from your aura.

This spiritual light will go up into the ring of ascension, and then that ring of ascension will collect it. This will help the whole planet to be filled with the energy of the light you are vibrating and Earth's aura can be filled. Begin to do this now.

The light that you are emanating is of the highest spiritual frequency. It is going into Earth's energy field and Earth's aura. It is going into the ring of ascension. This spiritual light is a light of harmony and unity.

From the perspective of modern astrology, when Saturn, Neptune, and Uranus enter certain positions, they correspond with global changes. For example, when these planets move into different positions, there might be corresponding changes in society. There could be changes in core values. There could be changes in how governments function. There could even be social upheavals. The movements of the outer planets seem to correspond to energy shifts in the universe that enter this solar system.

You have seen an effect known as the Arab Spring.[1] You have seen great social upheavals of consciousness on this planet. There are other aspects of dramatic change coming. These aspects of change are based on a new energy that basically declares things cannot continue as usual on the planet. The biosphere cannot continue to exist if everything is going in this current direction.

There must and will be a change in how Earth and humankind interact. This change can be dramatic. Some of you know that this phenomenon is also called earth changes. Please understand that Earth changes also include the

---

1 Arab Spring was a wave of revolutionary demonstrations, riots, and civil wars in the Arab world that began on December 18, 2010, in Tunisia with the Tunisian Revolution (http://en.wikipedia.org/wiki/Arab_Spring).

functioning of humans within society. People have often thought that Earth changes only included volcanic eruptions, hurricanes, and other aspects of global warming. Actually, Earth change also includes humanity and its actions toward the planet. Humanity is part of this planet. There could be upheavals on both the physical Earth and people in society.

In biorelativity, we take it to the next level and ask this: How do we transfer this spiritual light and energy into some type of action that creates a change? Clearly, things have to be different. People have to relate to the planet differently. That means that they must use a different approach. Humanity's behavior has to change. There has to be a limit to the amount of environmental destruction now occurring, such as a decrease in carbon emissions, ocean pollution, and marine life death.

Spiritual energy can be influential in causing change. Spiritual energy on Earth has to be demonstrated somehow. There are cases in history in which people have aligned with spiritual energy. Biorelativity is a spiritual force that can lead to some type of positive change that can lead to even a forceful action for positive planetary shifts.

What is the nature of this type of planetary action? That needs to be determined by you. It is the mission of the Group of Forty and all lightworkers to make a shift so that a certain type of action can be implemented. For example, one of the actions in the planetary cities-of-light work is to do activations in which people put crystals around the perimeter of a city and visualize a powerful electromagnetic energy field surrounding it. This energy field can even be quantum light or omega light. This will have a positive effect on people and the city.

People on Earth might experience short-term memory. Once they experience this activation, they might not think that they have to do it continually. They might not understand what exactly a planetary city of light is. You might have to do teaching, more activation, or more exercises so that this gets into human consciousness. When this gets into human consciousness, they as a group might decide that they are going to protect their valuable city with spiritual light.

Biorelativity exercises can create a spiritual energy field with a thought vibration. This will create an emanation of light. The power of thoughts are increased through various methods, including implementing group unity, visualizing the ring of ascension, and using etheric crystals. This boost will make the thoughts more effective. Then the energy field of the planet can be filled with powerful healing thoughts.

Implement Biorelativity for Balance

Now you will probably ask, "Juliano, tell us what to do. What is the next step? What do I do now?" My answer is that you are on the third dimension experiencing this third-dimensional energy. We are not going to recommend a specific action now. We are aware of the principle of noninterference. Fifth-dimensional beings will not directly interfere with the third dimension. More importantly, each of you is now moved to follow your wisdom and to receive your guidance. You know what is possible. You know what you can do and how you can influence people. You know what you can write and speak. You know who you can talk to and how you can organize events.

By implementing biorelativity, you are doing something measureable on the third dimension. Such activities could include teaching. People on this planet are hungry for a paradigm that will heal this planet. You all feel the imbalances that exist in your auras. Each person on this planet has different ways of coping with this imbalance. Some people use drugs. Some people are becoming sick, and some are becoming despondent.

Living on a planet in such imbalance affects your electromagnetic energy field in a major way. Biorelativity can help you to become more balanced because you personally benefit from sending healing energy to Earth. This is also going to be helpful because you feel more energetic when you have a plan. This works on many different levels, even the smallest. For example, some of you are creating special corridors in your backyards. This is doing something positive to heal the planet — using the energy of biorelativity. Some of you are creating spiritual force fields around your property. This does something on a small level and also contributes to a healing force. Some of you are working on the planetary cities of light, which contributes healing on a larger level. Some of you might be more motivated to teach and to spread these ideas.

Another key concept in biorelativity is that this planet has an aura; it has an energy field affected by your thoughts. If Earth's energy field is distorted, blocked, or has holes in it, then the bio-life-force energy of the planet can leak away. The work of starseeds like you can bring down an input of omega light. Omega energy can help to fill up the gaps and holes in Earth so that the bio–force field is at least revitalized and replenished. A new frequency can be maintained. This Earth has conscious beings like you who can bring down special life-force energies.

Blessings, I am Juliano.

Chapter 11

The Noosphere and the Etheric Energy Field of Earth

Juliano, the Arcturians, and Chief White Eagle

Greetings, I am Juliano. We are the Arcturians. The noosphere is the mental energy field around Earth. It is part of the etheric energy field and exists in another dimension. The etheric energy field is, of course, also connected and anchored into the third dimension. It has quite a dramatic and important effect on the events manifesting now on Earth.

The etheric energy field also contains the collective unconscious. The term "collective unconscious" was in part developed by the Swiss psychiatrist Carl Jung. He used this term to describe the ancient Earth archetypes and symbols that are used by cultures around the globe. The work on archetypes has been continued by other psychologists as well as anthropologists, and now you are beginning to see interest in the galactic archetypes and the galactic collective unconscious.

Earth's interactions with extraterrestrials have occurred physically and also etherically. Of course, many of you know that there have been extra-terrestrial manifestations, for example, the Nephilim, who are referred to in the Hebrew Bible in Genesis as "the fallen ones," or "those who came from above." Our studies reveal that the Nephilim interacted with Earth's energy field and decided to incarnate on Earth. When you interact with a planet's etheric energy field, you can choose to manifest from that field onto the planet. This is exactly what the Nephilim did.

Once you incarnate on the planet, you realize that you become involved with its incarnational cycle. For this reason, the Arcturians chose not to incarnate on this planet. However, in some cases, it is possible to interact on the etheric energy field of a planet without manifesting on it.

The Power of Higher Thought Patterns

The human energy field has many similarities to a planetary energy field. For a moment, visualize your aura and your energy field. You might become aware of it and realize that it is vibrating. Your energy field has multiple layers. You have layers of spiritual energy, mental energy, physical energy, and emotional energy. You are multidimensional beings. Many of you struggle to understand what it means to be multidimensional. Being multidimensional includes interacting with the etheric energy fields. The planet has an aura just like the human aura, but the planetary aura is filled with vast energies from the collective history of the planet and all its beings. This includes all the animals and plants as well as numerous other sources of energy.

The biosphere, for example, is also related to the etheric energy field of the planet, which can be described as the aura of a planet. It is divided into etheric layers that are uniquely related to the existence of humans inhabiting the planet. In comparison, the aura of a planet like Mars is different from Earth's aura. The main difference is that there is a collective energy field of human thought and energy stored throughout history within Earth's aura. This means that the thoughts, energies, emotions, and other emanations from the human spirit fill Earth's aura. Earth's aura is similar to the akashic records, the collective library of all thoughts and events for all beings throughout the galaxies.

Earth's energy field consists of layers. One layer is Earth's mental energy, which includes the collective unconscious. The collective unconscious includes many transgenerational animalistic and cultural symbols. This means that they occur in multiple generations across many cultures.

Visualize Earth's energy field in layers as I have just described. We are coming to the point of the mental layers, which contains higher thought and a higher level of light energy. You can readily understand that a mental thought could be higher than, say, an emotional thought of fear or anger. Mental thoughts are usually reserved for more evolved beings like humanity.

There is a special layer of energy in the mental layer of Earth's aura called the noosphere. This layer of energy is related to higher energy and higher thoughts. The noosphere is directly related to the overall evolutionary process of the human species. It has a relationship with the collective unconscious as part of the thought energy field of Earth.

The noosphere contains a special section of thought patterns that are related to higher light and to humanity's higher evolution. Higher thought patterns directly influence the evolutionary process, relating to such concepts as the fifth-dimensional Earth, the just society, the planetary cities of light, and the etheric crystals.

The Arcturian Etheric Crystals

We have downloaded and placed twelve Arcturian etheric crystals through-out this planet. They are in strategic locations directly related to the work of the starseeds. The starseeds understand on a deeply intuitive level that the etheric crystals have a special power to influence Earth's higher evolution. In fact, the etheric crystals bring in fifth-dimensional energy to Earth on a continual basis.

There are twelve etheric crystals. Their names and locations are (1) Lago Puelo in Patagonia, Argentina; (2) Volcán Poas, near San José, Costa Rica; (3) Serra da Bocaína, near São Paulo, Brazil; (4) Mount Shasta, California; (5) Mount Fuji, Japan; (6) Copper Canyon, Mexico; (7) Lake Moraine, near Banff, Canada; (8) Bodensee, Germany; (9) Istanbul, Turkey; (10) Montser-rat in Spain; (11) Lake Taupo, New Zealand; and (12) the Blue Mountains (Grose Valley), near Sydney, Australia. We have downloaded these etheric crystals with the help of the starseeds. These crystals are in a configuration directly influencing the noosphere.

The twelve Arcturian etheric crystals are now part of the noosphere. The purpose of these etheric crystals includes creating and holding a thought energy field of higher evolution for humanity. The etheric crystals have a special ability to be transdimensional, which means they can interact with fifth-dimensional energies, energies that you on the third dimension cannot interact with alone.

The etheric crystals have the ability to receive the input, light, and even instructions from the fifth-dimensional guides, masters, and teachers. These etheric crystals are like highly developed computers that are able to hold fifth-dimensional programs that can eventually be manifested into a third-di-mensional reality.

We, the Arcturians, know about the importance of the relationship of the noosphere to higher manifestation. We know that what is occurring in the energy field or the aura of a planet like Earth directly affects what is man-ifested. But the aura — the etheric energy field — of Earth has low levels as well as high levels. This means that you must comprehend that all levels of Earth's aura affect what is being manifested now. There are programs of a lower vibration manifesting on Earth. You are seeing many of these lower-vibrational manifestations now.

One of the layers on Earth's aura has to do with lower beings. These lower beings have been called ghosts and discarnate spirits lost in the astral world. There are also other energies and spirits in the lower parts of Earth's aura gaining strength and power that are able to negatively influence Earth manifestation.

One way to change lower Earth manifestation is to work with Earth's etheric energy field. This includes purifying the lower astral world. To change the course of evolution of the planet, you must go to the noosphere layer. The higher energy of the etheric crystals helps to bring fifth-dimensional energy into Earth's etheric energy field.

When you are able to connect to the etheric crystals, you can send them thoughts of high evolutionary healing. Then those thoughts are placed into Earth's noosphere. The exercise of placing those thoughts into the noosphere through the etheric crystals is a high form of biorelativity. Biorelativity is focused on telepathically communicating with Earth. The etheric crystals can relate to the noosphere. Remember, you can personally relate your thoughts to the noosphere because it is part of Earth's energy field. The noosphere's higher thoughts will go directly to Earth's feedback loop system and to the core of Earth's spirit known as Gaia.

Planet Earth knows how to relate to her noosphere. In fact, the noosphere is a planetary energy field that relates to Earth's evolution. You as planetary healers are working to ascend this planet, bringing it to a higher level. There-fore, the etheric energy field within the noosphere will help to manifest a higher reality on Earth.

Connect the Arcturian Crystals to Earth's Noosphere

Crystals have special powers on Earth and in the etheric world. What are these powers? Crystals can hold thoughts as programs. All crystals have the ability to amplify thoughts. That means that the arcan power [an Arcturian term for measuring thought power] of each thought that goes into the crystal can be multiplied or increased, sometimes on quite a dramatic level. It can go up exponentially, depending on the strength of the crystal.

Crystals have the ability to be multidimensional, so they are able to expe-rience energy from different dimensions simultaneously. Crystals are also inherently healing. That is, they resonate and send out higher energy. Crys-tals are able to communicate with other crystals and other planetary systems.

All twelve etheric crystals have these abilities. Equally important, these etheric crystals are now embedded in Earth's noosphere. From the meditations that we have done, they are now part of a higher thought pattern. You have helped to instill these etheric crystals into Earth's noosphere. Go now to the etheric crystal that you feel closest to. For the purposes of this exercise, I will use the Mount Shasta crystal.

Now connect with your thoughts, your third eye, and the Mount Shasta crystal (or the crystal that is closest to you). The crystal in Mount Shasta is rising up from the top of that mountain. As you visualize this crystal, you can remotely connect

with it because it is in Earth's energy field. Through your training and your sensitivity, you are able to connect easily with etheric energy and with the crystal. The
etheric crystal is multidimensional because it connects from the fifth-dimension to
you on the third dimension, and it holds energy for the noosphere in Earth's aura.
You cannot see fifth-dimensional energy at this point, but the crystal is able to receive
that information and light.

I, Juliano, with the Arcturians, am now downloading a heightened level of
energy for higher evolution on Earth, and it is now going into the Mount Shasta
crystal and the other crystals. Think of higher mental evolution. What does that
mean? It means that there is going to be a release of higher thoughts and that omega
light will now be downloaded into these crystals.

[Tones] "Omega light. Omega light."

The crystals are filled with this higher-dimensional light. Now you can send your
thoughts into the crystal, and say, "Let these higher thoughts of evolution and omega
light permeate Earth's noosphere. This higher layer of mental energy is only for higher
evolutionary thought. Let the omega light and all higher evolutionary thoughts now
go into the etheric crystal to be placed into Earth's noosphere."

Let each of these twelve crystals expand its influence into Earth's noosphere.
Use your arcan power to bring a great divine light for transformation and evolution
from these etheric crystals directly into Earth's noosphere. I, Juliano, send down very
powerful energy now into each crystal, for we have a direct link, a direct binding of
light between the fifth dimension, the etheric crystals, you the starseeds, and Earth's
noosphere.

To the best of your ability, visualize all twelve etheric crystals in Earth's aura.
You can see auras. Many of you can do that. You know what energy waves look
like around an aura. These twelve etheric crystals exist in Earth's aura. Now they
are above you interacting with the fifth dimension, sending light into the noosphere.

Remember, the central aspect of humanity's evolution lies in the fifth dimension.
The key ingredient that will enable humanity to make the next evolutionary step is
its connection to the fifth dimension. The ability of thought projection needs to be
strengthened and expanded in the noosphere. Send that thought now into the crystal
that you are working with. Send the thought of humanity incorporating the fifth
dimension into its next evolutionary stage.

The codes of ascension are opened up in you. It means that higher emotions,
higher light, and higher thought patterns can be received. It means that the reality
of the veils can be removed so that people can see interdimensionally. The higher
guides and teachers can interact more easily with you. It also means that humanity
can resolve many of these dense Earth problems in a great new energy of healing and
beauty. Send this thought, "Humanity is evolving toward a fifth-dimensional state
of evolution. Repeat it: "Humanity is evolving toward a fifth-dimensional state of

*evolution." As you send this thought into the etheric crystal, know that the thought
is going directly into the noosphere.*

Now we will do some specific healing for balance and removal of all contaminations in the environment.

*Visualize a fifth-dimensional planet. What does a fifth-dimensional planet look
like? A fifth-dimensional planet is pollution free. It does not have radiation contamination or any type of garbage or waste. A fifth-dimensional planet has no wars.
There is a harmony that we call the "just society." A fifth-dimensional planet has
many temples, yet there is no religious division. The people live in harmony, peace,
and spiritual light. Try to visualize other aspects of this fifth-dimensional planet.*

*Now, project the image of a fifth-dimensional Earth into the etheric crystal that
you are working on. Use the images you experienced when you were visualizing
an ideal fifth-dimensional planet. Remember that the fifth-dimensional planet also
interacts with the galaxy and other parts of the Galactic Council and higher beings
of light.*

*The etheric crystals have a beautiful connection to the noosphere and to the
spirit of Gaia. One of the key functions is that Earth can attract the fifth dimension.
Remember that the third dimension and the fifth dimension will be interacting. That
point of interaction is the ascension, a great downloading of light and energy.*

*What does it take to make the attractive force of Earth and its noosphere strong
enough so that it can attract the fifth dimension? It takes a strong noosphere, a strong
thought pattern, and electromagnetic light.*

*Now, send this thought into the etheric crystal, "Earth's ability to attract the
fifth dimension is increasing." Visualize the fifth dimension as a sphere. Visualize the
third dimension as another sphere. Visualize that these two spheres are attracted to
each other and interact.*

*Say, "Earth is able to attract the fifth dimension." Send that thought into the
etheric crystal you are working with. A fifth-dimensional planet is a planet that has
fifth-dimensional light and is able to balance all weather patterns. All droughts are
relieved, all volcanoes are put into rest, and all earthquakes are calmed. This is
what a fifth-dimensional planet looks like. As a fifth-dimensional planet, Earth will
become calmer and more balanced.*

*I feel the strong energy you are sending into the twelve etheric crystals. Those
etheric crystals send energy to the noosphere. The noosphere then sends that energy
into Gaia. Gaia responds because Gaia knows more strongly now that she has great
powers of attracting the fifth dimension.*

*The etheric crystals will remain in their places above each of these locations,
especially in the area of Mount Shasta. Let the balance of the drought in California
be reversed so that more rain will come to California, the Northwest, and the Southwest. Let the cooling temperatures and calming weather from the Blue Mountains in*

Grose Valley be over Australia and New Zealand and over the entire planet. Know this Gaia.

In particular, as we look at the Fukushima area, know that there is a fifth-dimensional healing light helping to disperse, delete, and correct the damage to that area, Earth's aura, and Earth's energy. We, the Arcturians, send a special healing to fill up the hole that is over Earth's energy there because of the extreme radiation leakages.

Now we are going to continue our work with the noosphere through the purification and energy work of Chief White Eagle. I am Juliano. Blessings to you all.

• • •

[Chants] "Hey ya ho ya heyyyyy, hey ya ho ya heyyyy, hey ya hooooh." All my words are sacred. Blessings to you all as I feel your power and your connection to Earth.

Purify with White Eagle Light

We know of the value of purification. Purification occurs on many different levels. There is a great need for purification on Earth now. That purification has been described in many different ways as great storms, fires, and earthquakes and are often called end-time events.

I would like to propose to you that the real purification first has to occur in Earth's energy field and in Earth's aura because they have accumulated over the centuries many negative spirits and many negative thoughts. Earth has accumulated a long reservoir of conflict and densities. We want to purify Earth's unconscious, etheric energy, and aura.

I, Chief White Eagle, am speaking to you with the White Eagle Light. Yes, this is the source of my power, the white light from the eagle. The white light is a special light of purification. We can purify Earth's aura, including the human thought patterns and the lower beings filling its dense parts. Then the great end-time events will not have to occur.

We go into our medicine wheel to help purify Earth's aura. This is why we go into the sweat lodge; it is for self-purification. It is how we do purification ceremonies. This is why we are talking to you about the healing light of the planetary cities of light. All of this is related to creating the White Eagle Light. Today, we all are connected to a great healing power, the twelve etheric crystals that surround this planet.

Visualize the Blue Jewel, the planet, as you see her in the great pictures from the Moon, the way you see her on the cover of the film The Blue Jewel. *See the layers of Earth's aura in this picture. Now you have x-ray vision, and you have the ability* to see interdimensionally. You can see the energy fields, and you can see all of the dark spirits around Earth. I could describe them, but it is not necessary because you see the results of the wars and the darkness that continually fills Earth with lower light and lower energy.

From your third eye, send the White Eagle Light into Earth's aura now. The White Eagle Light is the highest light of purification for Earth. The densities are diminished, and there is a new ray of hope and light in Earth's energy field.

The White Eagle Light is going through the entire aura of Earth for purification. Now, we will go up to the next level of higher thought in the noosphere. Just visualize a White Eagle in the noosphere. In the concepts of the collective unconscious, there are certain animal symbols that carry a great deal of energy. Place all of your healing thoughts for Earth into the noosphere. Visualize again the White Eagle coming into the noosphere. See the White Eagle now.

You have helped place the White Eagle and its healing powers into the noosphere. The White Eagle Light represents the evolution and the highest light. The White Eagle is a higher animal; it is a higher bird. Only those with higher consciousness are able to see the White Eagle.

Now bring the White Eagle into Earth's noosphere. All of the thoughts and all of the energy included in this healing are contained in this image of the White Eagle. Let the White Eagle come into your own energy field. Feel its power within you. Let the image of the White Eagle be placed in each of the twelve etheric crystals. The twelve etheric crystals now hold the energy of the White Eagle. The White Eagle Light is now filling the noosphere. It is in each of these etheric crystals and in your consciousness as well.

I am Chief White Eagle. Now you know of some of my powers of planetary healing. Good day. We are all brothers and sisters with the galaxy. Ho!

Chapter 12

The Omega-Time-Particle Dimensional Wave

Juliano, the Arcturians, and Chief White Eagle

Greetings, I am Juliano. We are the Arcturians. Earth is now passing through a threshold that can be described as a shift going to a different level. This new level leads to a period of imbalance. Remember, when you are looking at the situations of balance and imbalance, please understand that it depends on your perspective.

As a system, Earth is homeostatic, that is, it maintains a balance of different energies, situations, and requirements to sustain the complexity of the biosphere, which is a complex matter. Earth is crossing into a threshold characterized from the third-dimensional perspective as imbalance. Each of you is probably already experiencing this imbalance in your personal lives, and you can see the imbalance occurring on the planet. There are many extremes and many polarizations occurring.

We are very much aware of the weather imbalances occurring throughout the United States, Mexico, Europe, Australia, Asia, South America, and even in New Zealand. We are aware of the activity on the Ring of Fire. We are aware that Earth is going through a period of self-correction, and what is self-correction for Earth is a period of uncomfortableness for you.

By "self-correction," I mean that Earth is seeking to bring back a homeostatic situation. Certainly, you are aware of the previous normal seasons that have been characteristic of your springs and summers, your normal rainfall patterns, and the calmness and reliability of farming. Farming has been dependent on the certainties and predictions related to the food chains and food cycles — weather that seems to occur on a regular basis.

Earth has to consider all activities, all blockages in its meridian system, all thought patterns, and all energies that have to do with the oxygen content and the relationships between the atmosphere and the Sun, between the Sun and the Central Sun. Earth has to consider its relationship to the galaxy because it is part of a complex galactic system. The Sun, of course, participates in the galactic complexities as well. The Sun is going through a variety of different storms and activities that in part are due to its alignment with the Central Sun in December 2012, which began a period of imbalance. Earth has crossed a threshold. This threshold indicates that you are getting closer to an acceleration of events that is part of the pattern of predictions made around 2012.

Remember that some of the predictions of 2012 described periods of great imbalances and upheavals, blackouts and electromagnetic energies, more intense polarizations, and human-caused Earth conflicts. I have predicted that the greatest upheaval that is going to occur will come from a human-created event. Such an event could be described on the scale of the nuclear power accident that occurred in Japan. The major event could also be described as an upcoming arms conflict. All of these predictions are possible, and you might be surprised to think it is possible that another nuclear accident from a power plant could occur.

Our observations and our careful analysis of nuclear energy on Earth shockingly indicate that there has been no overall change. There has been no overall increase in safety. There has been no overall consideration of how to better protect this planet from nuclear accidents. There has been some movement toward shutting down some nuclear plants in Germany. Some plants have been closed in Japan, but they started up two more plants at the same time. When you look at this from a planetary perspective, you can see many nuclear plants in operation globally as dots on a map all over the planet. You can see nuclear radiation waste disposal sites and radiation leakages.

The Omega Light Time Zone

This is a time that needs increased biorelativity. You need to increase your spiritual powers and your spiritual practices of planetary technology. You need to ask the question at the center of all planetary healing work: "As starseeds and as planetary healers, how do we work together to bring down fifth-dimensional energies directly into this planet?" The maximum input of fifth-dimensional energy is needed now. The imbalance will not easily be rectified without an input of fifth-dimensional energy.

Great spiritual teachers and great spiritual prophets have been on this planet. These prophets and spiritual leaders have had a dramatic effect on the planet and its religious, economic, and political situations. Interestingly, their effects are often postponed; they can take centuries to become firmly rooted and directly show their most powerful influence. A simple example of this is that Jesus's influence on Earth didn't really become powerful until several centuries after his passing.

There is a difference now between the ancient times and the modern era because you are living in what I call an omega time zone, which is a zone in which time can be accelerated. It is an era in which multiple events that seemingly would take decades or years to occur can transpire in a month or two. In an omega time zone, you feel as if you have had several lifetimes in the past year or two. You may have already experienced this in your personal life. I am sure that there are times when you feel as if you have gone through a whole lifetime, but it has only been six months.

Earth is in the omega time zone. Planetary healers can take advantage of it by gathering their forces and energies and using the thought powers in a simultaneous manner to create a shift or change. This shift, or change, is amplified by the dimensional waves that are already occurring because Earth is closer to its intersection point with the fifth dimension.

Interdimensional waves are electromagnetically charged particles that contain the omega-time energy particles. That means that these waves can accelerate the shifting of energies. To take full advantage of the omega time zone and the omega particles, you have to use advanced spiritual technologies to interact with the omega time particles.

Repetitious meditative approaches consist of one group that meditates at 9:00AM while the next group meditates at 10:00AM, another group meditates at 11:00AM, and so on. Thus, there is a twenty-four-hour or twelve-hour cycle in which one person or one group seeks balance for Earth. This is what I call a synchronistic relatedness of meditations that can help to stabilize the planet and bring fifth-dimensional healing energy and light into Earth. When bringing in the fifth-dimensional healing and light, we are talking about focusing on bringing in an electromagnetic quantum time particle. This particle is a dimensional wave filled with the energy of planetary healing for rebalancing the planet.

There are technologies that can be unified with this synchronized meditation. For example, we can call on the dimensional wave of the quantum time particles to be merged with human thoughts. Healing thoughts can be focused on rebalancing the weather patterns and Earth's feedback loop system so that they are brought into stable positions.

Use the Planetary Tree of Life for Balance

Earth's feedback loop system is not in a stable zone because it is attempting to bring itself into a different balance that humankind might not like. Humankind is blocking meridians on Earth. When humankind creates undue pollution in the air and lots of carbon in the atmosphere, these blockages create a communication pattern to Earth's feedback loop system. It says, "Okay, humanity wants Earth to go in this direction." Now you can see Earth is complying. What more evidence is needed for the planet to understand that Earth's feedback loop system is responding to what appears to be blockages created by humanity?

Therefore, with a greater intensity and a greater usage of the omega time particles in the meditations, you can communicate to Earth that you want Earth's feedback loop system to become more moderate. You want Earth's feedback loop system to react and create a system that is in better balance with humanity's needs. At the same time, humankind can work to remove the blockages on the meridians. There needs to be a decrease in some of the extremes and polarizations.

We have downloaded the twelve etheric planetary crystals around the world. We have downloaded the information about how each crystal is located in a particular spot on this planet and involved in a chain of interactive spheres described as a new meridian system. The original meridian system is so blocked that it is unlikely it can be reopened. So you create a new system in which you bypass the blocked area to keep the energy functioning.

One of the Arcturian planetary healing technologies for Earth is based on the Arcturian Planetary Tree of Life. Humankind can work with this new meridian system to process, assimilate, rectify, and rebalance Earth's feedback loop system. This sounds like a high expectation for the Arcturian Planetary Tree of Life, but you have to consider that it is based on a paradigm originating from galactic sources.

The configuration represented by the twelve etheric crystals downloaded throughout the planet participates in a multidimensional, sacred energetic grid. It is able to process fifth-dimensional energy and disseminate it on the planet.

This Planetary Tree of Life grid can also take energies that are manifesting now on the third dimension and retransmit the energy of the blockages so that a greater and more harmonious balance can be instituted. We met with a powerful Arcturian starseed group in Santa Fe, New Mexico, to work with them in their beautiful creation of the Arcturian temple. We began this work of seeking to create and amplify a spiritually charged grid that bypasses the original planetary meridian system to work with a greater healing and a greater balance for Earth.

Part of this work in the Santa Fe Arcturian temple was based on the concept of loving kindness and compassion for Earth. In the Arcturian Planetary Tree of Life, it is shown that it is necessary to have a planetary balance. You can see this imbalance in Earth's weather patterns. This extreme weather pattern is an imbalance that might be described as a judgment or a punishment because of a variety of blockages, misunderstandings, and miscalculations resulting from human activities.

In our travels throughout the galaxy, we have seen planets fail to learn this lesson. We have seen planets that were not able to organize themselves sufficiently to respond to this type of feedback loop judgment, or punishment, represented in extreme weather patterns. You have stories of judgment expressed as extreme weather in your sacred texts in which gigantic storms or upheavals occured because of human actions.

The feedback loop system of the planet has certain safe points, and once you pass those thresholds of safety, there is a point of no return. You probably have even heard this in the discussions about the 2012 end-time cycle, which means that human activities might have crossed a certain point. This point could be based on not cutting back on nuclear energy or carbon emissions. This could mean that the weather, volcanic activity, and tectonic plate activity are now also reaching new levels.

Electromagnetic Communication from Earth

Many people might be surprised to learn that Earth is communicating with humanity, even though humanity may not think so. It is a very responsive and sensitive planet. Earth might be going through a warning period. Things could remain like this unless you make some changes. This is a time for deep reflection; you need to intensify your biorelativity activities, your spiritual interventions, and your group connections with each other.

There is a danger that the imbalance apparent in Earth's feedback loop system is being energetically and electromagnetically distributed throughout the planet. Remember that everything on this planet and all planets consist of electromagnetic particles. These particles contain different energies. Earth's feedback loop system is communicating and sending out charged particles, sending out a new imbalance from the human perspective. Those charged particles of imbalance are also being distributed throughout Earth's energy field. Certain conflicts and polarizations might intensify during this period because of the particle acceleration. The omega time particle dimensional waves can counterbalance the energy waves coming from Earth's feedback loop system.

Starseeds can use their spiritual technologies now and intensify their work with the Arcturian Planetary Tree of Life. It is necessary and helpful to increase the energies of the planetary cities of light and work with greater devotion to create more sacred spaces on this planet — spaces devoted to holding fifth-dimensional light. It is important to visit the etheric crystal sites and work with the activations of energy. Talk about them. Have connections with them through people's interactions with each other. Continue working with the Arcturian temple. Have people hold energies of loving kindness that say to Earth, "Yes, I understand this judgment. I understand why there needs to be a harsh response. I understand why there needs to be these harsh storms. I understand why there needs to be this harsh heat wave. I understand why there needs to be intense rains."

Also call on the energies of compassion and the energies of kindness to the planet. Earth is a kind planet. Earth is a loving planet. Earth wants to live in harmony with humanity. You even call Earth your mother, which she is. The mother is compassionate.

I would like for Chief White Eagle to speak with you about Mother Earth. I am Juliano. Blessings.

•   •   •

[Chants] "Hey ya ho! Hey ya ho ya hey! Hey ya ho." All my words are sacred. Greetings, I am Chief White Eagle. I send my blessings to each of you who are planetary healers of the highest light. Know that you are in a higher evolutionary position.

This concept of the planetary healers helping Earth still refers to an elite group of starseeds — lightworkers — who are devoted to shifting the energies of the planet. Believe me, Mother Earth is compassionate. She knows how to act.

Humankind's Relationship with Earth

One of the greatest assumptions humans can make is to say Earth is not affected by humanity. There is a parallel between your relationship with your mother and humankind's relationship with Earth. Your mother is affected by what you do. She has great loving kindness, compassion, understanding, and acceptance for you. Also, when there is danger, your mother will act appropriately. You know that most mothers go to extremes to protect their children. Humans are the children of Earth.

Earth at this time is extremely receptive to your prayers and sensitive to humanity's input. Earth desires to receive spiritual input from you, the children of Earth. We, of the ascended Native peoples on this planet, know that the medicine wheel is one of the most powerful tools for beginning communications with Earth's feedback loop system. The medicine wheel can receive the dimensional omega light time particles, and those waves of light can be sent directly into Earth.

The planetary ladders of ascension can also serve as receivers of the omega time particle dimensional waves. The ladders of ascension can act in the same way as the medicine wheel; that is, the ladders of ascension can receive and download light. The idea is that you have to pray and bring down light and bring down the energy into the ladders of ascension.

"O Father/Mother Creator, we the Arcturian starseeds and planetary healers are gathered here today to help rebalance Earth. We are here to communicate with Earth and Earth's feedback loop system. We are gathered in a great circle of light, for we now reside on many parts of this planet, and we join in the ring of ascension around this planet in our spirits.

"O Father/Mother Creator, we open up our crown chakras to receive these omega time particles of light. We will go into silence as we each receive this light, the omega time particle dimensional wave. Then at the end of the meditation, we will send this higher energy back into Earth."

[Pause in silence for a few minutes.]

[Chants] "Hey ya hoohh. Hey yaa hooohh."

The omega time particle wave of dimensional light is received in the ring of ascension, and now it goes to each of your medicine wheels and your planetary cities of light. It goes to each of the twelve etheric crystals and the places that are holding them. The ladders of ascension receive this. Together we send a healing balance, a healing thought, to Earth's feedback loop system to create a better harmony of weather and balance. Let the consciousness of the entire planet open up to this powerful energy that Earth's feedback loop system is now demonstrating.

When you reach these types of crisis situations, go into ceremony more often. Practice spiritual exercises and say more prayers. Spend more time in the medicine wheel and seek purification. Spend more time working to transmit your energies around to the planet. Most important, attempt to listen to what Earth is saying. Also, do more chanting.

A Powerful Balance Is Coming to Earth

The Earth feedback loop system is an energy vibration, an electromagnetic wave vibration. Some of the new vibrations coming to Earth are because Earth is in a different position to the Sun and in the galaxy. There is different electromagnetic energy. It is not only humankind's activities that affect the planet but also the energies Earth experiences on its path throughout the galaxy.

I, Chief White Eagle, call on the highest energy from the Central Sun to be part of this omega time particle wave energy. Accelerate this light into each person and into each medicine wheel. Accelerate this light into each ladder of ascension and each planetary city of light. Accelerate this light into each of the twelve etheric crystals, and learn to connect with the highest fifth-dimensional energies. Know that the grandmothers and grandfathers, the great spirits overlooking this planet, are working together with you.

[Chants] "Hey ya hoohh. Hey yaaaa hoooohhhh." White Buffalo Calf

Woman is coming to Earth. She is going to lead a new movement on this planet that will bring a powerful balance and a powerful energy. She will bring an energy of a new, just society — a new way of justice and a new way of doing business on this planet. This will bring new economic, political, social, and healing energies. You are bringing the pathway for her entrance. Welcome her. I am Chief White Eagle. All my words are sacred. All my relations. Ho!

Chapter 13

The Intersection of the Dimensions

Juliano and the Arcturians

Greetings, I am Juliano. We are the Arcturians. The intersection between the third and the fifth dimensions is the basic energy vibration that will set the ascension in motion. Please understand that the intersection occurred in other planetary systems in this galaxy and in other parts of the universe. So the intersection of dimensions is not a new or unique event to the Blue Jewel. Nonetheless, it is significant.

The Pleiades, as you know, is a fifth-dimensional planet. The main planet on that system in the fifth dimension is Era. That Pleiades system is inhabited by humans who are part of your heritage, and they look almost exactly like you. Before they were in the fifth dimension as a planet, the Pleiadian scientists experimented with space-time travel. They were going through the planetary evolution cycle quite similar to what Earth is now experiencing. But they were more advanced than Earth. During this scientific and space exploration period on Era, they discovered the secrets to dimensional travel through hyperspace.

In fact, it is clear that when you travel from one dimension to another, you must travel through hyperspace. The entry and the reentry from hyperspace back into the third dimension or forward into the fifth dimension is complicated and must be done with precision. In moving from hyperspace into a dimension, a tremendous amount of energy is exerted and unleashed. It is really difficult to describe. Think of an airplane or a spaceship breaking the sound barrier. There are waves of sound that are almost visible, and you can feel and hear the results of the spaceship or the jet breaking the sound barrier. If you are on Earth when this happens, you will hear the sonic boom, and it might even rattle your windows.

Traveling into hyperspace requires accelerating to extreme speeds that are much faster than sound waves. For example, an airplane might need to travel faster than the speed of sound, which may be more than 800 miles per hour. In fact, the speeds needed to reach the entry into hyperspace come close to the speed of light, which as you have heard, is approximately 186,000 miles per second.

When you want to return to Earth or the third dimension from hyperspace, you will travel at a tremendous speed. When your ship is in hyperspace, it might not feel as if you are traveling at a high speed. This is similar to flying in an airplane; you could be flying at a speed of 600 miles per hour. You have no concept of how fast you are going until you look at a speedometer. On a spaceship, you will feel the effects of gravitational pull and the energy around you when you begin to leave hyperspace and enter the third dimension.

So when you leave hyperspace and come back into the third dimension, you enter that dimension with huge force, a huge wave of energy similar to the sound wave I just described. That is when you break the sound barrier on Earth.

During this earlier period, the Pleiadian scientists did not have a total understanding of reentry protocol and the necessity for precise calculations. For example, when extraterrestrial higher-dimensional beings come to Earth or your solar system, they reenter from hyperspace at the huge Jupiter corridor because it is far enough away from Earth. The Jupiter Corridor provides enough space so that the force coming from hyperspace into the third dimension will not overwhelm Earth or even another planet, such as Mars. Earth or Mars could receive a huge pulse of energy from the entry of the spaceship. Such a reentry too close to Earth would cause a huge disruption in every aspect of dimensional life on the planet. If Mars were thrown out from a hyperspace reentry, that would affect the gravitational energies of Earth and create problems on your planet. So exact and precise reentries are paramount when reentering Earth from hyperspace.

Now, by coming into the solar system at the Jupiter corridor, there is more than enough space to make up for any errors and miscalculations. It gives the space traveler a buffer, a nice margin of comfort.

Dimensional Boom Causes Planetary Catastrophe

Pleiadian scientists and the astronauts made a miscalculation many eons ago when they were traveling through hyperspace. Remember, traveling through hyperspace is the preferred way of traveling throughout the galaxy. There are certain techniques of acceleration used to go into hyperspace. Once space travelers attain a certain speed, they can use a certain method in which thought forms are integrated with the thought waves. This integration, based on special computer technology, allows the spaceship to enter hyperspace. Earth's scientists are close to developing this technology. You will see recognize it when you hear scientists talking about telepathic communications with computers. That is, the computer can read your thought waves and perform tasks based on what you are thinking. This is the initial step toward space travel using hyperspace and thought waves.

The Pleiadian space travelers were coming back to their planet, Era, from hyperspace, and they made a miscalculation. When they came in from hyperspace, from the fifth dimension back into the third dimension, they came in too close. They produced a wave of energy and life force that threw the Pleiadian planet totally out of balance. Try to understand the overwhelming force of a starship coming out of hyperspace and entering the third dimension at a speed that is perhaps equal to one-half or maybe one-third of the speed of light. That would be an incredible 60,000 miles per second. Imagine the huge sonic boom made when a jet flies at that higher speed on Earth. Now imagine the sonic boom — or perhaps as you might call it a "dimensional boom" — made when you come back into a dimension. The planet can be thrown totally off balance by a dimensional boom.

In this instance, the Pleiadian planet Era was thrown off its rotational axis. The planet stopped rotating. Perhaps you have even heard speculations of what could occur if Earth just stopped rotating for twenty-four hours. It would be catastrophic. So there was a planetary crisis on Era because of this mistake, because the spaceship reentered from hyperspace too close to the planet.

The Galactic Council and the ascended masters intervened. They were aware before this incident that the Pleiadians were making great advancements toward peace through spiritual work. They had integrated their spiritual wisdom with their planetary technology in an effective way. So the Galactic Council made a decision that Era could move into the fifth dimension. The decision was made for several reasons. It was decided that it was not in the interest of the karma or the evolution of the planet and its inhabitants to suffer such a catastrophic event. There would have been a great loss of life and an extreme disruption in their ability to evolve as a society. So the Galactic Council and the ascended masters performed a planetary intervention, creating the conditions necessary to move Era into the fifth dimension. This, in effect, saved the Pleiadian planet from catastrophe, and it also provided the necessary intervention to create a better harmony for the planet.

The error resulted from a computer malfunction. There are special types of software that must calculate reentry protocols. The time factor must be taken into consideration, because the entry and reentry into hyperspace is based on time measurements. For example, you cannot reenter at a time before you started your journey. I know that sounds obvious or maybe even confusing, but in hyperspace, it is possible to leave the third dimension at 10AM, and then you could reenter at 9AM that same day. Well, that distortion in time travel is not allowed, because that creates undue time waves and disruptive energy waves.

When you are in hyperspace, time loses its third-dimensional meaning. The measurement of time is not possible in hyperspace as it is on the third dimension. When you are in hyperspace, when you are traveling at such extraordinary speeds, any type of time-measurement device would not operate in the same manner. In hyperspace, time can be slowed down, and in some cases, time can actually begin to move backward.

You cannot reenter the third dimension at a time before you left. The reason I'm explaining this to you is that I want you to have an understanding of the power of the intersection of the dimensions. We talked about a spaceship coming from the fifth dimension through hyperspace to the third dimension. If that is not calculated at the right time, then there could be problems, and the planet could be thrown off its axis. Rotational problems can result, and catastrophic planetary events are possible.

The Intersection Cycle of the Ascension

The intersection of dimensions is a necessary step for the ascension. You are closer to this intersection of dimensions now. The necessary calculations are being prepared, and the foundation is being laid for the intersection with a force that is totally beyond the normal comprehension. Yet the force created when this intersection occurs has to be calculated so that there is a smooth intersection. It has to be calculated so that the entire planet is not destroyed by a catastrophic event. Even a relatively small spaceship that comes in at this huge speed from another dimension can totally disorganize and throw a planet out of balance.

Can you imagine the power that would come to Earth when the dimensions intersected? What does that mean? What kind of force? What kind of calculations? Where does the intersection have to begin? It is necessary to provide a buffer that would ensure that there are no harmful effects from the intersection. At the same time, the intersection would have to be smooth enough and effective enough that it would allow the ascension to occur. [Tones] "Oooooooo."

This is a galactic event. It is an event that calls for many people, many starseeds, choosing to incarnate on Earth now. They became involved in Earth's incarnational cycle, and they know that it is beneficial to incarnate now to experience this intersection of dimensions.

Many ascended masters and higher-dimensional beings are coming to observe this event in the same way astronomers would observe the eclipse of the Sun. People want to observe the intersection of the dimensions. In fact, the intersection of the dimensions has a lot of parallels to an eclipse because it is also an alignment. December 22, 2012, was an indicator of the type of alignment necessary for the ascension. Third-dimensional planets are more capable to experience the intersection of the fifth and the third dimensions when there is a type of galactic alignment such as 2012.

Try to imagine the huge distances we speak of. For instance, the intersection of the Sun, which is 93 million miles from Earth, and the Moon, which is 239,000 miles from Earth, creates an alignment called a solar eclipse. But a dimensional intersection involves galactically aligning with the Sun, the solar system, and the center of the galaxy. The center of the galaxy can be as far as 35,000 light-years away. So the ascension is a very precise alignment, and from many aspects, you are now in the alignment cycle. You are in the intersection cycle of the ascension.

The Importance of Spiritual Resonance

Earth and its energies are in a state of huge polarization and turmoil. You are aware of the end-time predictions. There have certainly been many polarizing events on Earth. There are indications that these polarizations will continue. However, the energy polarization is creating a shift, an imbalance. This indicates that the energies of 2012 reflected a shift from old thought forms, values, and standards. This shift will affect the old ways of doing things in terms of religious, spiritual, economic, military, environmental, and ecological systems. Methods that are part of the older system are not going to work anymore. You have seen these systems breaking down now in a more intense way, and it is clear that as you move into the coming years, there will be more examples of how these old thought forms and patterns will not be able to hold the energy of old systems.

Therefore, the polarizations are creating different camps, or different sides, indicating that there will be breaks in patterns of doing things. These breaks are intensifying greatly now, and they will reach a peak soon. This will be seen on a global scale. Older social and political patterns cannot sustain the energies. Breaking old patterns is frequently a precursor to the ascension and the intersection of the dimensions.

Imagine again the idea of the jet breaking the sound barrier and the waves of that sound coming to the ground and causing a sonic boom. The predicted intersection of dimensions includes the initial steps that have already occurred on Earth and now include the creation of these dimensional waves coming into this planet. To withstand these waves, you must be in spiritual resonance. To have spiritual resonance, you need to develop your spiritual energy and spiritual wisdom. It must be understood that these dimensional energy waves are powerful and helpful. But if you are not in resonance with them and do not understand them, then they become disruptive and can throw you into a greater polarization.

One of the dangers of polarization is that people are thrown into their locked positions, and they become almost protective and aggressive in holding them. People often hold on to their polarized positions even in the face of seeming defeat. You are seeing examples of this now. When you are in spiritual resonance with this dimensional energy, you can immediately go into higher states of consciousness. You are ready to ascend. You are ready to experience this elative and joyful occurrence known as the intersection of dimensions. This experience is to die for (pardon the pun), because you will give up your ego and embrace this remarkable transition and transformation.

We have been helping you and the planet prepare for many years now. We know that the final process necessary for the ascension is found in the attractive magnetic energy force field of the third-dimensional Earth. Earth must be emitting an electromagnetic frequency that attracts fifth-dimensional energy. This emission allows the fifth dimension to lock on to Earth to create the beautiful experience of the intersection. Yes, the intersection of dimensions is a fantastic force field far beyond what can be described or imagined in normal consciousness.

At the same time, with the assistance of the ascended masters, Jesus, and the Galactic Council, the dimensional intersection will take place with such precision and such loving kindness that it will allow a smooth ascension. It will be a beautiful, relaxing, harmonious, and balanced intersection. It will not be a shock. This is a beautiful testimony to the preparation that you, the starseeds, are helping to provide as the planet works toward making the intersection and alignment of the dimensions happen. The work that you have done with the etheric crystals, the ladders of ascension, and the planetary cities of light are helping to create the magnetic resonance that allows the ascension and the attraction to the fifth dimension to occur smoothly. In fact, each person who is thinking and working with fifth-dimensional energies is part of this magnetic spiritual resonance.

Deployment into the Third Dimension

Living in the third dimension now requires that you develop a sensitivity that exceeds the normal third-dimensional sensitivity. To perceive and experience these fifth-dimensional energies and energy waves, you need to have a higher degree of sensitivity. This would be normal because you are increasing your psychic powers — your third eye powers and crown chakra energies. Unfortunately, many of you still have to function in the third dimension. You might find that as you experience these fifth-dimensional energies, you can become off-balance when you are in the third dimension. This feeling of being off-balance comes to you because there is often a dramatic contrast between the higher fifth-dimensional energy and the lower energies from the third dimension.

Remember, this is a time of great polarization. So when you are working on the ascension, you are in fact working to increase your sensitivities to polarization energies. When you return to the third dimension with heightened sensitivities, sometimes the contrast can be unbalancing to you unless you are properly prepared. You have to take some steps to prepare yourself for "deployment" into the third dimension.

Now, some of the interesting steps that the higher-dimensional beings use are very instructive. Billy Meier (the Swiss man who had direct contact with the Pleiadians)[1] interacted with Semjase, a guide and teacher from the Pleiades who came to Earth to instruct Billy. She and her Pleiadian crew were able to develop thought-field protective waves, which means that only certain people were able to see them. Even though Billy Meier was able to see Semjase and her crew, other people who were 30 or 50 feet away could not. Semjase used a protective device that prevented others from experiencing them. Now, this would be an interesting device for you to use; however, you do not have such technology available on Earth.

There is some benefit to protecting yourself and your aura. Remember that I have given the instructions about the Pung energy. Pung is an energy in which your aura would only allow higher vibration to enter your energy field. The lower vibrations would harmlessly bounce away from your aura. At the same time, your energy field maintains a highly charged energetic state so that negative energy bounces away. Also your energy field would not collapse or experience an indentation in the face of negative energy. So these are other ideas for protecting your energy.

We repeatedly remind you to do the cosmic egg exercise. Without protection, it is easy to go from a heightened state back into lower energy. This could cause a disorganization of your aura. You need to maintain the total integration of your aura. You don't want your aura to be disorganized. If it becomes disorganized, then it is okay to withdraw in order to strengthen it.

Living in a planetary city of light can help to strengthen your aura. The

---

1 To learn more about Billy Meier's extraterrestrial contacts, go to http://en.wikipedia.org/wiki/Billy_ Meier.

idea of the planetary cities of light is based on the concept of improving and protecting your energy field by living in a higher energy place, creating a safe haven for your energy work by creating an attractive energy force that will resonate when the intersection of the dimensions occurs. Further, we have explained in detail that the interaction with the galactic sister cities provides a more powerful downloading of fifth-dimensional energy. The fact is that the sister cities are all fifth-dimensional cities, and they have all experienced the ascension. Therefore, they can send the ascension energies and the dimensional resonant energies to you.

There is a way to be more in resonance with these dimensional waves. These waves that some of you are experiencing will become stronger now because the intersection of the dimensions is getting closer. But there are also powerful energy waves of dimensions that you can receive, and they can activate you to a higher frequency.

Direct the Dimensional Waves Coming to Earth

The ladders of ascension, the etheric crystals, the subcrystals, and the ring of ascension are all spiritual tools to use for creating integration with the dimensional waves. There are many global systems on this planet that are becoming overburdened, and they aren't able to hold the energies. I am referring specifically to the economic, religious, and political systems. You can use the dimensional energy waves to increase your thought power for biorelativity.

Biorelativity occurs on several levels and has primarily been taught on the third-dimensional level. So when discussing the Native American ideas of biorelativity in talking to Mother Earth, these can be considered fifth-dimensional biorelativity exercises. One of those exercises that will help to balance this planet is to work with receiving the dimensional energy waves. Sometimes those waves come in every twelve hours, six hours, or even more often. You can attract and use the wave to help you experience more fifth-dimensional light.

These waves are like an ocean of spiritual fifth-dimensional energy coming to this planet in anticipation of the ascension, of this intersection. The intersection of the dimensions will lead to the ascension and will be a positive experience for those who are ascending. You can use biorelativity with fifth-dimensional energy to quantumly affect the stability of the Fukushima power plant, for example, so that it doesn't collapse and its rods don't fall. Use the fifth-dimensional waves to focus on bringing moisture to the Southwest and to creating a balance with weather patterns to stabilize the plates on the planet.

Focus these dimensional waves into the etheric crystals. The focus of the etheric crystals is significant, because they have the power to absorb and defuse these dimensional waves in a positive way. Remember, the dimensional waves cannot be integrated by those who are polarized. Those who are significantly polarized don't have the openness and the sensitivity to work with or understand this kind of energy.

It is hard even for the starseeds to store or use this energy. Sometimes you don't know what to do with so much energy. You might feel uncomfortable having that much high-level energy. You might feel unbalanced because there are waves of energy coming to you. The etheric crystals have the ability to store this energy and defuse it. They can refocus it for you. When doing the biorelativity exercises, focus on the dimensional waves coming into the closest etheric crystal, your planetary city of light, or the ring of ascension.

I, Juliano, see a huge fifth-dimensional wave of beautiful power and energy coming to Earth. See that wave being absorbed by the ring of ascension, and see it being distributed to the twelve etheric crystals. These twelve etheric crystals are like new meridian lines throughout the whole planet distributing balance and fifth-dimensional power. Hold that thought for one minute.

You have just integrated a beautiful fifth-dimensional wave into this planet. That wave also integrates with your energy system now. All this creates a greater attractive force for the coming dimensional intersection.

I am Juliano. Good day.

Chapter 14

The Ring of Ascension

Juliano, the Arcturians, and Jesus

Greetings, I am Juliano. We are the Arcturians. Welcome. From your perspective, you have witnessed several years that have been a roller coaster ride for the planet. If you think that the first years after 2012 have been dramatic, remember that it was just the introduction and the preparation for what is still to come. We strongly acknowledge that the full spectrum of planetary healing activities and technologies must now be implemented on Earth.

When we designated 2011 the year of the planetary healer, we knew that there would be a much more intense need for your work and intervention. We knew that the polarizations you see would become more intense. We knew that Earth changes or global changes in weather patterns were going onto become more active and that the opportunity for telepathically connecting with Earth is stronger now than any other time before.

It is truly an amazing time to be on Earth. It is truly an amazing opportunity to use your skills as planetary healers. Many of you have incarnated onto Earth at this time to explore, practice, and contribute to the planetary healing experience, which is the key factor in the biosphere's survival and Earth's rebalancing.

We speak about your personal ascension, but we also constantly speak about the planetary ascension. We know that Earth as a planet will ascend. One of the major tools for the planetary ascension is the ring of ascension. We will now explore in greater depth the meaning of the ring of ascension. How can you, as planetary healers, use the ring of ascension to more effectively work your biorelativity exercises for the healing and rebalancing of Earth?

It is time to work with the whole planet as one unit. It is time to realize that one part of a climate, one part of a continent, communicates with and is in balance with other continents. What happens in Australia affects what happens in the United States and in Canada and so on.

Earth Imbalances Are Human Caused

The Ring of Fire is a long chain of energy that extends to many countries and continents and across oceans. The most effective approach to biorelativity is to work with the entire planet. However, it is not the only approach. There are circumstances in which you would work specifically with one area. But even when you work with one area of the planet, you have to take into consideration how the change that you are requesting will affect other parts of the planet.

Say a hurricane is coming to Louisiana and you asked for that hurricane to be stopped. You would have to consider that because of the forces being expressed, that hurricane would go into another state and cause damage there. So another approach is to ask that it be dispersed over a wider area. An even more intensive approach would be to look at the ocean currents coming from the Southern Hemisphere and the warming in the oceans there to observe how this affects violent weather.

Earth's feedback loop system is so complex that you have to be very cautious. Praying for rain to come to one area could negatively affect other areas. At times there are many complex factors going on. For example, the movement of tectonic plates causes earthquakes and volcanic eruptions. The Ring of Fire extends for thousands of miles. So it is difficult to say, "Well, let's block the energy of this eruption," because then you would have to think about whether there is going to be an eruption somewhere else along the Ring of Fire.

There is the approach of admitting in all humbleness that you do not understand all of the mechanisms of Earth's feedback loop system. There are many factors that contribute to Earth's energy field that also affect Earth's meridians and Earth's feedback loop system. It is difficult to know how the blockages that humanity has imposed on Earth's meridian systems affect Earth's feedback loop system. It is difficult enough to try to understand Earth's feedback loop systems without considering the effect of the placement of nuclear reactors, without the holes in Earth's aura from numerous nuclear aboveground tests, which still has an effect on Earth's aura even though these tests occurred thirty or forty years ago.

It is difficult to assess how dams blocking key rivers on Earth affect the feedback loop system. It is logical to say that the rivers have been affected. In the principles of biorelativity, Earth seeks homeostasis — balance in a certain range so that certain levels of oxygen and nitrogen are maintained, as well as many other chemical factors, so that the biosphere and the life forms that it supports can be maintained. It is truly phenomenal that over thousands of years Earth has maintained a homeostasis that has allowed humans and many other living creatures to survive. Never before has one species (namely humankind) influenced — either consciously or unconsciously — Earth's feedback loop system so.

Previously the dinosaurs, who were perhaps the most predominant creature on the planet, did not really influence Earth's feedback loop system. Actually, they lived in harmony with Earth. Now humans challenge Earth's feedback loop system, and Earth is having difficulty maintaining the homeostasis necessary to support humankind. There has to be a way to send biorelativity communications to the whole planet at once. There has to be a way to transcend the smaller mind and connect with the supermind of humanity, the supermind of the planet. You can start with the ring of ascension.

[Tones] "Ooohhhmmm. Ooohhhmmm. Oooooohhmm."

The Intersection of Ascension

The ring of ascension was downloaded with the help of the Arcturians and ascended masters working with us. The ring of ascension is like the ring you see around the planet Saturn in your solar system, and it is for Earth's ascension. It is like an etheric halo, and it has a unique ability. This ring interacts simultaneously with fifth-dimensional energy while it downloads it to the third dimension.

This ring is inhabited with the thoughts and the love of the ascended masters. There are many ascended masters who contribute to and work diligently for Earth's ascension. The ring of ascension serves many purposes, and one is to allow the guides, the ascended masters, and teachers to more easily bring down fifth-dimensional information, fifth-dimensional energy, to Earth.

Many of you already know that you have been in contact with masters and teachers now more than any other time. There are more people channeling guides and teachers and connected with higher energy than any other time on Earth. I know that sounds like a fantastic assertion, but numerically, there are more starseeds on Earth than any other time. There are more ascending masters and more students of ascension on Earth now.

In ancient times, there were several prophets and teachers preparing for the ascension. But even then, there were only several prophets who would be able to ascend, and never would there be more than several prophets in a lifetime on Earth ascending at the same time. It would be an individual, unique event.

Now here we have a situation on Earth in which hundreds of thousands of starseeds and ascending masters [masters who are working toward their own personal ascension] can and will ascend. So of course there is a great need to interact with them because we know that ascension is like birth. During a birth in the hospital, there are many people around, such as doctors and nurses. There are special preparations, and families are waiting. In the same way, during the ascension, there are many guides and teachers on the other side waiting for you. They are helping to prepare you for this transition.

The part of this preparation is to provide an accessible energy, mainly the ring of ascension, that will help you to access fifth-dimensional energy. This is for planetary ascension as well. Many of the guides and teachers — particularly Jesus, Sanat Kumara, and Ashtar — are gathered in an interaction with the ring of ascension to facilitate the uplifting of the entire planet.

Biorelativity Intervention

The ring of ascension surrounds the entire planet. You might think of the ring as having just one location, a two-mile diameter going around the equator. You could also compare the ring of ascension to the rings around Saturn or Neptune. From your vantage point on Earth, you could use a telescope to measure the width of the ring and say that the ring has a certain dimension, covering a certain width around the planet.

But this ring of ascension is a fifth-dimensional, holographic ring. It has special powers and abilities. What are those special abilities? The ring of ascension can translate and interact with third-dimensional messages and at the same time receive messages and energies from the fifth-dimensional masters.

Imagine you are sending healing thoughts for Earth's weather patterns and seeking balance for the end of a drought in the Midwest of the United States. Imagine that you are praying for the many animals and people who are suffering. You send these prayers and thoughts to Earth to the feedback loop system using the ring of ascension. The energy you send travels around the entire Earth. It interacts telepathically with all of the different systems around Earth involved in supporting and creating the shift that led to the drought in that area. Many areas and ocean currents need to be shifted to end the drought, and it must be done in a way that is in balance with the whole planet. It must be done in a way that supports and brings harmony to the whole planet, not just one area.

The ring of ascension takes the energy you send and travels around and influences all of the places that need to be changed so that a new balance can occur. What is also beautiful is that starseeds, who might be sitting in Australia, Germany, or Philadelphia, all have equidistant access to the ring of ascension. So the ring of ascension receives information from all places around Earth. It is not limited to a certain geographic bandwidth. But it is limited to the thoughts of the starseeds, and it can be as wide as the number of starseeds who are supporting it around the planet. Or it could be narrow if you want to be more focused. But wide can also be focused.

The ring of ascension is holographic. The fifth-dimensional ascended masters also participate in the ring of ascension simultaneously. They monitor the ring of ascension all the time. They listen to what you and the planet need. Earth's feedback loop response can sometimes occur right away. Other times, it might take a short while or might even be longer because you do not know all of the factors in the feedback loop system that need to be shifted and changed in order for the request to occur.

To successfully do a biorelativity intervention, you would need to have a certain level of arcan thought power — 10 arcans or 20 arcans. The more arcans there are in your power of thought, the more likely that the changes you are asking for will occur. By going through the ring of ascension, you interact with the fifth-dimensional masters, and their thought patterns and their energy can also be measured in arcan power. They have the ability to emanate much higher arcan power than you can imagine.

But for their arcan power to be effective, it must interact with yours. This is one of the laws of fifth-dimensional planetary spiritual healing. Fifth-dimensional masters' and teachers' thoughts and healing powers must interact with the third-dimensional inhabitants of a planet. The ring of ascension offers that important medium, which allows the fifth-dimensional masters to interact with your requests for telepathic healing — for planetary healing — for Earth.

[Tones] "Oooohhhmmm. Ooohhhmmm."

Together we can send a request for planetary healing to the ring of ascension, which will be wherever you are, wherever your thoughts are. Choose what healing thought you want to send to Mother Earth through the ring of ascension. Request that the ascended masters closest to you hear this and send their thoughts into the ring of ascension.

The arcan energy power of your thoughts for planetary healing is strong now. The guides and teachers actively process and use your energies to distribute new healing light for the biosphere so that ring of balance of light can be distributed throughout Earth. It is one very powerful tool.

Imagine what a beautiful energy it would be to paint an image of the fifth-dimensional ring of ascension around the planet — 1,600 people around the planet, sitting in a circular fashion, sending light to the ring of ascension with their crown chakras. On top of the planet in the etheric world, there are fifth-dimensional masters and teachers simultaneously sending their thoughts and light into the ring of ascension.

Then the twelve etheric crystals from the planet are raised to interact with the ring of ascension. This amplifies the power of your thoughts. Then at the end of the exercise, the etheric crystals are brought back down into Earth, and they hold the energy of the ring of ascension in crystal formation. The etheric crystals can hold fifth-dimensional energies in their healing powers to an extraordinary degree. It is as if you are storing the healing powers. You are able to store that energy in the etheric crystals. The etheric crystals interact directly with the ring of ascension.

[Tones] "Oooohhhmmmm. Ooohhhmmm."

Iskalia Mirror Energy

Another powerful tool for planetary healing is the Iskalia mirror. The Iskalia mirror is like a gigantic ethereal mirror over the North Pole that has the ability to collect energy from far distances of the galaxy. Given the right circumstances and the right openings to the sky, even a telescope with a 200-inch- diameter mirror can receive light millions and billions of light-years away, though the light is faint. Telescope mirrors from the astronomical world can be so sensitive that they receive light and energy from the beginning of the formation of this universe.

Now imagine that there is a fifth-dimensional etheric mirror — a mirror that can not only receive light in this dimension but also in other dimensions. The fifth dimension now interacts on many different levels with the third dimension. The Iskalia mirror is in a particular alignment to receive fifth-dimensional light from the Central Sun. We know that Jesus originated from the area of the Central Sun, and he is one of the founding fathers of universal light, which include Moses as well as Buddha and many other ascended beings.

The light and energy from the Central Sun is now in a fifth-dimensional phase of knowledge and wisdom. The healing light is particularly focused on Earth. The 2012 alignment, or the solar alignment, was not just the end-times energy. It was not just the energy of upheaval. It represented an energy of change. It also represented a time for new fifth-dimensional energy to come to Earth. This fifth-dimensional energy is already on its way.

The energy of the Central Sun is coming to Earth, but it must be gathered and focused. It must be directed toward Earth. To this end, the Iskalia mirror has been placed over the North Pole by the Arcturians. It is an etheric mirror at least one mile in diameter, even larger in your Earth terms. But the size is not as important as the fact that it has the potential to gather fifth-dimensional light from the Central Sun, which can be focused to particular areas on Earth in need of planetary healing.

It is also especially suitable to direct the energy and light from the Iskalia mirror to the planetary cities of light. The planetary cities of light are special cities set up to be receptive to fifth-dimensional energies. They are sensitive to the new fifth-dimensional energies coming from the Central Sun. These are new solutions, new ideas, and new energies that perhaps have not been sent before. There are going to be new sounds, new tones, and new musical energies coming to Earth through the Iskalia mirror, which is receiving light from the fifth dimension.

[Tones] "Iisskaalliaaa liigghhtttt. Iiskaaaliiaaa liigggghhtttt." I, Juliano, am calling on the Iskalia light. It is coming from the Iskalia mirror and is directed toward the ring of ascension. [Tones] "Iisskaalliaaa liigghhtttt." Iskalia light from the Central Sun, the highest fifth-dimensional light, is now being downloaded into the ring of ascension. It is being transferred directly into the planetary cities of light. [Tones] "Iisskaalliaaa liigghhtttt."

The omega light is also available for planetary healing. We are calling on all planetary healers to unite and to use their powers of meditation, organization, speaking, and creation. This is the time to activate and use the strongest arcan power possible for planetary healing.

I will ask Jesus to speak with you briefly. I love you all.

I am Juliano. Good day.

• • •

The Interaction of the Ascension

I love your ascension work and your abilities to interact with the fifth dimension. I love your desire to be on the fifth dimension. And I am very pleased that the Arcturians have helped to establish this ring of ascension around Earth, especially at a time when many people see nothing but darkness and polarizations. You are seeing the destruction of many biospheric treasures on Earth. The ring of ascension serves an important role in holding together a fifth-dimensional downloading mechanism.

The ring of ascension also connects the ladders of ascension. The ladders of ascension can reach up to the ring of ascension in your practice. We are calling on you to work with us to download a ladder of ascension at Lago Puelo and St. Martin de Los Andes in Argentina, where a group of devoted starseeds has been working diligently for the healing of this planet. We will extend this ladder of ascension to the ring of ascension. By doing so, we will ensure that all ladders of ascension will be connected to the ring of ascension.

We, the ascended masters, are committed to working with you for Earth's ascension and for your ascension. We send love to you, for you love Earth. This is a great service to us and to the Creator, for the Creator has told us that Earth is going to ascend. So we work together for the preparation of this interaction energy. The ascension is an interaction of the highest magnitude with the fifth dimension. Nothing pleases our Father more than to have the fifth dimension interact in the third dimension and to send starseeds like you up to the fifth realm. Blessings from the ring of ascension.

I am Jesus. Good day.

Chapter 15

Folding the Space-Time Continuum

Juliano, the Arcturians, and Tomar

Greetings, I am Juliano. We are the Arcturians. Arcturian spiritual technology is devoted to helping you in your ascension and planetary-healing work. It can also help you to advance your spiritual practice and evolution. Our spiritual technologies, including shimmering and thought projection, are useful on many different levels, particularly for protection and as a practice for your ascension.

Traveling in the Fifth Dimension

The folding of the space-time continuum is an enhancement technique based on the principles of the corridors. You have worked with us in interdimensional traveling, which often occurs through corridors. I compare the concept of corridors to tunnels. When you seek to go to a higher astral or interdimensional realm, there needs to be some pathway that will help you get there.

A corridor is a tunnel that connects you from one realm to the other. That is to say, if you wanted to go from the third dimension to the fifth dimension, then using a corridor would be useful to you. The corridor, in a sense, transcends the space-time continuum. The corridor allows you to travel distances that are immeasurable in normal third-dimensional terms. Also, the corridor can provide a sense of protection.

When you travel from the third dimension to the fifth dimension, you will find that there are areas in the fourth dimension through which you must pass. These areas in the fourth dimension, especially the areas in the lower fourth dimension, often have lower spirits, ghosts, and other lower-energy beings. Indeed, the fourth-dimensional beings often try to attach themselves to unsuspecting third-dimensional travelers. In many cases, they are able to come down into the third dimension and cause great mischief. They are able to do this kind of mischief by attaching to the energy fields of unsuspecting people or people who have low-vibrational energy.

Many acts of violence, distortion, and strange events occur because of the bleeding of the lower fourth dimension into the third dimension. I use this term "bleeding" because, in a sense, it can be compared to the concept of a hemorrhage. Dimensional bleeding can occur when there are no protections between dimensions. The corridor or tunnel allows one to travel through the fourth dimension without worry about being accosted, attached to, damaged, or harmed in any way by these lower fourth-dimensional beings.

There is another technique that enhances traveling through the corridors: the folding of dimensional space. The first principle of this technique is that space and the space-time continuum are objects. Space in particular is an object that can be manipulated. There are various methods to do this. Imagine space as a large piece of cardboard that can be folded up like an accordion. This image is a beautiful metaphor for the folding of the space-time continuum.

The space-time continuum as you know it in the third dimension does not exist on the fifth dimension. There are significant differences. You might have a difficult time imagining how it is to live in a world that has no space. You would probably think that everything is sitting on top of everything else. There is a type of space in the fifth dimension, but the principles of space function with different rules. For example, in the fifth dimension there is still a space between you and another person. You are not on top of another person.

When you want to be with somebody in the fifth dimension, you can connect with that person. You are able to fold the space-time continuum between you when that person is in agreement to be with you, and then you are immediately together. In the third dimension, I'm sure you have discovered that oftentimes you are with people you do not want to be with. You might be in places that you do not want to be, and you might have experiences that are not in your desired outcome. This would not happen in the fifth dimension.

In the fifth dimension, you can go anywhere you want just by thinking about it. If you wanted to go to a mountain area or a lake, then you could be there. It is as if there is no space barrier, or the space is folded up so that you could be there immediately. These principles are relevant to the practice of folding the space-time continuum in the third dimension.

Space Is an Object

In higher-order space travel, the practice of folding the space-time continuum plays a central role in traveling throughout the universe and throughout the galaxy. Everyone knows that there are huge distances between star systems and planetary systems. In the third dimension during a normal lifetime, you would not be able to go to a planet that is far away and return within a normal life span.

The technology of the Arcturians and the Pleiadians has advanced to a point that I can compare our space system technology to biofeedback. In biofeedback technology, you interact with the computer. In fact, the next big development in the Earth computer technology will focus on telepathic communications between the observer and the computer. The computer will be able to read your mind. Of course, the computer is not actually "reading" your mind but picking up, from a biofeedback position, your eye movements, your temperature changes, and your energy patterns. These patterns are related to your thought waves. Therefore, you and the computer are in a synchronization that is, from our standpoint, still primitive, but it forms the foundation for later development.

In the Arcturian technique of space travel, the engine of the space vehicle is similar to a biofeedback relationship in which the engine and the person operating the ship become telepathically connected. The space traveler will practice and visualize the folding of the space-time continuum. As the space traveler does this, there becomes an instant link to hyperspace. The space traveler must practice advanced meditations to do this successfully.

One of the key practices for the space traveler is the folding of the space-time continuum. When the captain reaches the point of successfully folding the space-time continuum, then his or her interaction with the computer on the ship and on the engine brings the captain into hyperspace, the place in the galaxy or the universe he or she is destined for or wants to be. If you watch the movie Contact,[1] you will see this principle of folding the space-time continuum demonstrated. The ship seemingly did not travel anywhere through three-dimensional space but actually traveled to a distant location in another dimension.

You can travel to any place on this planet instantaneously by folding the space-time continuum. You can project yourself to a faraway place, transcending the laws of the space-time continuum; you fold up the space-time continuum so that you are exactly where you are focusing. You think it, and you are immediately there.

When you want to be with somebody on the higher levels, there are other rules that apply. Namely, the person you want to be with must also want to be with you. There is a positive attraction. This can occur by transcending

---

1 *Contact*, written by Carl Sagan and directed by Robert Zemeckis (Burbank, CA: Warner Home Video, 2009) DVD, 149 minutes.

the space-time continuum. When you wanted to visit somebody who is in Germany and you are in Arizona, you each would need to visualize where the other is on the planet. You could visualize a globe and see a dot where you are on the globe. Then you can visualize Germany and where Germany is, and you will experience the space between the two areas. It is an enormous amount of space from a planetary standpoint.

As I said, space is actually an object. Visualize the space begin to fold just like a piece of cardboard. Space is like an accordion that is beginning to fold up. As it folds up, you move closer and closer to the object. During this process, it appears as if no time is transpiring. If there were someone on the outside observing you, that person would not see time advancing. Yet you would experience space folding. When space folds, time becomes nonexistent from the third-dimensional perspective.

Practice Traveling to Arcturus

Time as you know it is nonexistent in the fifth-dimension. It is more of a sense of eternity with an expansiveness that is not measureable, and it is difficult to describe. Sometimes you will find people who have what is called a near-death experience (NDE). During the NDE, they also experience a folding of space. They are able to travel to other realms, other locations on Earth, and even other places in the galaxy. When they return, they often find out that their friends observed them in a semi-coma for days or even weeks, but from a time perspective, his or her own experience felt like a few minutes or an hour. This demonstrates that when space is folded, when there is a transcendence over space, the time differential becomes difficult to measure using third-dimensional standards.

This technique of folding the space is also used by remote viewers in their travels. Astral traveling is based on the principle of collapsing space and also thought projection. When you travel using thought energy, travel is instantaneous. The fastest energy in the universe is the speed of thought. The speed of thought is faster than the speed of light.

The speed of light is 186,000 miles per second. This is the fastest speed that one can physically attain in the universe. As you know, the distances to the nearest stars are light-years away. The nearest star may be 3.8 light-years away, so if you are traveling at the speed of light, it would still take you 3.8 years to get there and 3.8 years to return.

Many of the planets inhabited by higher beings are much farther away. Some of them are 500 light-years away. Some are 1,000 light-years away. Outside the Milky Way galaxy, the closest galaxy is the Andromeda galaxy, which is 2.5 million light-years from Earth. No one has a life span of 2.5 million years. There is no way that a spaceship could travel at the speed of light and expect to get there in a lifetime. This is why these techniques of folding the space-time continuum are used.

You can imagine the distance between Earth and Arcturus, which is around 36 to 37 light-years away. Visualize the large space that is there. Yes, it is an immeasurable and unimaginable space, but still it is space, and you can imagine two points, one representing Earth and the second representing Arcturus.

If you are sitting in your house, say in Chicago or in Florida, then try to imagine sitting in a chair on the surface of the planet. Have an image of the planet, and see yourself sitting there on the planet. Imagine that you had a tremendous telescope that was able to zoom with 10,000 times the power. If people were in a satellite above Earth and looked down on you, they would see you sitting in a chair on Earth. Hold on to this image. You are sitting in a chair on Earth, and you see this great circle of the planet. This image helps in folding space. If you were going to travel to another part of the planet, then you would visualize the point where you would like to go. Remember, in the folding of space and time, you have to use two points: the point that you are in and the point where you want to be in the future, your destination.

When traveling to Arcturus, visualize a point there. We have Arcturian schools. We have the Arcturian crystal lake. We have the Arcturian crystal temple and other powerful points where you can practice traveling to by using this methodology. Choose one of these points to travel to.

I will turn the next part of this lecture over to Tomar, an Arcturian temple teacher. Many of you are connected to Tomar. He has many friends among you.

I am Juliano. Good day.

• • •

Greetings, I am Tomar. I am an Arcturian spiritual teacher and close friend of Juliano's and yours. Some of you are my students in other incarnations. Some of you visit me in my school on Arcturus, and I recognize your energy and devotion.

Our entire planet is devoted to spiritual practices and spiritual development. Many of you long to return to Arcturus to be with us. You would like to be able to spend 100 percent of your time working on your spiritual development. This would be a great blessing. Some of you are used to devoting yourself to spiritual practices full time. I know some of you suffer from being in the third dimension where you do not have the same time to devote to spirituality. In fact, in the third dimension, you have many tasks that you must complete that are "not really spiritual." You have work to do that you might not like but must do to earn money. You have to commute through traffic and endure other experiences that are not very spiritual.

Time-Travel Visualization

The method that Juliano is teaching you is directly applicable to your being on Earth — the folding of the space-time continuum. You can use this to your benefit because it is our goal to make your life easier and more spiritual.

Suppose you are on an airplane traveling from Buenos Aires, Argentina, to Phoenix, Arizona. This is a long trip. It might be twelve hours by airplane. The plane has to take off and then travel over certain countries. There are weather patterns to pass through. The trip lasts a long time.

How can you experience this trip without being tired? How can you experience this trip without being weakened by the traveling? The answer is that you can use the experience of folding the space-time continuum.

Visualize yourself in Buenos Aires; see yourself on Earth, and then visualize going to Phoenix. You see the trajectory. Then as you have those two points, use the technique that Juliano just described. See the space as a piece of cardboard, and then visualize that the cardboard begins to fold. As it folds, it is helpful to see it fold evenly. You move closer between the two points, and then they are touching. Then you are there, and you get off the airplane.

When you do this exercise while you are flying, you will experience that the trip happens very quickly. You will find that your body will not feel tired when you arrive. This same technique can be applied when you are traveling from your workplace to your home when there is a great deal of traffic. It might take thirty to forty minutes to travel a short distance because of traffic.

Before you begin to drive, visualize where you are on Earth and where you want to go. Then see the space between as a cardboard-like object that begins to fold up. This exercise will help to subjectively experience the actual traveling in an accelerated manner so that you will soon be there. Even though it may be the same length of time, it will seem shorter. You will experience it as space-time folding, and you will not be as tired when you arrive. It will seem exhilarating.

Travel to the Arcturian Temple

Come to our Arcturian Temple. I am known as the temple master, and I will describe the room where I would like you to join me. In the center of the room is a beautiful circular crystal. It is a multidimensional crystal. Being a multidimensional crystal, it connects with other realms, and you can travel into the crystal and then appear in our temple. Our temple is in a circular formation. There are many of us sitting around the circle, wearing very simple white and blue robes. There are many Arcturians and Pleiadians in the room as well as other advanced beings from Earth who come here regularly.

Beautiful music is playing; it is vibrational and emphasizes toning and cleansing the energy into a harmonious, accelerated light form. Our temple has beautiful windows that look out into the galaxy. Each window is like a powerful telescope. This means that the window itself has the ability to look out into the galaxy and interact with your mind. When you want to go deeper into the galaxy, your thought is received by the window, and the window then accelerates and magnifies where you want to go and what you want to see.

You can see Earth from our temple. You can also see the galactic center. You can see outside our galaxy, the Andromeda galaxy. You can see the Central Sun in our galaxy and the moon-planet Alano. This is an example of the telescopic power of the beautiful windows that are around our temple.

Visualize now where you are on Earth. Then leave Earth. Go past the Moon, past Mars, and past the asteroid belt. Go to Jupiter, Saturn, Uranus, Neptune, and the area around Pluto. Then go one light-year to the outer edge of the solar system. It is estimated that from the Sun to the outer edge of your solar system is one light-year. There is the belt called the Oort Cloud, which contains many comets and different solar debris. Go beyond that and begin to travel at the speed of thought past all of the close stars, past Sirius, past Alpha Centauri, and advance 36 to 37 light-years to the great giant star Arcturus. You can see there are different planets in our system that are also in different dimensions. Our planet is a fifth-dimensional planet.

You are able to see all different dimensions, and you can see the beautiful planet Arcturus that, within a reasonable distance, perhaps a half light-year from the star, is our planet Arcturus. You see our planet, a beautiful blue planet. You feel the energy vibrations from me, Tomar, and from all of the other spiritual students with us now in the temple. Bring your consciousness here, and see our beautiful temple. Now you feel the space between you and my temple on Arcturus. The space is like a piece of cardboard, and it begins to fold. It folds rapidly, and suddenly you are here. You are here in Tomar's temple on Arcturus.

The space between your place on Earth and your being here has now collapsed. The space has folded, and you are now here with me and with our great spiritual friends in Tomar's temple. You see me levitating above this crystal, and you enjoy the vibrational light that is here in the temple. Experience being with me in the temple with all the other masters together in meditation. We will now go silent. [Pause.]

You experience an expansion of your energy field. It is a contraction to incarnate on Earth. You were required to confine your energy to a more condensed version of yourself. Here in Tomar's temple, experience yourself in expansion. Experience yourself in a higher frequency. As you experience this expanded self, your chakras open wider, and your abilities to be psychic and to heal are increased.

Now look into this beautiful circular crystal that is in the center of my temple, and feel your true, multidimensional self. One of the problems with experiencing your multidimensional self on Earth is that it is hard to integrate these higher aspects in your Earth mind. There are a lot of contradictions in the Earth way of thinking about how you can be in two places at one time. Here, in Tomar's temple, your mind is in a whole different level. Experience your multidimensional self now.

Your multidimensional self is able to fold space instantaneously. You can be in two places at the same time, three places, even. You can be in different aspects of yourself simultaneously. This is the power of the crystal and Tomar's temple.

Now, let us begin the journey back to Earth. See yourself above our planet. See yourself sitting in my temple. Now visualize the place on Earth where you were, and see the space between Earth and Tomar's temple, and begin to fold the space like a piece of cardboard. Now, shoohsh! You return to Earth.

As you return to Earth and to your body, you retain this special energy, the multidimensional presence that you experienced in my temple and the many higher beings who were there with us. Integrate this now and come into full consciousness on Earth, integrating all the principles of the folding of space. Remember, the folding of space also means the acceleration, or the shifting, of time. Time does not make any sense unless there is space. If space is transcended, then you are in a totally timeless place.

Blessings to each of you. I am Tomar. Good day.

Chapter 16

Heal Your Immune System with Higher Consciousness

Juliano, the Arcturians, and Quan Yin

Greetings, this is Juliano. We are the Arcturians. The issue of your immune system and the major developments of viruses and parasites and, of course, the well-known problems with the Ebola virus are all symptomatic of a major planetary shift. We need to put this entire epidemic in the perspective of the planetary shift. You are experiencing a phase known as planetary extinction. This planet has gone through five extinction periods throughout the 4.56 billion years of its history.

The genetic codes and structures of humanity have evolved according to a certain period. Generally, a genetic change in a species takes 400, 1,000, or even 1 million years. You are now witnessing genetic changes on a more rapid basis. These changes are occurring through all the species, including insects, mammals, and reptiles. More complex organisms take a longer period to change. In fact, genetic changes often occur more rapidly during a crisis, meaning the species must either change or suffer dire consequences.

It is clear that rapid changes are occurring on Earth in a short time. Many species have become extinct in the past forty years. Beyond that, environmental changes are so rapid that the genetic structure and shifting cannot keep up with the rapid changes on the planet. What does this mean for those who want to survive and continue to have a stable existence on this planet? Those people must adjust and must be prepared to become cocreators of their genetic systems. In particular, they must cocreate and influence their immune systems. Your immune systems must evolve and be strengthened. The attacks and the intrusions on the immune system are quite dramatic now. Your immune system can interact with your spiritual energy to create shifts in your body.

Vibrational Healing

The overwhelming amount of radiation in the atmosphere now compared to fifty years ago is one of the main factors in the degradation of the human immune system. The prominent radiation factors include, but are not limited to, radio waves and high frequency waves. I am not suggesting that you stop using your cell phones, so don't become too discouraged, but please understand that such radio wave contamination is one of many factors causing what I call distortions in the energy field of the immune system.

The immune system is not limited to your biological organs or lymph node systems. The immune system must be visualized as your whole energy field. This view is a major advancement in spiritual healing; that is, the immune system is viewed in terms of an energy field, which is the basis of the new type of healing now necessary on this planet. This type of energy-field healing has been referred to as vibrational healing. Vibrational healing is based on the premise that everything is a vibration, that diseases, parasites, and viruses have a certain vibrational frequency.

The human body has a vibrational energy field referred to as the aura. The aura is the frontline of the immune system. The aura has certain vibrations around it that protect your human structure and your organs. These are actually waves and vibrational energy fields. Some of these immune system vibrational fields are located in the chakras, but many of them are actually embedded in the patterns of your energy system. For example, we often refer to energy as representative of the helix form, and the helix form is one of the key ingredients or shapes of the correct DNA structure. There are other key shapes, such as cones, swirling circles, and vibrational circles, part of the protective immune system in your energy field.

There are factors that can distort your energy field. Radiation and radio wave emissions in particular have the ability to distort and suppress the vibration rate of your energy field, much like plaque in your arteries or brain cells. It is well known that plaque on the brain cells is the primary symptom of Alzheimer's disease. Plaque suppresses the life of the cell and eventually kills the nerve or brain cell, leading to Alzheimer's disease. Nuclear radiation has a similar effect on the vibrational frequencies in your aura. It suppresses the aura; it wipes out certain auric cells. It has the ability to distort your field.

The cosmic egg is an ideal shape for keeping your aura in optimum health. It is described as a perfect egg shape. The egg shape maintains your aura and has the ability to repulse energy of a lower vibration. The cosmic egg has the ability to block viruses trying to enter your energy field as well as to retard parasitic activity of all sorts.

Parasitic activity is not limited to the little microbes called parasites.

Certain people emit darker energy forces, and sometimes these forces harm others. These darker energy forces can contain hooks, similar to the hooks found on fishing line, that can go into your energy field. The goal of such activity is to parasitically attach to you and then to drain your energy. In fact, a parasite is just that. It lives off another organism's energy. Parasitic activity in your aura from lower-vibrational beings who wish to take your energy can contribute to the degradation of your immune system. Such hooks actually take your life-force energy, which sometimes is referred to in Chinese medicine as your chi. The chi energy is the strongest component for keeping your immune system healthy.

In regard to the Ebola virus, there are several things you should be aware of: The virus first comes into your aura energetically, and the manifestation of the virus in your physical body is secondary to the intrusion of the energy of the virus in your aura. This is an important distinction because you can strengthen your aura. You can do certain exercises to work with your aura, and those exercises can block the lower-vibrational frequency of such viruses and such parasites so that the energy of the virus does not penetrate your aura. If the energy of the virus cannot penetrate your aura, then the physical manifestation of the actual virus cannot enter your physical body.

The Environment and Your Immune System

There are ongoing experiments on this planet to overcome the space-time continuum, and some are not known to the public. These experiments have to do with time travel and distorting the space-time continuum so that people can collapse space and thus travel long distances throughout the galaxy. When you collapse space, you also collapse time. There are certain safeguards that must be done for these exercises to occur so that they are not harmful to the planet.

Many years ago we mentioned to you that the Galactic Council and the hierarchy of ascended masters in the galaxy felt that humanity was close to exporting nuclear technology into the galaxy. It may appear that humanity is not close to overcoming the speed of light and space travel, but they are, which means there is the possibility that they could export some of the technologies, including nuclear technologies, throughout the galaxy.

Some of the military experiments damage the auric space-time configuration of the helix, the conical shape around Earth. Earth has different complexities of auric energies that hold the third-dimensional energy in a configuration so that the space-time on Earth can be stabilized. You need this stabilization in order to function. Distortions have occurred over the past forty to fifty years. These have created leaks and distorted patterns in Earth's energy field and have also degraded the human immune system.

The human immune system is primarily centered in your auric field, and your auric field is sensitive. It responds to the energy field of the whole planet, including shifts in Earth's radiation field. Sometimes you notice dramatic changes in your mood, uncontrollable crying spells, feelings of confusion, and other distortion symptoms directly attributable to the holes that have been created in Earth's aura.

The toxicity of Earth's environment is well known. The contaminations in the oceans, rivers, forests, and air have an accumulative effect on Earth's meridian system. It also has an accumulative effect on your neurons and nervous system. Many people have been asking over the years, "Where should I live to be the most protected?" It's becoming more difficult to find those perfect spots because even they are suffering from genetic degradation due to the ocean and air currents movement around the planet.

This global environmental problem directly relates to the primary attacks on your immune system through the nervous system. Environmental contamination has a direct effect on your nervous system. This includes making you more sensitive to chemicals. It also includes affecting and lowering the protective effectiveness of your nervous response from the toxic environment. This can create distorted thinking patterns and digestive problems.

Environmental toxins can create holes in your aura, which can allow lower-vibrational parasites and viruses to come in. The toxins can affect your outer aura. You can think of the aura as being outside of the body, or you can view the body as being inside the aura. The outside of the aura affects the body. The reverse is also true. What is inside the physical body and what the body picks up chemically from toxicity can also affect the aura. So let it be said that this is a two-way street.

The good news is that the toxicity you are accumulating can be purified and expelled from your system. This is a good time to move into a discussion of healing energy, and then I will return to the idea of vibrational energy, the aura, and balancing yourself for maximum health on Earth. I am Juliano.

• • •

Tones to Protect Your Aura

Greetings, dear ones, I am Quan Yin. Healing sounds are very important in balancing your vibrational field. Even though you might feel as if you are accumulating many contaminants and being exposed to viruses and parasites, do not despair. There are advanced methods of purifying your energy field and protecting yourself from these dangerous intrusions.

Let's go over some healing tones that you can use to protect your aura.

These tones are advanced and can have a dramatic effect on healing. The first tone I'm going to use with you is the healing sound "haaaa." [Tones several times] "Hhaaaaa." This is one of the most powerful sounds in vibrational healing, and we use this sound to expel unwanted energy in your aura, your immune system, and your energy system in general. Visualize as you're toning the word "haaaa" that all of the lower-vibrational energies, such as the parasites and viruses, are like projectiles being thrown out of your aura. They are just sent out into the ethers away from you.

We're going to do this exercise very slowly. Sit comfortably, take a deep breath, and relax. Know that you are in a calm, energetic state and that you have tremendous powers to heal and bring your immune system into its highest balance. Visualize that you are bringing a small ball of light, like the size of a marble, into your stomach. This small ball of light is able to expand at a tremendous speed and vibration. On the count of three, the ball will become a larger ball of light, and it will expand and accelerate. It will look for all lower vibrations, parasites, viruses, and bacteria in your system, and it will push them out of your physical body. Then it will push them out of your auric field away from you.

I repeat: You have a small marble-sized light ball in your stomach. At the count of three, I will emit the sound "hhaaaa," and I want you also to emit the sound "hhaaaa." Listen and try to resonate this sound as deeply as you can: "Hhhhaaaaaa, hhhhaaaaaaaa." Try to go to that deep place inside your stomach where you can feel this powerful energy.

Okay, let's begin: One, two — the ball is small but is ready to explode into beautiful white light — three. [Tones two times] "Hhhhhaaaaaaa." The ball of light explodes inside you, and it pushes all lower vibrations, all viruses, all parasites, and all microbes out of your aura. Again, one, two, three [tones two times]: "Hhhhaaaaaaaaaa." Lower vibrations are removed from your physical body and removed from your aura.

You might feel a tingling, and now we are going to rebalance your aura with the sound "oooohhhhh." Ready? All of the energy is now rebalanced because the lower vibrations are removed, and now you're back into rebalancing everything. When you rebalance, there are no holes in your aura or energy field. Your balanced aura interconnects energetically and blocks viruses, parasites, and bacteria. This is a new type of balance and harmony. We will just sing this tone together [tones three times]: "Oooohhhhh." Now feel the rebalancing and reharmonization of your aura after everything has been expelled. A new harmonic light is going to be created in your aura. We will be in silence for a while. Just listen to these sounds again: "Hhaaaaaa. Ooooohhhhh." [Pause.]

Reintroduce Elasticity into Your Aura

Here is a third sound: "Hhhhoooooo. Hhhhooooo." This sound relates to what we call the pung energy[1] of pushing out, of pushing energetically. Imagine a stone is thrown into a beach ball. This beach ball has great elasticity, so as the stone goes into the beach ball, it makes a small indentation. But then it bounces out and is thrown off the ball. This is what we call pung energy.

The auras of people who have become overtaxed lose their elasticity, and because of this loss of elasticity, when an intrusion comes in, they cannot repel it. I am going to help you reintroduce this elasticity in your aura with the sound of "aahh, aahh."

Visualize your aura in the shape of a gigantic ball, and try to see it with a color. Perhaps it is orange, blue, red, and white. When I make the sound "aaahhh," the energy ball around your aura is going to become elastic. It's a strong and very powerful characteristic that we will call "elasticity." Affirm: "My aura has elasticity. My aura has elasticity." On the count of three, I will make the sound "aaahhh." I would like you to do that also, and your aura will become more elastic. One, two, three [tones three times]: "Aaaahhhhh." Experience the elasticity of your energy field. We will now take a moment of silence. [Pause.]

Now we are going to lock in this work. We will be able to hold this energetic ability so that you can have this available at any time. We will use the following sound [tones three times]: "Lay oh ah. Layyyy oooohh haa aahh."

Let the light of "lay oh ah" lock this energy in your aura now so that you have elasticity and also so that you are able to expel any intrusion at any time from your aura using the "hhhaaaaa" sound. Listen to this tone again [tones three times]: "Lay ooohh haaa ahhh." You are part of the new humanity who has the ability to interact in a new way with your energy field. Juliano will talk to you again. I am Quan Yin.

• • •

The Placebo Effect

Greetings, I am Juliano. The placebo effect was discovered a few hundred years ago and consists of the idea of giving sugar pills to patients. The patients are told they are being given special, powerful medicine, perhaps even a medicine that may have come from deep in the Brazilian jungles and has great healing powers. But the pill itself has nothing healing in it. It only contains sugar. It is the mind and the energy and the intention of the doctor giving the pill to the patient that activates the special quantum healing energy.

Quantum healing energy can be triggered through special circumstances that can results in a placebo effect. The right circumstances include being in

---

1 "Pung" is a Chinese word used to describe a type of energy in tai chi.

a healing setting, such as a doctor's office, in which you can open your belief system. A miraculous shift of energy can occur in a biological system when quantum energy and thinking are introduced. The truth is that there is a quantum energy. You will not think that quantum energy is just a sugar pill. The doctor can project a special quantum energy force into the person's aura through the pill, which can act in a way that transcends the space-time continuum and normal logic. We, the Arcturians, also use these methods, only we send etheric healing energy.

Visualize an etheric crystal. It's also good to have a physical crystal with you in the room. If you have a physical crystal, please hold it in your hand. If you do not have a physical crystal, then visualize an etheric crystal in any size or shape you desire. Visualize and remotely thought-project yourself to the crystal lake on Arcturus now. See yourself sitting at the Arcturian lake sitting on the shore.

You are now in your fifth-dimensional body, which has great healing powers and is able to easily overcome the dense energies on the third dimension. Your fifth-dimensional body is able to calibrate a special healing light specifically adapted for your body and your special needs.

As you sit on the lake in your fifth-dimensional body, look to your right and see an etheric crystal that's maybe twelve inches tall and has suddenly appeared at your right side. Take that crystal, and pick it up and hold it in your right hand. You'll see and feel its great healing energy. The crystal has a fantastic blue light. Now with your higher fifth-dimensional thoughts, send special quantum healing power into the crystal and calibrate that healing power for the specific needs of your third-dimensional body. Calibrate it now! [Tones] "Tatatatatatata, tatatatata, tatatatata."

This crystal is filled with special calibrated, fifth-dimensional healing light. It can heal your mood. It can heal your disposition. It can heal any specific needs that you have. Calibrate it now using your fifth-dimensional mind and the powers of the crystal lake, sending in quantum healing light that you now have access to on the fifth dimension. That crystal is now in your hand. At the count of three, we are going to shimmer, and you are going to return to your third-dimensional body with that crystal in your hand. One, two, three — shimmmeerrrrr back into your third-dimensional body with this crystal, this beautiful etheric energy crystal, in your hand.

If you have an actual crystal, merge the energy of the etheric crystal into your physical crystal on Earth. If you don't have a crystal with you, at the end of this exercise, look for a crystal and merge it with this etheric crystal. If you don't have a crystal at all, know that this etheric crystal is available to you.

Allow the crystal to emit healing light into your aura. [Chants] "Tatatatatatata, tatatatatatata, tatatatatatata." The healing crystal emits quantum healing light now. [Chants] "Tatatatata tatatatata tatatata." It is especially calibrated for the needs of your physical body, and it fills your aura now. We will go into silence while you allow all this to integrate. The quantum healing light from this etheric crystal has filled your aura now, and the etheric crystal will be available to you for personal use. Remember, it is calibrated for you to bring the greatest and most effective healing!

Blessings to you all. I am Juliano. Good day.

Chapter 17

Intermediaries and Expanded States of Consciousness

Juliano, the Arcturians, Sanat Kumara, and Chief White Eagle

Greetings, I am Juliano. We are the Arcturians. Throughout Earth's and the galaxy's history, there have been many different intermediaries. Intermediaries are spirit guides, prophets, and other beings who are able to bridge the energy gap between dimensions. There is a good reason why intermediaries are necessary. Now we are in a time when the messages, information, and energy from intermediaries are vitally important to your development and even to your survival on the planet. Intermediaries are essential to your ascension and your soul evolution. Intermediaries are able to go to higher levels of dimensional experiences.

Dimensional Hierarchy

The nature of reality is hierarchical, a hierarchy of dimensions. For example, the fifth dimension clearly is above the third dimension, and the sixth and seventh dimensions are above the fifth. I know that this concept of hierarchy seems to contradict the circular time and space of the fifth dimension, but the assumption is that the third dimension is based on linear thinking. In the fifth dimension, dimensional time and space interact in a circle. So when I talk to you about hierarchy, it is a linear description, not a circular model. Linear can be, of course, horizontal or vertical; nonetheless, vertical is still a linear progression.

How is it that we can reconcile this difference when describing the concept of hierarchy? Frankly, the answer is a paradox. To explain how you can have a vertical linear hierarchy that is fifth dimensional and incorporates the characteristics of fifth-dimensional ideals seems illogical. Yet the vertical model seems to express the basis of reality because you experience a different and higher hierarchy as you go to a higher realm. In fact, the whole basis of ascension rests on the fact that you are going to a higher level.

You can dispute this paradox. You can say that everything interacts on the same level and all is one. I would agree with you, actually, because by the very nature of this reality, of this universe, everything is one. However, from the perspective that you now experience in the third dimension, there appears to be a hierarchical system. One aspect of this hierarchy system is the different and higher dimensions. Another aspect is the different levels of dimensional beings, including the angels and the angelic hosts. There is a hierarchy of angels with a head angel who is also called an archangel.

These levels of dimensions present a paradox. The paradox has some points of unity and resolution because by the very nature of your being (as part of the Adam species), you are able to experience both parts of the dimensional hierarchy simultaneously. You are able to experience the top of the hierarchy and the bottom of the hierarchy. But you can only have this experience in expanded consciousness.

Intermediary Communication

The angelic world is only one part of the hierarchy, and as you know, it is also part of the sacred triangle energy because the angelic world includes fifth-dimensional beings. The angelic world is considered an intermediary world because it is between the third and fifth dimensions. The angels can exist between dimensions and also in the fifth dimension.

Understand that there are different levels of intermediaries. There are intermediaries living in the fifth dimension who are able to bridge the gap and come down to the third dimension and appear to you. These beings include the sightings or apparitions of, for example, Mother Mary, arch-angels, and higher-dimensional extraterrestrial beings sometimes observed through UFOs.

There are prophets and masters who have accepted intermediary roles on Earth, such as Moses, Buddha, Confucius, Lao Tzu, Jesus, and Mohammed. Numerous other beings can also be considered higher intermediaries. They come down from the order of a hierarchical system to bring information and healing energy to Earth.

This is a time when there are many intermediaries coming to Earth. There have been periods of spiritual darkness in Earth's history. There have been times when there were no intermediaries or when there were very few, and they were only available to certain people. Now you have unparalleled access to intermediaries. Even though this is a period of great change, disruption, and upheaval, intermediaries have been able to manifest through various techniques, including the ability to appear in this reality. That is, fifth-dimensional beings can appear on Earth through visions and channelings.

Other ways intermediaries interact with the third dimension is through walk-ins, cohabitation, or the sharing of the spiritual presence with higher Earth beings. There are now spiritual beings on Earth who are able to have prophetic visions and communications. There are starseeds who have the ability to telepathically communicate with the fifth-dimensional hierarchy. This telepathic communication occurs through various methods, including channeling and intensive meditations.

There are many spiritual masters and gurus on the planet who have direct access to intermediaries. The hierarchical energy of spiritual teachers from the higher realms is working to bridge the gap between the higher light and the third-dimensional life here on Earth.

Why is it necessary to have intermediaries? The answer lies in the dense nature of the level of reality you are experiencing, the third dimension, which has duality and polarization. The third dimension is in many ways the bottom rung of this hierarchy of dimensions. This third-dimensional experience on Earth is very special. Earth is a special planet, as you know. We refer to Earth as the Blue Jewel. One of the reasons Earth is such a special planet is because its energy field, which allows for duality, also allows for the experiences of higher-dimensional beings to manifest and to communicate on this planet.

You might take intermediaries for granted. You might think their existence is natural. This is not the case on other planets. Not all planets that have higher life forms in the Milky Way galaxy have the experience of intermediaries. There are examples of civilizations on Earth and other planets that do not accept and will not work with intermediaries. These are planets of darkness, and because of their particular energetic configuration, they do not have the opening and the ability to experience other realms and other communications.

I want to explain another important fact about intermediaries. This planet, this Blue Jewel, cannot evolve and resolve the current conflicts and situations without the intervention and communication from fifth-dimensional intermediaries. The intermediaries' energy is necessary to overcome Earth's duality and polarizations.

The idea of communicating with intermediaries is important for your development and evolution. You each have personal intermediaries — spirit guides and teachers — around you. Not just one channel or one prophet has the ability to communicate with these higher beings. Rather, each person has at any one time ten to fifteen and sometimes even twenty guides around them. Spirit guides are also considered intermediaries.

Why would you consider a spirit guide an intermediary? Because most spirit guides exist on the fifth dimension. Spirit guides come from higher realms. These beings can see things that you cannot, and they can have communications with other beings that you cannot. Of course, most important, they can bring you special messages from higher realms.

You are close to ascension. There is great upheaval, conflict, and polarization. And there are many intermediaries working with humanity through all this. You need to be able to access your spirit guides now. Accessing your guides is not as hard as you might think.

Accessing Higher Guidance

Some of you might feel closed to accessing higher guidance. You might say, "Oh, I cannot talk to my spirit guides. I cannot talk to my intermediary." There definitely are intermediaries you can relate to. This planet has a long history of many beautiful ascended beings who have worked as intermediaries. They are very plentiful. One of the great gifts on this planet is the existence and the ability of intermediaries to work and communicate with humanity. Certainly, there must be one of two intermediaries that you feel connected to. Try to work with the guides that you feel drawn to.

I, Juliano, am an intermediary. I come from the planet Arcturus. We are a fifth-dimensional planet. We are home to the Arcturian stargate. Our planet has ascended, and we accept our ability to be of service to Earth as intermediaries. We have certain abilities, ideas, and technologies that we are able to communicate through messages to those on Earth who are receptive to our information and to our energy.

I am happy to report that our role as intermediaries to Earth has been successful. Some of you have already asked, "Well, is the fifth-dimensional work we are doing helpful? Is the Arcturian work helpful? Are the spiritual energies coming down through the Arcturians and other powerful intermediaries helpful to Earth?" The answer is yes. We are helping to create an awareness and consciousness of a higher dimensional level, and our communication to Earth is verifying the existence of the fifth dimension.

Part of our foundational work is the essential task of placing in the consciousness of humankind the existence of the other dimensions and the higher realms. The existence of the consciousness of these realms creates a thought field that shapes the development of this planet.

From your perspective, you might think that Earth is going into deeper chaos and that the spiritual work and spiritual energy you have been working with do not seem successful. You might not see obvious signs of spiritual transformation on this planet. That view is coming from a more confined third-dimensional perspective. Your higher consciousness and your fifth-dimensional energy work is permeating Earth's noosphere. You can visualize that you are establishing a foundation of strong spiritual light that will shape the evolution of this planet.

There is an overwhelming body of intermediaries here to work with you. Some of you know of them from the Ashtar Command. Others know them from your work with the White Brotherhood-Sisterhood, Jesus, the Pleiadians, and P'taah. Some of you know my work. Some of you know the work of the ascended Native peoples, such as Chief White Eagle.

The Galactic Kachina

The intermediary can bridge communication between a higher energy field and the third dimension. Higher beings often communicate directly to humankind. You might ask, "How can we communicate with the Blue Jewel?" There are various techniques that many of you practice, including creating medicine wheels, performing ceremonies, and praying or talking to the spirit of Earth. Some of you have even heard the spirit of Earth speak to you or through others.

There are intermediaries between the spirit of Earth and humankind, such as Sanat Kumara. He is known as the planetary logos. He is like a bridge between the spirit of Earth and humanity. Native Americans have intermediaries called kachinas. They bridge the gap between the third-dimensional world and the spirit world as well. Kachinas have a home on Earth in the Native American Southwest in the San Francisco Peaks, outside of Flagstaff, Arizona.

There are different levels of kachinas. Some focus on agriculture, and some focus on other realms and even other dimensions. There are warrior kachinas as well. The Galactic Kachina is a new kachina. This kachina was downloaded into this realm several years ago through the work of David and Gudrun when they were working on the powerful area of the San Francisco Peaks, which connects with the higher kachina energy. They were able to assist in bringing the energy of the spirit of the Galactic Kachina to that mountain. Now the Galactic Kachina is there and accessible to all of you.

The Galactic Kachina is the intermediary between the Central Sun and Earth. It is like a messenger in which energy, ideas, and thoughts from the Central Sun are bridged. Through this bridge, you can connect with higher galactic energy. You can learn what information and ideas need to be brought forth from the Central Sun to this Earth. This illustrates an important idea in the concept of intermediaries: a higher energy field exists. This higher energy field is not exactly logical. It does not necessarily speak in sentences, and it does not necessarily speak with duality and polarization.

Intermediaries can be compared to high-voltage electrical lines. A higher electromagnetic energy field (high-voltage line) might be beyond what your normal electromagnetic energy field (your fuse box at home) can tolerate. Remember that you are an electromagnetic, vibrating energy field, but you have limitations. If a stronger pulse or stronger spiritual electromagnetic energy field comes to you, you have to be ready to process the energy from that higher force. Sometimes the energy is so heightened that you are not able to bridge it, and you might not be able to experience it.

I know that many of you have difficulties seeing spirits and connecting with spiritual energies or spirit guides. This has to do with how your electromagnetic energy field is configured. It has to do with whether your electromagnetic energy field can tolerate certain higher light force fields. It has to do with whether you have the right mental belief system to process this type of energy (higher voltages).

I think you have the basic picture. The Galactic Kachina is difficult to describe, yet you can feel the effects of the Central Sun. Remember that the Central Sun, which is located in a dimensional space approximately in alignment with the center of this galaxy, came into a galactic alignment with your solar system on December 22, 2012. That means that there was an increase of galactic spiritual energy coming to Earth from the light and energy field from the Central Sun. Some of you have experienced this downloaded energy but in a way that you cannot easily explain.

Some of you might be experiencing confusion or uncomfortableness as a result of the new galactic energy. You might even be feeling a little agitated. Some experience this new energy as a general feeling of unrest. Maybe you are having difficulty making decisions. The things that used to be normal and give you pleasure in the third dimension do not provide satisfaction anymore. There are various ways of interpreting this type of reaction. But I think the important thing is that you are intuitively sensing some other spiritual force that has come to Earth, and you are reacting to it.

You might not be able to define the nature of the force. You might not be able to say what its message is, but you know on an intuitive level that there is something different going on energetically. This is felt as some other spiritual energy, a newer, powerful energy. It is even unsettling in the sense that it disrupts traditional social and political models.

This unsettling energy is affecting everyone, even nonspiritual people. Even those people who seem to have really third-dimensional perspectives still experience and feel the effects of the energetic field known as the Central Sun energy coming to this planet.

The Galactic Kachina can bring messages and information to you from this energy. It is able to download this energy so that you can bridge it and comprehend it. You can experience this energy in a form that you are able to process. That is the exact and perfect role of the intermediary. The Galactic Kachina intermediary bridges that gap from the Central Sun and brings that energy to you in a way that you can begin to comprehend it, integrate it, and use it.

I want to compliment your third-dimensional mind because you need it. All these different energy fields from the higher realms need to be transposed into a workable form that you can integrate and process. I, Juliano, see this higher light. I see these higher-dimensional realms. I see the many intermediary guides and teachers, including the Galactic Kachina and Sanat Kumara, around all of you. Please welcome them as well as your ability to speak to them and receive their messages.

Welcoming the guides is one of the most important tools in the new spiritual technology from the Arcturians. Welcome and accept the higher dimensional spirit guides and intermediaries working with you and working with the planet. Accept them aloud or in your thoughts, and this will help to produce the right energetic configuration to open your higher thought powers, which will help you to receive their messages. This is one of the foundational exercises necessary to increase your receptivity.

A Halo of Spiritual Light and Harmony

The ring of ascension is an etheric halo around Earth, an etheric energetic ring composed of the thought fields and higher-energy blessings from the ascended masters. The White Brotherhood-Sisterhood and the great ascended teachers are sending higher energy to Earth through the ring of ascension.

This fifth-dimensional thought field helps to form the ring of ascension. I like to compare this ring to a halo because the halo is a sign and manifestation of unity and harmony. The halo is a sign of spiritual development and unity with the oneness that exists. A halo around their heads and shoulders is what all of the ascended masters have when they manifest and appear on Earth.

You work hard to purify your energy field. You have worked hard to remove illness, darkness, and congestion. The halo is the culmination of your spiritual work and represents harmony with higher dimensions. It implies that you have reached a point of acceptance and integration. It implies that you have reached a point of interaction with the higher dimensions and know that you are in communications with other dimensional beings and are receiving their higher energy. It implies that you have a certain level of personal power and protection.

Being in a halo is a wonderful experience on the third dimension. The ring of ascension offers humanity a halo around Earth. It is a force field, a thought field, composed of spiritual light and harmony. The ring of ascension is a thought field and energetic ring demonstrating that there can be harmonic communication with the fifth dimension. It is unique because it might not be physically observable to you, but it does interact and exist etherically with the higher-dimensional realms. This ring of ascension interacts with you, the starseeds. This ring of ascension is set up so that you are able to access the fifth-dimensional guides and teachers more easily.

How do you access the ring of ascension? In your meditation, visualize a golden halo that looks like the ring of Saturn around Earth. Thought-project yourself to this ring of ascension so that you can more easily meet your intermediary guides and teachers. Remember, there are great intermediary guides and teachers that transcend individual eras. Work with the ring of ascension.

I am Juliano. I now turn this over to Sanat Kumara. Good day.

• • •

The Blue Jewel

Greetings, I am Sanat Kumara. Blessings to you. You, as I, love the Blue Jewel, planet Earth. It is a planetary spirit of high development that has great spiritual abilities. The Blue Jewel is reaching out to you.

The Blue Jewel has survived for 4.56 billion years in this part of the galaxy and has experienced transitions too numerous to list. The Blue Jewel has experienced many different life forms, including higher life forms, even before your civilization. There have been higher life forms on this planet before you.

The Blue Jewel has the ability to communicate intergalactically with the Central Sun and other advanced planets telepathically, such as Arcturus. It even communicates with planets in other dimensions. This is a multitalented planet. It would have to be to survive this long and to deal with the profound changes now occurring. The Blue Jewel is adjusting to humanity. But I am not sure that humanity is adjusting well to the needs of the Blue Jewel.

Earth's Crowning Jewel

There is one important message that I, as an intermediary, am here to tell you. There must be some adjustment on the part of humankind. Planet Earth, with all of its capabilities — its feedback loop system and its intergalactic communication — wants you, the Adam species, to remain on her. Remember, the crowning jewel of Earth is humanity.

It sounds strange when we anthropomorphize Earth, saying that she is proud of you, and you are her crowning jewel. What happens on the third dimension is communicated in higher realms. Earth communicates to other planets. This communication occurs partly in the form of electromagnetic energy.

The electromagnetic energy field of Earth is transmitted throughout the galaxy. Earth receives energy from the galaxy and from the Central Sun. Earth transmits to the galaxy different electromagnetic particles, energy fields, and vibrations. So when I anthropomorphize Earth, I say that Earth is communicating that she is proud that you, humanity, are her crowning jewel.

You all know that Earth is being stressed and is at the point of creating some major changes. Earth has the responsibility of maintaining the ingredients for a biosphere to exist. Earth is looking at it from a long-term perspective. The biosphere may not continue. It could collapse and then humanity dies. All life forms might die. But from Earth's perspective, from the perspective of the Blue Jewel, she already has different ways and means of ensuring that life forms will exist, even if humans destroy themselves.

If humanity destroys the biosphere and cannot continue to live on this planet, it won't be the end of the Blue Jewel. It won't even be the end of life forces because there will be other adjustments made by Earth. It could take another 25,000 or 50,000 years. It could take another million years. Earth knows how to maintain or re-create a biosphere on her surface. She's done it several times before.

This is not meant to be a negative message. It is just a message that says Earth knows how to survive and hold life forces. But Earth prefers humankind to survive and to continue. Earth is pleased with your spiritual energy and development — the starseeds, those who work with her. Earth is pleased with the spiritual development achieved by the advanced beings here.

Earth notes this spiritual development in her responses. One factor in Earth's response to this spiritual development is that greater catastrophes could be occurring but are not. There could be greater volcanic eruptions and earthquakes. Earth is aware of some of the difficult situations occurring now. Some of them are frightening. The message, though, is that Earth is responsive to humanity. Earth will listen. She is particularly sensitive to those who respect her. Earth is a great spiritual planet with higher powers, and she wants you all to know that. She is a planet with extraordinary abilities. You are very gifted to be part of her experience.

I am Sanat Kumara. Good day.

•   •   •

Central Sun Energy Interferes with Old Thought Forms

[Chants] "Hey ya ho." Greetings, I am Chief White Eagle. I have the honor of speaking about the Galactic Kachina. The Galactic Kachina says to me that she is working to download the new light into the minds and thoughts of the starbeings and the star sisters and brothers on this planet.

She is on the San Francisco Peaks near Flagstaff, Arizona, which is receiving much light from the central part of the galaxy, from the Central Sun. She said that this light, this energy, has many different facets. The first message is that many of the old ways for working with human-made systems do not work. The old systems based on polarity, dominance, and abuse are not going to work any more. But those ways, she says, are deeply embedded in human consciousness. Even those who do not follow those kinds of beliefs still possess the old patterns from primitive times in their DNA. Those older patterns are now being disrupted. There is a new energy field that is interfering in the old patterns. Think about receiving a radio signal and then suddenly there is interference.

The Galactic Kachina says that an energy wave from the forces of the Central Sun is coming here and interfering with these older systems. This causes disruptions, which causes upheavals. The Galactic Kachina says that there is going to be more social upheavals coming to this planet. There are many upheavals now. No country is going to be spared from the social upheavals because the old system is based on an unsustainable energy pattern. The older ways are not able to be planted into a foundation.

You are seeing social change now. New weather patterns are also a reflection of the need for shifting the old. The Galactic Kachina recognizes that sometimes disruptive weather patterns are not the most helpful way to stop the old patterns. The Galactic Kachina is also communicating with Earth. Earth is an advanced spiritual planetary being that has basic planetary instinctual reactions. You are seeing some of those instinctual reactions now in terms of storms, earthquakes, and volcanoes. Yes, Earth can respond in a more heightened spiritual way too.

Part of this communication from the Central Sun and from the Galactic Kachina is for Earth's growth. The Galactic Kachina says that Earth as a planet will have to stretch her abilities. The Central Sun energy is being downloaded now into Earth, and the Galactic Kachina is helping. The Galactic Kachina also wants to bring new ideas of ways of being to you and to help Earth to personally expand its systems. This means your beliefs about yourself need to expand. The system of energy you've used to maintain your configuration of self must expand. You must expand your personal power.

All of these aspects of your self are being shifted right now. You are receiving a different and new electromagnetic frequency coming from the Central Sun. It is difficult to integrate this new energy, but it is also something that you have wanted. It is something that you have come here to experience and to foundationally download into the planet. Part of the planetary healing work focuses on downloading this kind of frequency into the planet, and part of the work is to download new energy from the Central Sun into your personal energetic system. You are going to become a new you, which is something you all want anyway. Manifest the new part of you now.

I, Chief White Eagle, again welcome the Galactic Kachina. Know that she is going to be working with you and with the spirit of Earth. All my relations. Ho!

Chapter 18
Protect Your Spiritual Energy Field

Juliano, the Arcturians, and Chief White Eagle

Greetings, I am Juliano. We are the Arcturians. Many of you are experiencing vulnerability in your spirituality and in your spiritual energy field. There are many reasons for this. Basically, the planet is in crisis. It is going through an unprecedented, rapid shift in many of the systems that are necessary to keep a stable biological environment.

One of the major dangers to the planet is the radiation permeating it. The permeation of radiation became a problem even before the Fukushima power plant accident. There have been rapid exposures of damaging radiation in the oceans and throughout the atmosphere for many years due to nuclear testing and the dumping of mass amounts of radiation wastes. It has been estimated that over 50,000 tons of dangerous radiation has been dumped into the oceans. What you are seeing at this point is a major addition to the rapidly deteriorating situation regarding the exposure to radiation.

However, the human body is very adaptable. The biological organisms on this planet have great adaptability. Earth throughout its history has experienced catastrophic events, but it has been able to survive. Many species have died, but others have adapted.

Adapt to the Changing Times

You are living during a planetary crisis. You are being called on to make major changes in yourself and your energy field. Extreme releases of radiation create holes in Earth's atmosphere. Overexposure to radiation creates holes in Earth's energy field that can cause leakages of life-force energy. You can also experience leakages in your energy field if you are overly exposed to radiation. Unfortunately, everyone on the planet is being overly exposed to radiation — everyone!

This might come as a shock, as some of you think that you are living in a safe area. Many of you have developed sacred energy fields and sacred sites around your living areas. I am proud and happy about this. The key to maintaining your protection is through a strong spiritual energy field. The key in maintaining your survivability during this unprecedented shift is to create a protective energy field so that you can adapt.

Adaption is a multidimensional process. Adaption includes protection so that you are not overly bombarded with dangerous energy. Also adaption includes making the shifts in your DNA to adapt to what is becoming the new normal. The new normal on this planet is an increased amount of radiation.

There are factors other than radiation that are considered dangerous, such as the many types of environmental pollution that can affect your energy field. The different methods I have explored with you to protect your energy field involve creating the cosmic egg (see appendix A) using colors, and shielding. Shielding can include placing a cone of light around you that is the spiritual color known as Arcturian blue (see appendix B), or layered white light. The idea is that your spiritual energy field needs to be protected.

You know that you will take your spiritual body with you when you leave the planet, and you do not want your spiritual body to be damaged or distorted. You have mental, emotional, physical, and spiritual bodies. Primarily, the spiritual body has those aspects of you that will ascend and transfer to the higher dimensions.

Logically, you would agree that it is most important to protect your spiritual body from assaults. Assaults from external forces can include radiation. Many people on the planet have become mentally unbalanced. You are witnessing unprecedented wars, social upheavals, conflicts, and polarizations creating imbalanced energy fields. This is a time for acceleration. Suddenly people are realizing that there are limited resources. Unfortunately, this is a time in which people generally, from a social and political standpoint, are becoming hardened in their positions. They do not want to compromise. You have seen this a great deal in recent years. This kind of polarizating energy is going to continue. There is a lot of distorted energy. People are hypercritical in a negative way toward people who do not agree with those in power or those who have a certain view. Polarization has been a problem on Earth for many centuries.

In previous lifetimes, many of you have had negative experiences in groups. You have either been, shall we say, prejudiced or abused by groups. On the other hand, you have been part of good groups. The negative groups somehow have been betraying you; some have even become cults. There are many different scenarios that have occurred in the group energy on Earth. However, this does not mean that groups by themselves are bad. It just means that there is a typical force that can use the group energy for selfish purposes. At this time, it is not necessary to worship one leader. Everyone must come into his or her own self-mastery. This is a time when it is necessary to find the master within you. This is one of the interesting lessons now on Earth.

The Biggest Challenge on Earth

One of the biggest challenges on this planet focuses on how to bring fifth-dimensional energy down into the third dimension. Perhaps it might be fair to say that many of you have had previous lifetimes on other planets. Some of you have had previous lifetimes as fifth-dimensional beings. I think it is also correct to say that you might have underestimated the density of the third dimension. Even the ascended masters, who have come to this planet bringing great gifts and energy, have underestimated the densities on this third-dimensional Earth. These masters have led exemplary lives. They have access to what is considered miracles. Yet some of the masters who have incarnated on Earth have had difficulty in overcoming the third-dimensional density. Their teaching and energies still have not helped humankind to overcome this current planetary crisis.

There are many lessons for you to learn in order to graduate from Earth. Some of these are personal lessons. You will want to know the secret to bringing fifth-dimensional energy into solving your personal problems and protecting yourself. In your history, there are examples of masters who have brought down fifth-dimensional energy to this planet. You have seen this on a personal level and also on a group level.

There are surprising ways of bringing down fifth-dimensional energy. There were two Native Americans, Chief Crazy Horse and Geronimo, who were able to bring down fifth-dimensional energy around them through their special powers. During their lives, they seemed to be very well protected. For example, Geronimo was able to go into battle and never suffer defeat. Bullets would fly around him, and he was never wounded. Chief Crazy Horse also had special powers of protection.

There are also examples of this in your religious stories. You have the story of Moses, who used fifth-dimensional energies to move a group across a waterway. He was able to survive for many days without food or water. Many experiences he had on Mount Sinai were fifth dimensional. Jesus demonstrated fifth-dimensional energy in a dynamic way. He demonstrated bilocation, the ability to rise and re-create his body and ascend — which is of course one of the major gifts he gave to humanity — and he left behind an energy field his followers used to create a force for teachings of higher wisdom. Unfortunately, later some of his teachings were distorted or limited.

Some groups, such as the Essenes, were able to use Jesus's teachings in a way that allowed them to also experience fifth-dimensional energy. The Essenes, as a group, chose to experience this fifth-dimensional energy in their isolated caves as part of their withdrawal from the normal life and social ways.

There are many other examples of masters, teachers, and famous people who have brought down fifth-dimensional energy. What was their secret? Why isn't fifth-dimensional healing energy manifesting more quickly? Why isn't everything changing? Why is it that the whole planet has not received and accepted fifth-dimensional energy? These were questions asked by all the ascended masters, and there are no simple answers. The ideas and energy that you connect with in the fifth dimension do not always immediately manifest. Wouldn't it be wonderful if they did? Wouldn't it be wonderful if you envisioned your city as a city of light and it immediately raised its vibration so that everyone was living in peace and with social justice in a just society?

Planetary healers must learn how to accelerate bringing down fifth-dimensional energy into Earth. An important lesson from the teachings of Geronimo and Chief Crazy Horse is about acquiring personal power. Bringing down fifth-dimensional energy to Earth requires you to learn how to use personal power.

Your higher self already knows how to bring down fifth-dimensional energy, but you need further instruction on how to acquire personal power so that you can manifest that fifth-dimensional energy on this planet. The key paradigm for Earth's transition into the fifth dimension lies in the sacred triangle. The teachings of the sacred triangle focus on the unity of three spiritual paradigms. I have spoken about this so many times. Each paradigm (galactic spirituality, the White Brotherhood-Sisterhood, and the Native peoples' teachings) standing alone is not strong enough to bring down and manifest in an accelerated way the fifth-dimensional energy. If each paradigm could do it by itself, then, for example, the White Brotherhood-Sisterhood energy field would have transformed Earth. If the Native peoples had been strong enough, they would have been able to bring peace and balance to the planet. If the starbeings were able to do this, they would have done it already.

Many of you know from past lifetimes that other planets have not resolved the type of planetary crisis Earth is now experiencing. I know from my dream-time connections with you that some of you have personally experienced the destruction of the third-dimensional planets you were on. You have directly seen, tragically, how a planet can destroy itself while experiencing the same type of crisis now on Earth.

The teachings of the sacred triangle say that all three paradigms must come together to resolve the current planetary crisis. To answer the question about how to bring down and accelerate the manifestation of fifth-dimensional energy into Earth, into the third dimension now, we turn to Chief White Eagle.

I am Juliano.

• • •

Personal Power

[Chants] "Hey ya hooooo. Hey ya hooooo." All my words are sacred. Greetings, I am Chief White Eagle, and I welcome the spirits of Geronimo and Chief Crazy Horse. We welcome all of you to our great powwow in our great medicine wheel, our great circle of light. You and I are brothers and sisters, and we gather here to learn the great teaching of personal power.

Personal power in the spiritual world is the ability to connect with higher energy and use that higher energy on Earth for a specific purpose. There are a great many people who attain spiritual wisdom. It is a difficult task to become spiritually wise and to understand what is going on in your lifetime. It is a great challenge to live in peace and harmony with yourself.

You also know that it takes something beyond personal harmony to change a planet, city, or country, let alone Earth. What is it? That is where the example and the teachings of Chief Crazy Horse and Geronimo come in. These masters exhibited great personal power. They have exhibited the ability to protect themselves energetically and to change others around them.

Personal power requires creating a magnetic energy field around yourself. There are many different ways of describing an energy field. It could be in a perfect shape, it could have holes in it, or it could be parasitic. You can describe an energy field as being dark or light.

People with personal power can clear their energy fields. By clearing their energy fields, they rid themselves of parasitic attachments. People with personal power can bring down their higher selves and their masters and teachers. In a vision quest, you can bring your power animals, guides, and teachers into your energy field. With that force, you are able to effect change.

A strong magnetic energy field will attract others who share the same vision. This means that personal power can be adapted in creating a group energy. Chief Crazy Horse, for example, had many followers. Geronimo also had many followers. I know that they were warriors fighting forces that were sometimes ferocious. I am not here to judge the path they chose to manifest on Earth. I was not in their shoes — or moccasins — so I do not know how I would have acted if I were there. But I do know that they fulfilled, to the best of their abilities, the gathering of personal power to protect and maintain their lifestyles. Going "on the warpath" is not necessary now. There are other ways of using your powers to gain influence on this planet.

Magnetic energy attracts people. Connect with your personal power. Consider what type of personal power becomes increased in a group. Geronimo and Chief Crazy Horse could not achieve anything without group support. What group power is there in the Group of Forty? What magical or mystical powers lie in forty members in one group? What mystical powers lie in forty groups of forty? What mystical powers lie in having groups around the globe?

It is time to evaluate your personal power on two levels. The first level is your individual life, and the second level is being part of a group. A group has an energy of its own that is magnetic and can attract many people. There are energy fields and forces that you can work with more powerfully when you are connected with other people. This is a basic teaching not only of the Native people but also a well-known fact throughout Earth.

Connect with fifth-dimensional energy. Higher-dimensional concepts, such as divine wisdom, divine judgment, the just society, divine mercy, divine compassion, and divine endurance are all energies that can lead to victory over the darker third-dimensional forces. You now have the ability to stand up to darkness with higher wisdom and higher teachings.

White Buffalo Calf Woman represents a powerful force in the world of personal power. She shows us the path of justice, balance, personal integrity, and planetary balance. She helps the planet transcend the lower third-dimensional polarizations now destroying the beloved Earth.

There is a planetary force of rectification. Earth has been out of balance. The negative forces that can destroy this planet will be overcome by a greater spiritual force that lies within your ability to attract personal power and to unite with the group. [Tones] "Hey ya hoooooo."

Connect with your own personal power to feel that you can protect yourself. Feel that you have a strong energy field. Juliano spoke to you about the dangers at this time and the fact that your spiritual energy field is vulnerable. A vulnerable spiritual energy field can be affected by darker forces. Your spiritual energy can be withdrawn from you. There are many results of being spiritually vulnerable. Part of that vulnerability occurs from living on a planet that has a great deal of imbalances from many sources. Having spiritual power in the Native tradition is connected to being a spiritual warrior. Spiritual warriors are able to emit a great energy.

Connect to your inner self; connect to your inner spiritual warrior side. Connect to your spirit guide. If you so feel chosen, connect to Chief Crazy Horse; connect to me, Chief White Eagle; connect to Geronimo; connect to Chief Buffalo Heart; and connect to White Buffalo Calf Woman. Invite them into your energy field now. When you connect to your personal power guide and teacher, your energy field becomes more powerful. You feel able to throw off these lower and darker energies. I will chant very softly while you connect with your personal guides.

[Chants] "Hey ya hooo. Hey ya hooo." Bring these guides into your energy field. Invite them into your energy field. Invite these spiritual warriors into your energy field now. [Chants] "Hey ya hoooo."

Know that you can have these spirit guides with you whenever you want. They can be with you as you walk the planet as you are exposed to different levels of negativity. The spiritual warrior within you and your power guide and teacher will help you to build a strong energy field. Lower negative energy will not be able to penetrate your magnetic power. Feel your pulsing aura push out with the strength of a powerful warrior. Remember Geronimo and how he was able to use this technique. Even bullets could not touch him. This is how powerful your energy field can become!

Do not be afraid to shout. Do not be afraid to make a loud noise. That is why we use drums in our ceremony. That is why we use rattles. That is why we are shaking the energy field to tell the self that this is the new way. This is the way to activate personal power. This is the way of the spiritual warrior.

Now with your ability to have personal power, connect to the fifth dimension. The ideas and the solutions of healing Earth lie in the fifth dimension. Juliano has given great lessons in traveling to the crystal lake and to the Arcturian temple [see chapter 6]. The idea is that when you are in these places, you connect to your supermind. You connect to the higher level of consciousness that sees so much more and that feels so much more. In the supermind, you are connected with super powers, super energy, and new ways of using your personal power on Earth.

So, you see, we are all gathered together now in a great etheric circle of light, in a great medicine wheel fifty miles above Earth. We are sitting around this beautiful circle. It is like a beautiful tepee. After you hear my words, go into your medicine wheel and feel the power. We, as a group, are in a big circle above Earth.

[Chants] "Hey ya hoooo." O Father/Mother Creator of all, we are gathered in this beautiful medicine wheel. The medicine wheel is a circle of power. It is a place in which we can gather the powers of the galaxy, the masters, and the teachers. Let all who hear these words and who are participating in this circle be activated in their own personal power. Let them become the spiritual warriors that they are. Let them connect to their guides and teachers so that they can follow their paths of planetary healing. Let their teachings, thoughts, and words be powerful. Let them have great courage and strength, for they are following the way of the White Buffalo Calf Woman. They are following the way of the Galactic Kachina in bringing through, in a courageous way, a new teaching to this planet. [Chants] "Hey ya hoooo. Hey ya hoooo."

I ask that you accept these gifts — the gifts of your power animal: the deer, the buffalo, the eagle, the bear, the whale, and the dolphin. The healing of this planet *depends on you as starseeds fulfilling your mission. Part of that mission is to accept and use your personal power for planetary and personal healing. Let your energy fields be more magnetized and more powerful. A powerful energy field can push off negative energies that come to you. Fill up your energy field now with strong, beautiful white light. We are all brothers and sisters on this Earth, brothers and sisters in this galaxy.*

This is the great teaching. The ascended masters are Native teachers coming to help you activate your power as planetary healers and spiritual warriors. All my words are sacred. All my relations.

I am Chief White Eagle. Ho!

Chapter 19

The Medicine Wheel

Juliano, the Arcturians, and Chief White Eagle

Greetings, I am Juliano. We are the Arcturians. The concept of the medicine wheel is a galactic symbol related in many cultures. For example, the mandala is also in the shape of the circle. In the Native American cultures, these mandalas also have corresponding energies to the medicine wheel.

The medicine wheel is a gift from the star family to the people of Earth. A star family is a group of higher masters similar to the Galactic Council. They oversee the evolution of Earth energies as well as other planetary energies throughout the galaxy. You are not the only civilization in this galaxy, but Earth is a special civilization with a high number of starseeds.

Starseeds are those people who have had previous incarnations on other planets and have had contact in Earth lifetimes with starbeings from other planets. Many of you have had contact with your star family in other Earth incarnations, which has opened you to connections with them. The star family includes the Pleiadians, Arcturians, higher Sirians, and Antareans.

Unique relationships have been established between the star family and the native peoples of the planet as well. The star family has ongoing contact with receptive people on Earth.

The Blue People

Your sister galaxy Andromeda has many parallels to Earth and your gigantic, beautiful galaxy you call the Milky Way. The Andromeda galaxy is home to the Blue People. The Blue People are highly evolved spiritual beings who exist in thought form without incarnations in physical bodies. This development is an evolutionary step that you are on the track to achieve. It is difficult at this time, in this physical body that you are in, to conceptualize an incarnation without a body. Imagine that it is possible to have a presence without a body, but you would exist only in a thought form. This is one of the powerful levels of evolution that the Andromedan Blue People have achieved.

The Andromedans have taken an interest in Earth's population and starseeds. What is beautiful about the starseed energy is it attracts other starseeds, other star-family members. The star family members include all of the higher evolved beings in the Milky Way galaxy. This means that the star family includes you! You are part of the star-family, and you are able to connect on many different levels with its energy.

The star-family has interacted with native peoples for many centuries. There are many stories of the star family giving them information and energies. In earlier times, people lived and interacted with the sky at night. They interacted with the star family energy directly on a nightly basis. Civilization has created large cities, and that has contributed to fewer nightly interactions with the star family and with the sky.

Sometimes the historians and the scientists are surprised that native peoples such as the Maya had so much knowledge of the sky and astronomy. But this is easier to understand when you can picture people interacting with the beautiful sky on a nightly basis. You can connect Earth energies with the night sky. I encourage you all to interact with the night sky as much as possible. You can meditate in an open area to connect with Arcturus, even though there are parts of the world where Arcturus is not visible.

Living in the Southern Hemisphere, you might decide to connect energetically with the Southern Cross or with its nearby star system known as the Magellanic Clouds. Telepathically, you can also connect with the star family during your meditations under the sky. [Tones] "OOOhhhhh."

The Wheel of Incarnation

We, the Arcturians, are part of the star family. We are also involved with the Pleiadians in the gifting of the medicine wheel and the circle. The mandala has contributed to the formation of the medicine wheel, or the medicine circle.

The idea of the medicine wheel, as given to the earlier native peoples, focuses on creating telepathic communications with planet Earth and to the galaxy. The medicine wheel can be used to create a telepathic link to the wheel of incarnation. This is quite an expansive energy and tool. The wheel of incarnation represents your histories. You've had many earlier lifetimes on Earth. Some people will refer to the medicine wheel as representing the wheel of incarnation, as it is represented in the Hindu philosophies. This is a good comparison.

You can also look at the wheel of incarnation holographically. One of our primary teachings relates to holographic perception. We are helping you to expand your perceptual field so that you open to the holographic world. The third-dimensional world is linear and more confining. The higher perception always includes holographic energies so that when you use this perception, you begin to see multiple levels. In incarnational terminology, the term "multiple levels" refers to cosmic karma and cosmic incarnations: The wheel of incarnation is related to your Earth incarnations, especially for you, the starseeds.

The wheel of incarnation also relates to your cosmic incarnations and to the fact that you have incarnated on other planets, some even in the third dimension. You have also incarnated on planets in the fifth dimension. Of course, you will wonder, "How can it be that I have incarnated on a fifth-dimensional planet? Why am I here now on this third-dimensional planet?" To understand that, you have to use the holographic energies to look at the concept of what I call coiled incarnations.

When looking at a coil, you notice that it goes up and around, and there is a part of the coil that seems to be somewhat flat. This flat part symbolically refers to multiple dimensional incarnations on a plane. You are moving up in your evolution. You are moving up the coil. There are places on the coil where your development stays on one plane. On one part of the plane, you are in the third dimension, and in the other part of that plane, you can be in the fifth dimension. Eventually, you reach a point where you are totally fifth dimensional and you never (unless for some reason you choose to) have to return to the third dimension.

Some of you have lived on fifth-dimensional planets, and in that life you went on excursions to Earth. During one of those excursions, you either had an accident or were involved in the third dimension and experienced the cause-and-effect of karma on Earth. Therefore, you were unable to return to your fifth-dimensional life. The best way for you to return to the planet you came from is through the ascension. Your star family knows of the ascension and knows that starseeds like you will want to participate in it because many of the starseeds will take this opportunity to return to their home planets.

Some of you in your star-family work were sent here on certain missions. You were already fifth dimensional, but you volunteered or were asked to come here to participate in this Earth ascension energy and light.

The medicine wheel can be used as a wheel of incarnation. Do not limit the use of the medicine wheel to the incarnations on the third dimension. Also, holographically, use that beautiful symbol to relate to other cosmic incarnations, which you can access through the center of the wheel. The center of the medicine wheel represents a holographic corridor that will allow you to go to other medicine wheels in other realities. You can even use a medicine wheel to connect to the fifth dimension.

The wheel of incarnation is powerful when it is used for this lifetime, such as for gaining greater insight into your personal life. Many of you feel that this lifetime seems equivalent to five or six lifetimes because you are going through so many life experiences and phases. You have gone through so much work. It may seem as if you have had one complete lifetime in the earlier part of this lifetime. Some of you had earlier experiences in this lifetime that are totally removed from the spiritual work you are now doing. Of course, this means that you have been doing third-dimensional work to prepare for this highly spiritual time.

Some of you have even allowed walk-ins. In this incarnation, you completed certain tasks, and then you decided to allow another spirit to come in. Being a walk-in has allowed you to enjoy the opportunity of working in this spiritual energy of the 2012 energy field.

Harmonic Energy

Previously, I compared the medicine wheel to crop circles because it is our understanding that crop circles are highly advanced medicine wheels that contain geometric patterns related to deeper energies within Earth. Fifth-dimensional beings work with crop circles to create these energy configurations, which are telepathic communications with the spirit of Earth, Gaia. These telepathic communications give instructions to Gaia, telling it that Earth is in transition and coming into fifth-dimensional energy.

Crop circles are also communications about Earth's feedback loop system. Earth's feedback loop system is set to maintain a certain relationship between the chemistry in the atmosphere and on Earth. If the chemistry on Earth shifts, then the atmosphere makes a corresponding adjustment to maintain levels that allow everyone to breathe. There needs to be a certain percentage of oxygen and nitrogen.

Earth's feedback loop system is not well understood by Earth scientists. They do not know how to communicate with it, and that is for a good reason — because Earth's feedback loop system is a secret code that has a powerful function. The secret code cannot be easily broken. It is not to be easily accessed. If people accessed the code for nonspiritual reasons, they could produce havoc and perhaps use it for military purposes.

Using Earth's feedback loop system can be a way of controlling weather patterns in certain parts of the world. For example, it could affect volcanic eruptions or create earthquakes. In fact, the highly militaristic scientific project called HAARP[1] is working to crack the codes of the feedback loop system, and they are coming close. They now understand that there is a basic harmonic frequency on Earth. All planets — all stars — have a radio frequency vibration. The people doing the HAARP experiments want to explore whether it is possible to shift Earth's frequency and the results of doing so. That is what I call playing with fire, because scientists don't understand all the reasons why a planet vibrates at a certain harmonic frequency.

The Harmonic Convergence of 1987 was a big doorway for you. Many of you were sensitive to the 11/11/11 energies because it was also a time of harmonic energies and communications with Earth. Harmonic energies can be opportunities to communicate with Earth's feedback loop system. The 12/12/12 is another example of planetary harmonic energy. Even 12/12/11 was a powerful time to communicate with the harmonic energies.

Harmonic energy activations can become part of Earth's feedback loop system. The medicine wheels and the crop circles can be tools to interact with the harmonic energy field of the planet. They are tools through which many people in group meditations can telepathically communicate in a harmonic way with Earth to restabilize her energy system.

Earth's feedback loop system is being affected by the disharmony on the planet, which creates irregular vibrations that affect the harmonic vibration of the planet and therefore affect the feedback loop system. Harmonic convergence and harmonic energies are ways of stabilizing the harmonic energy field of the planet. This is one of the most powerful tools in biorelativity: the stabilization and creation of harmonic light.

Harmonic light has different cycles so that you can be on resonant cycles or frequencies with Earth, which will help create harmony. This is also found in music as you have some people sing a resonant tone in an octave above or below the main score. It all harmonizes. Harmonic energy is one of the most powerful tools in biorelativity. The use of the medicine wheel, the medicine circle, can accelerate harmonic energy and light. The mere creation of the medicine circle establishes a harmonic energy field where you built it. That harmonic energy field can be utilized multidimensionally to send harmonic energy to Earth's feedback loop system. It can also be used to connect with other medicine wheels around the planet. The crop circles are harmonic tools for fine-tuning Earth's harmonic energy.

Earth has a complex harmonic pattern. Adjustments of Earth's harmonic

---

1 The High Frequency Active Auroral Research Program (HAARP) is an ionospheric research program designed and built by BAE Advanced Technologies to analyze the ionosphere and investigate the potential for developing ionospheric enhancement technology for radio communications and surveillance. For more information, see http://en.wikipedia.org/wiki/High_Frequency_Active_Auroral_Research_Program.

frequency can only be expressed in complex geometric patterning, such as in crop circles. The medicine wheel also has the ability to do harmonic adjustments to Earth, and it is not built as complexly as crop circles are. The medicine wheel is a relatively simple geometric pattern. Some crop circle patterns have never been seen before on Earth and might not be easily reproducible.

These patterns are set up so that they correspond to human communication. Thus, the medicine wheel can easily increase its power when you step into it. It can also increase its healing and communication powers to the harmony of the feedback loop system.

The medicine wheel functions as an interactional tool through human prayers and telepathic communications with Earth, and it can hold spiritual energy. The crop circle might exist for one planting season, holding its spiritual energy during this time, but the medicine wheel can hold your energy for a more sustained time. It can hold your healing thoughts and communicate them to Earth.

Many medicine wheels could be built by the Group of Forty starseed members. Medicine wheels can and should be built in all the planetary cities of light. Medicine wheels have multidimensional abilities; that is, they can communicate with Earth and with other medicine wheels. They can also increase in power logarithmically. Ten medicine wheels around the planet are far more powerful than two. The whole planet can learn about and use the medicine wheel.

Galactic Energy

Many of the Native peoples in earlier times knew that Earth was receiving galactic energies. This has been expressed by the exploration and discussions of the Maya, who believed they were in communications with the galactic center.

What does it mean to communicate with the galactic center? It means you are receiving and sending galactic energies. Galactic energy is complex because Earth is in a solar system far from the galactic center. Earth's solar system is primarily directed by the Sun, and the Sun is on a path going around the center of the galaxy, which takes (according to recent calculations) 250 million years for one cycle. We are now approximately halfway through that cycle.

You go around the Sun in 365 days. You have autumn. You have summer. You have four seasons. You know that each position creates different weather patterns and energies. Those energies and weather patterns are designated in the medicine wheel. In referring to the phases of your life, you talk about the early years, the middle years, and the sunset years.

Earth's precession, or wobble, affects what angle of energy is received from your Sun and the center of the galaxy. On 12/22/12, Earth was in an approximate alignment with the galactic center. Earth is in this galactic align-ment because of the wobble of its axis and because you are approximately at the halfway point of a galactic revolution. These alignments provide an oppor-tunity for new, intense, higher light and energy. You need newer thoughts and newer vibrations to change and repair Earth.

I want to emphasize the word "repair," because by all scientific observa-tions, Earth is in quite a fix right now. Earth has problems that seem irresolv-able. These problems are already creating damage that seems irreversible. But in this alignment, the new, higher vibrations and energies help solutions to emerge.

In one sense, the path of the solar system around the galaxy is a gigantic medicine wheel. You see, the medicine wheel is representative of inherent patterns in the galaxy. Perhaps it is more difficult to understand how the solar system and Earth are feeding back information to the center of the galaxy. The center of the galaxy is sending energy to Earth, and there is a new vibra-tional field coming. Earth and the solar system have come into a new position in their 250-million-year path around the center of the galaxy.

What kinds of communications emerge from Earth and your solar system? That is where the star family enters the picture. Your vibrational energies are picked up by the star family members, the ascended masters, and the Galactic Council. For example, the Galactic Council and the star family knew when the first atomic bomb went off. They know when experiments are done in the space-time distortions. You cannot do a space-time distortion exercise with-out many other energies in this galaxy picking up on it.

What happens on Earth is communicated to other parts of the galaxy, partic-ularly to the center, especially events involving nuclear energy. Nuclear energy also affects the time-space distortion field. On occasion, a time warp is created in different energy fields on Earth. That time warp is like a wrinkle in the space-time continuum, and that wrinkle is picked up by other parts of the galaxy.

The star masters, ascended masters, and the Galactic Council know that there could be potential problems here on Earth. They are picking up the waves of energy created by the space-time distortions in some of the scientific and military experiments you have done.

The medicine wheel also has the ability to harmonically communicate to the galaxy. It can harmonically receive the highest light from the center of the galaxy and send it outward. This is a good practice because you want to attract higher-dimensional energy and beings to Earth. One of the reasons why the fourth-dimensional Grays came to Earth is because of the disharmo-nious energies that were sent out. Many ascended masters are coming to Earth now because you are sending out higher harmonic energies.

The reason for harmonic convergences (11/11/11, 12/12/12, and other harmonic dates) is to reinforce sending out harmonic light so that higher beings will continue to come to this planet. That is one of your main missions: to contribute to and develop new techniques for using harmonic energy and the harmonic attraction force. One of the greatest tools for this is the medicine wheel.

Now, I will turn the next part of the lecture over to Chief White Eagle. I am Juliano. Good day.

• • •

Harmony Is the Opposite of Polarization

[Chants] "Hey ya ho ya hey ya! Hey ya hoooo." Greetings. All my words are sacred. I am Chief White Eagle. I welcome this opportunity to be together. I want to acknowledge that we are creating with you a beautiful circle above the planet. We, the Native peoples, the ascended masters, and the higher grandmothers and grandfathers are continually participating in a great medicine wheel above this planet.

We are in the fifth dimension, and with our work, we are interacting to bring down the power of harmonic light that Juliano talked about. Continue to build medicine wheels around this globe in all the areas you can reach. Increase the power of your planetary cities of light to attract more people and more lightworkers.

In our teachings, the medicine wheel is a sacred space. It is a great gift, and you can create a sacred space by building your own medicine wheel. You can use that sacred space to bring your powers into it. The medicine wheel can amplify and increase your powers of harmonic thinking. It is a wheel of harmony. Harmony is the opposite of polarization.

You have experienced enough polarization. I know that many of you have discovered that polarization is tiring. It wears out the systems. Welcome any opportunity to be able to experience harmony. Know that the medicine wheel can assist you in experiencing harmony with your personal incarnation cycles, with Earth, and with the galaxy. We are particularly interested in working with the medicine wheel in creating harmonious energy to Earth. We know that our prayers can be more powerful when they are done in the medicine wheel. I see many new medicine wheels being developed around the planet. I see many connecting the Group of Forty.

Think now of your own medicine wheel. Think of it at this moment. If you don't have a medicine wheel, visualize where you would want to put it (your living room or your backyard). Visualize the medicine wheel, and connect with that harmonic light and energy. Let that light and energy emanate throughout the planet. Let it emanate off Earth into the ethers so that you are able to attract your higher personal energies of healing in this incarnation and also higher planetary powers for Earth healings. Use the medicine wheel for attracting the great powers you are developing to experience galactic connections and for attracting a greater galactic energy. [Chants] "Hey ya hoooo. Hey yaaa hoooo. Hey ya hooo."

Using the medicine wheel will help you come into a powerful harmonic energy field.

We are all related. I am Chief White Eagle. Ho!

Chapter 20

Cellular Memory and Expanded Consciousness

Juliano, the Arcturians, Chief White Eagle, and Archangel Metatron

Greetings, I am Juliano. We are the Arcturians. Cellular memory transcends lifetimes. It even transcends eras. The cellular memories you have from your childhood dramatically affect you. Many have used reincarnation as the great clearing. Some people believe that when you die, you go into the intermediary realms, and from that position, you are reborn. The belief is that there is a cleansing of the cellular memory. Therefore, you come back into this lifetime with a clean slate.

From our study of your cellular biology and evolution, we have noted that when there is a reincarnation, it does not mean that there is a total clearing. It means that all cellular memory is erased. When observing other galactic civilizations, we have found people often repeat mistakes. Some civilizations, despite their best intentions as higher beings, seem to repeat patterns that result in their destruction.

There was a psychologist in Europe [Alice Miller][1] who postulated the idea of repetition compulsion, which states that people tend to repeat earlier incidents based on their memories of that incident. Cellular memory transcends lifetimes. So what you bring into this lifetime is often based on what happened in a previous lifetime. That could be both a positive and a negative. You might have had high talents in previous lifetimes. You might have penchants for the understanding of languages or music, for example. These gifts were probably brought with you to this lifetime from previous incarnations. Those cellular memories enable you to access those traits successfully in this lifetime. That certainly seems to be very positive.

On the other hand, you have also faced particular problems in this lifetime

---

1 Learn more about Alice Miller and her work at http://www.alice-miller.com/.

— health problems, relationship problems, and financial or career problems. The cellular memories from previous lifetimes have been reloaded into your mind and into your genetic codes. The energies in this lifetime will bring you to situations in resonance with your cellular memories. These renewed situations (coming from the resonance of your previous lifetime cellular memories) are done for a specific purpose. It is in part your evolution and in part your need to complete certain lessons.

Cosmic Memory

Cellular memory operates on a planetary basis. When looking at the millions and even billions of souls now incarnated on this planet, you see how cellular memory plays a major role in some of the conflicts, tragedies, and upheavals happening. Cellular memory plays an important role in cosmic justice, or what I would prefer to call cosmic memory. "Cosmic justice" is a term that has been used to describe the rectification of events from other lifetimes or planetary systems. It is an attempt to describe karma on a cosmic level. Cosmic justice describes karma in a way that takes into consideration people's energies and experiences from other planetary systems and galaxies.

Cosmic memory is a more encompassing concept. It is related specifically to cellular memory. Cosmic memory states that the energies and events people are attracted to are related to their previous experiences locked into their cellular structure; therefore, these people attract that energy together. This can become complicated when you are looking at a planet like Earth that has 6 or 7 billion people. If you consider that many of those people are bringing in cosmic memories from many lifetimes and many parts of this galaxy, then you would be overwhelmed in trying to understand the energies and events occurring on Earth. The many Earth events occurring now might seem without logic and without reason, yet they do have energy related to cosmic memory.

The evolution of a planet also depends on the cellular and cosmic memories of its inhabitants. The concept of cosmic memory relates to the origins of the starseeds on Earth. They bring memories from previous extrasolar planetary incarnations. Cosmic memories influence DNA. There are also extraplanetary influences on the Adam species. This includes beings such as the Gray beings or the Orion people from that planetary star system known as Sirius. I am referring to influences from earlier conflicts on stars distant from Earth.

Star civilizations have been in existence millennia before humankind appeared on Earth. These star systems and planetary systems went through many advanced stages technologically and spiritually. They also went through some disastrous and catastrophic energies that, in some cases, led to severe destruction of entire planetary systems. Some of you have cellular memories from these catastrophes, and they are embedded in the cosmic memory of Earth.

Why is there such diversity of beings on this planet? Earth is a freewill zone, and because of the energy of free will, many have been attracted to Earth for rectification of certain cellular cosmic issues. Earlier planetary civilizations have reached a point similar to where Earth is now — the point of evolution. Become aware of your own cosmic memories. Expand the cosmic memory idea to include cosmic justice and cosmic karma. Use this perspective to understand what is going on now on Earth.

What appears so confusing on Earth now is actually a reenactment of earlier dramas that have occurred on other planets. You as starseeds have the cosmic memory of these events and thus are attracted to Earth at this time. Some of the starseeds are returning to observe this cosmic drama, which can only exist in a freewill environment. That environment has to do with the energies of ascension. There is a tremendous spiritual freedom paralleling the cosmic drama you see being played out on Earth.

Clearing Cellular Memory

There is a German word that can be used to describe cellular cleansing: *reinigung*. This word describes cleansing and clearing at the same time — purification. In the Arcturian spiritual system, we look for this cleansing, or this reinigung, in several different ways. Cleansing and clearing can include memories and traumas from earlier reincarnations. We also know that clearing and cleansing happen as you are reborn. However, when you are reborn, everything in your conscious memory could be lost, but the imprints of previous events from past lives still remain in your DNA memories.

Your energy and knowledge and mistakes from past times remain as imprints. All of the previous events, including the wisdom and the mistakes and the folly, were erased from your memory. You will not incarnate with the benefits of those experiences. But you could come back with the energy and resonance to attract similar situations to reenact them — replay the dramas — in ways that lead to resolution and transcendence of unlearned lessons and dramas.

There are pitfalls in trying to learn lessons during your incarnational cycle. Some of those pitfalls relate to the concept I mentioned previously: repetition compulsion. In the theory of cellular memory, you tend to attract the situations that were important to your soul's development, whether positive or negative, and there is a tendency to repeat them until you learn the lesson. You need to repeat experiences so that you can choose the correct way to transcend and move on to other places that contribute to your soul evolution. These principles also work on a planetary level. People can return to a planet and come together on a planetary level in order to bring forth new energy and new choices. The choice now on Earth is transcendence of polarization versus catastrophic implosion due to an inability to resolve polarities. Having these choices offers the opportunity for evolution.

The word "compulsion" in the English language has a strong connotation. Compulsion implies force. You are compelled to do something. Cellular memory can come through with a compulsion for repetition. It is a strong force that will require huge effort to overcome.

One of our missions is to provide new spiritual energy. We have studied the entire situation, and we have learned that you can have a cellular memory clearing while you are still in an incarnation. In fact, to uplift and maintain your spirituality to the highest level (especially in these times of cosmic unfolding and manifestation of karma), the ability to work on a cellular level and do the cleansing while you are in this incarnation becomes paramount.

Memory cleansing can occur in this incarnation; you can completely remove your memory compulsions, earlier memory programs, and memory programs from other incarnations. However, you must consider that you could also lose many positive memories. For example, you do not necessarily want to remove your memories of other languages or talents from other lifetimes. Maybe you would like to remove the cellular memories of illness and their manifestations of cosmic drama on the planet. Maybe you wish to remove memories of your time in Atlantis where you might have contributed to the energy of high-technological weaponry. At that time, you believed that the weaponry was the way to balance the planet. Now you see that building weaponry is not the way to do it. You would like to cleanse these memories but keep the awareness of consciousness in this incarnation. You want to preserve the positive parts.

Many of you are familiar with the cone-of-light technique [see appendix B] in which you place a cone of light around your auras that allows positive light and energy in. This is the same method as self-protection. Negative thoughts or negative energy will not be able to penetrate that wall of light. But you will want a shield to have a certain permeability to allow in light, Christ love, higher Kabbalistic energy, and energy from the Arcturians and other angelic beings.

When clearing cellular memory, you will want a similar type of shield to be in place. That shield allows the positive memories to come through but not the negative. Remember, we are also talking about memories from other lifetimes of a lower vibration and have a certain compulsion for repetition within your system. Those would be cleared. You would have a fresh start, a fresh perspective. That would enable you to be in a far more powerful position mentally, physically, emotionally, and spiritually on this planet. In some ways, this clearing would be a true spiritual cleansing, a spiritual healing. That would allow you to be free of these lower programs and memories that still could be affecting and influencing you.

• • •

The Sacred Shields

[Chants] "Hey ya ho ya hey!" Greetings, I am Chief White Eagle. All my words are sacred, all my brothers and sisters! We bind our light and love together.

Know that it is time to bring out your sacred shields. Do not neglect your etheric shields. They are a necessary part of working on the third dimension in spiritual transformation. Shields are a tool used in cleansings and protecting yourself from the many negative energies that are erupting on this planet now.

Visualize a shield. If you do not have a shield, then create one or find someone who could help you make or draw a shield. Visualize that shield now in front of your physical aura here on the third dimension, and let that shield be reinvigorated. Let that shield stand as a guardian, as a lightbeing, at this sacred time at this sacred place. You must have a shield in place. It is just part of your expansion.

You can have many different shields. You do not have to use the same shield each time. Some of you as spirit workers are also shamans. Shamans use different shields. Use the image of the shield that sings with your heart, that you know is the right shield for you. When you are in resonance with your spirit shield, you are impenetrable to lower vibrations, to lower energies. Even the lowest of the spirits cannot touch and go through the shield. I, Chief White Eagle, at this moment, activate and empower each of your shields now so that when you pick them up, you will feel a new sense of protection and spiritual resonance.

I am Chief White Eagle. Ho!

• • •

The Cleansing

Bring yourself to the highest vibrational energy now as we embark on a cleansing and clearing. Bring yourself to your highest light frequency, and bond with all who are participating in this exercise so that you will gain an upliftment energetically in your vibratory light. You will now be able to participate to the fullest extent possible in this exercise.

Feel a blue corridor of light above each of you. This blue corridor of light connects you and your energy to the fifth dimension. Your spirit body lifts out of your physical body from the crown chakra. As your spirit body, the spirit astral body, lifts out of your body, it will carry the imprints and memories of your emotional body, your physical body, and your mental body. All those memories stay with your spirit astral body. Even those memories that might not be in your awareness now are still being called to come on this journey.

Your spirit astral self rises out of your physical body and follows the blue corridor of light to the starship Athena. As you connect with the starship Athena, you enter our huge healing room. Your personal holographic healing chamber is in the healing room. Enter your personal chamber programmed especially for you. Each chamber looks somewhat like a telephone booth. It has a comfortable chair and a computer screen and other advanced spiritual technologies there. Enter your own holographic booth.

Become aware of the cellular memories in your four bodies. You can energetically project these memories into our holographic computer. These are cellular memories, so they are directed by your thought projection and commands. As they are projected into the computer and appear on the screen, notice the many images simultaneously downloading. Look at them with intense interest. Process them with lightning-like speed. Take a moment to allow this fantastic energetic light to pass through the screen. Some of these images are from other planetary systems and other lifetimes that you may not even remember participating in. You are, for the most part, old souls.

Rest assured that all of these memories are now in the computer, and I, Juliano, am bringing down a beautiful, light, cleansing energy into your crown chakra. This cleansing energy is tied to all of your cellular memories. The older negative patterns, the compulsions that lead to lower vibrations and lower energies, can be cleaned and cleansed. They are not removed or forgotten. Rather, the compulsion energy to repeat them in any way is neutralized. The energy of wisdom and transcendence that would come from that memory is enhanced and integrated with this light as you sit in your holographic chamber.

You have received and integrated this cleansing energy. The cosmic ones that are of a lower vibration are neutralized and cleansed. Now as you look at the screen, only those higher images, higher vibrations, and transcendent energies come to the forefront. Perhaps some of you who are knowledgeable with computers know of the process called defragmentation in which the computer attempts to put together certain files and patterns. Defragmentation is one possible image you can use to understand the positive images, memories, and experiences as now "defragged" and placed together into a beautiful pattern of light. The ones of lower vibration with compulsion for repetition are moved into an area without power. This allows you to be in the highest vibrational state.

If there is a necessity for you to recall those memories, you can still do that. You do not need them at this point, because you have gathered all the learning and higher perspectives from those events. Now your computer screen is filled with the positive memories. Hold that vision now. [Pause.]

You have integrated and balanced this beautiful energy from the cleansing, and you have done it while you are still in this incarnation! This brings you a step closer to a higher evolution, through what we have called the reinigung. Prepare to step out of the holographic chamber. As you step out, you feel the light and energy of the healing chamber from our fifth-dimensional ship Athena. You will take with you this memory of being in the fifth-dimensional spaceship and the healing chambers.

Follow me as we leave the starship. Come down through the corridor, following the blue light. Then travel through a corridor back to Earth and come to a place about twenty feet above your body. We will do a realignment, recalibration, so that you will come into your physical body in the correct perfected alignment. Remember, as you come in, all of the higher energies and higher memories will come back, giving you new healing energies and abilities. You have a greater perspective and protection now. While in spiritual form, align your physical body — rebalance and download — then come back into your physical body.

It will take several days for all of this energy through spiritual osmosis to go through your system and upgrade everything. In cellular memory, the higher vibration transcends the lower vibration. All of the memories in your structures are now being updated from the beautiful work we have done in the holographic healing chamber.

The Complexities of Earth's Ascension

In working with cosmic justice and cosmic memory, we could make the argument that you are returning to complete your positive karma for your ascension. There are peculiar circumstances in this ascension energy. First, there is the energy of potential catastrophic implosion of a planet. Yet at the same time, there is the doorway to ascension. You are planetary healers as well. The exercise that we just did for your personal benefit also can be used to cleanse the planet's memory. Planetary cleansing is more complicated because there are so many sources and energies intermingling on Earth.

You have heard it said before that extraterrestrials have tampered with human DNA, which created impurities in what was once a pure human program. Now your DNA has energies from other planetary systems. This tampering helps in understanding why there is so much upheaval on Earth now. Earth life would be a lot simpler if there were only 10 million people on the planet, just the energy of the one Adam species, and the original programming was not tampered with. To deal with just that one system would actually be relatively easy compared to the complexities now on the planet.

Earth now has multiple influences that are often contradictory and polarized. They can be harmonized and transcended, but the effort and energy needed to overcome polarizations requires quite an effort.

I will turn the next part of this lecture over to Metatron. I am your beloved friend and teacher, Juliano.

• • •

The Sacred Codes of Ascension

Greetings, I am Archangel Metatron. You know that the DNA is a sacred code and the codes of ascension are sacred. Working with cellular memory and energies, reconfiguring them for higher light, requires an attitude of sacredness and holiness. You have done some powerful shifting. You can shift the DNA and the code. Cellular memory has to do with DNA codes because cellular memory is also part of a program. Anytime you shift a program, you should approach the task with the highest light, the highest vibration. You want it to be surrounded with the right holiness.

I, Archangel Metatron, am now going to bring in that light of holiness to each of you through these sacred sounds. [Chants twice]: "Kadosh, Kadosh, Kadosh, Adonai Tzevaoth. Holy, holy, holy is the Lord of Hosts." Let the light of Kadosh, the holy light, fill your cells. Let the memories that are of the higher light, the holy light, fill you now, the Aur Hakadosh. Let the holy light stand in your presence. Let it be projected from your present self to your future self on Earth so that you will walk in the holy light, and you will be able to send holy light to the planet. Each of the ten etheric crystals downloaded into Earth are now being filled with the energy of this holy light. This is an aspect of the golden harmonic balls of light. The sacred holy light and the awareness of that light becomes part of the activation of your cellular memories of the planet. The planetary energy is now being filled through the etheric crystals with holy light.

Pure light — pure energy — cleanses and purifies the cosmic and cellular memories. Blessed is the Holy One, and may each of you be blessed. You are beings of holy light. I await you on the fifth dimension.

I am Archangel Metatron. Kadosh, Kadosh, Kadosh, holy, holy, holy. Shalom.

Chapter 21

Preparing for the Ascension

Juliano and the Arcturians

Shalom. Shalom. Shalom. Greetings, this is Juliano. We are the Arcturians. The idea of shimmering is based on the concept that you are a multidimensional being: You live in several dimensions simultaneously. This is a difficult concept to understand from the third-dimensional perspective because you are in a linear time frame based on cause and effect.

You have perceptual blinders on, just as a racehorse, so there can be no distractions to the left and no distractions to the right. The horse just goes straight down the track. From an evolutionary standpoint, these perceptual blinders are useful and necessary for humanity. To survive primitive dangers, you do not want to be disturbed by energies coming from the other dimensions except during ceremonies, dances, or special meditations. It is interesting to note that ancient people would not only devote time to their multidimensional energies and presences but also honor the people able to experience multiple dimensions, calling them shamans. Now in your culture, the idea of being able to experience multidimensionality somehow seems foreign. The truth is that everyone can experience his or her own multidimensional presence. This is healthy, and it expands your energy field and even your abilities.

Now you have to go to a special person or shaman to have this experience. Shamans can access certain energies from other dimensions for healing. They bring back special energy and special light. So in many ways, it is more abnormal to not be experiencing your multidimensional presence. It is healthier and more expansive for you to be aware of and to experience your dimensional abilities.

The Etheric Body

Shimmering is a way of projecting into your multidimensional presence. The first spiritual technology necessary for you to understand shimmering is thought projection. Thought energy is the fastest energy in the universe, faster than the speed of light. The speed of light is 186,000 miles per second, which seems very fast, but it isn't fast when you think of the great distances in the universe. If you traveled to Arcturus at the speed of light, it would take you more than thirty-six years to reach our planet, and our planet is relatively close to yours.

The higher technology that uses special methodologies for interplanetary travel combines the technology of intergravity and intermatter propulsion systems with thought projection, which creates a special curve in the space-time continuum. When traveling at a certain acceleration, your thought projections can send you where you want to go instantaneously. Even now you can project yourselves thought-wise and energetically to remote places. You can thought-project yourselves to the Moon as well as other parts of the planet.

Your military uses a technology called remote viewing, which is based on thought projection. You project yourself astrally to another location where you are able to see, read, and in some cases, even send energies to people there. The military has used this type of technology for gaining military secrets. They have tried to gain access to secret plans or codes. Now, it would be one thing if they were doing this to attain the codes of ascension, but they were trying to find their enemies weaknesses. Combining psychic energy with psychic technology for military purposes is not well thought of in the higher dimensions. Psychic gifts such as remote viewing are meant to be used for humanity to improve themselves, not to be used for darker purposes such as military advantages.

In thought projection, you visualize your astral body traveling through a corridor, going to a desired destination. This all sounds simple, but there are several things to mention. First, let's talk about the astral body. The German term "doppelgänger" means that there is a double, or duplicate, of your body. Your astral body is a duplicate of your physical body. When you do thought projection, you work with this doppelgänger, this duplicate. Another term for this is "etheric duplicate," which has abilities far beyond your physical body. Your physical body has limitations because it is in the third dimension. The etheric body does not have limitations. It is able to bounce around. It can travel, it can walk through doors, and it can do all kinds of fun things. The etheric body is attached to you by the etheric cord, the astral cord.

You can astrally project yourself to the Moon or to the Andromedan galaxy, but you will always come back because the etheric cord will bring you back. If for any reason that etheric cord is cut, you would not be able to find your body, and you could not come back. When we do this exercise with thought projection, we always tell people they must agree to come back.

Now, you might ask: "Once I am in this really high place, why should I want to come back?" Because you are karmically tied to Earth, what you do here and how you finish this life relate directly to whether or not you have to return in another incarnation. So, yes, you can go into a very high place, but you are still karmically connected to Earth, that's why, when you go through the ascension, you graduate from Earth and become free of all your karmic attachments so that you do not have to come back. Thought projection, then, is based on the principal of where you think you can project your astral body. That is pretty powerful.

Through the Corridor to the Fifth Dimension

To understand shimmering, you also need to know about corridors. We often talk about traveling through the fourth dimension and going to the fifth dimension. As we mentioned in a previous chapter, there are many different levels and beings on the fourth dimension. There are ghosts and lower astral beings who are happy to attach themselves to you.

When your astral body is in the shape of a cosmic egg, you do not have to worry about lower astral beings attaching themselves to you. They cannot attach themselves to someone whose aura is in the shape of the cosmic egg. Illegal drugs and other types of lower-vibrational activities disturb the aura, making it possible for lower energies to attach themselves to people. Some of these lower astral spirits are naughty, and they take great pleasure in creating chaos on the planet.

For example, you have seen quite an increase in school shootings in which students, for some poor reason, decide to kill their teachers and classmates. In almost every case, these students were possessed by lower astral beings. Their auras were distorted and weakened. Lower astral beings can attach themselves to people with weakened auras and encourage them to do things they might not normally do. It is possible for people to have inclinations to do evil things, but they would never act on them without significant influence. The lower astral beings can take advantage of any weakness in your aura.

When you travel through a corridor, the corridor goes through the lower astral realm to the higher realm. Lower astral beings cannot penetrate the corridor. We encourage people to travel through a corridor when doing thought projection and shimmering. We, the Arcturians, have set up a corridor over you to protect you when you decide to work with us. Some of you have images of corridors. You can imagine entering a tunnel in which there is an attractive fifth-dimensional light and go through the tunnel to reach that light.

You travel through the corridor at the speed of thought. What is the speed of thought? We have already referred to the speed of light. How much faster is the speed of thought? The speed of thought is instantaneous; that is, when astral traveling, you just think and you are there, no matter the distance. It is very powerful. You can thought-project yourself to powerful places, such as to the top of the San Francisco Peaks, which is also known as Mount Humphreys, near Flagstaff, Arizona. There are many kachina spirits there. Ultimately, you can learn to thought project yourselves to the fifth dimension.

I have to point out that a dimension is a place of immeasurable size. It is also difficult to describe because the space in the fifth dimension is totally different. In fact, as mentioned earlier, there is no space in the fifth dimension. How can you live in a dimension with no space? I cannot really give a logical answer. The fifth dimension is primarily indescribable, but we can tell you it is a place with beautiful light, and all colors are intense. Also, there is a great love on the fifth dimension, because to enter the fifth dimension, you have to have a certain frequency.

In a previous chapter, I spoke about the rate at which your energy, your cosmic egg, vibrates. To enter the fifth dimension, you have to attain a certain resonant frequency, and you have to vibrate at a certain higher rate. On the fifth dimension, you do not feel the constraints of space and time, logic and causality. You feel a great sense of relief, like a burden has been lifted from you.

The third dimension is beautiful. There is great work that you can do here, but because you are starseeds, your true beings are more expanded than in this reality. To come into this third-dimensional reality, you had to contract yourselves. When you come to the fifth dimension, you are in a more natural, expanded state. We decided to make a special place for those of you who want to practice traveling to the fifth dimension where you can feel comfortable and experience the right vibrations. It has complete energy linkages with the Arcturians, and it will be safe to travel to. It is the Arcturian crystal lake.

The energy in the crystal lake is fifth dimensional, and inside the lake is a huge, spiritually powerful etheric crystal. There is no crystal comparable in Earth terms. The power of the crystal is so immense that we had to place it in deep water to attenuate its energy. This helps Earth starseeds tolerate it. Experiencing the crystal's power is similar to coming to an outdoor area of great white light or great sunlight. You might say: "Oh, it's very hard to adjust to this bright light." You feel overwhelmed by it and start blinking. Well, the power of the Arcturian crystal is so intense that it overwhelms you as well. For this reason, we put the crystal in the water. Later, after you adjust to the power of the crystal, we can raise it and gradually allow you to experience its full intensity.

We, the Arcturians, are working with the stargate, the fifth-dimensional transformation station where people come after they complete their Earth karma. By passing through the stargate, they are finished with all karma. When you open the huge doorway, you see a great, beautiful, intense light like you have never seen before. You have a huge attraction to this light. But you cannot go through the stargate until you are finished with your Earth lesson. Thus, the Arcturian crystal lake is set up almost like a training center for you to gradually experience fifth-dimensional energy and light.

The lake is one mile in diameter. It has a huge dome over it, so it is self-contained. You, in your astral presence, can travel through the dome. The etheric crystal has super-fantastic fifth-dimensional powers. It has the power to send you healing light. The etheric crystal also can be used to project you beyond the lake to other places in the fifth dimension. As you know, the etheric crystal is able to create etheric duplicates of itself that can be transported back to Earth. When the etheric duplicate crystals are transported back to Earth, they are downloaded to places they can be used for fifth-dimensional activations. Downloading etheric crystals is a methodology for helping to energize and set up fifth-dimensional grids on other third-dimensional planets as well as on Earth.

Your Fifth-Dimensional Body

Contemplate this: You have a fifth-dimensional body waiting for you at the Arcturian crystal lake. You can visit and cohabit with your fifth-dimensional body. You can download your third-dimensional, etheric body into your fifth-dimensional body. You might ask: "Well, why would I want to do that, Juliano?" For many reasons. Namely, when your astral body leaves your Earth body, it carries the imprints of your third-dimensional life on Earth. It carries the vibrations of your Earth presence, including all of its expansions and limitations.

When you go to your fifth-dimensional body, your astral body receives a beautiful upliftment. It receives purity of light, healing, and an amplification of fifth-dimensional energies. All these beautiful traits are integrated and processed in your Earth aura. When you put your aura into your fifth-dimensional body, it picks up those higher vibrations and frequencies.

When you return to Earth, you have the opportunity to download those astral impressions and vibrations into your third-dimensional body using spiritual osmosis. Spiritual osmosis refers to the integration and downloading of your astral body when it returns from the fifth dimension. Osmosis, in a biological sense, happens when a semipermeable membrane expels or admits nutrients and water, eventually equalizing the formula on both sides, but this is somewhat of a slow process of transfer. We like the term "osmosis," because it implies a purposeful and slow integration of energy.

One of the essential ingredients in our teachings about returning your astral body into your physical body is that you must reenter your physical body with your astral body in perfect alignment. Your astral body perfects an exact alignment so that you come into your physical body in just the right way. There are many examples of people who left their physical bodies in dream states who did not reenter their physical bodies with the proper alignment. There are mental illnesses related to improper alignment, including schizophrenia and bipolar disorders. Many of these disturbances can be rectified by having people leave their physical bodies astrally and then come back in perfect alignment. Reentry in perfect alignment is crucial in thought projection and shimmering.

There have been cases of people who experience traumas from car accidents and military experiences in which they were suddenly jolted out of their physical bodies and didn't come back correctly. We combine thought projection with astral traveling to return you into your third-dimensional body in perfect alignment so that you can experience the maximum spiritual osmosis.

We use an exercise called the merry-go-round technique for leaving your body and traveling with your astral body. Basically, you visualize a merry-go-round. There is a horse on the merry-go-round. You go around in a circle, and it is very relaxing. You know how children become very calm and in harmony with the merry-go-round. This is the feeling we want you to create when you to leave your body astrally while in a relaxed state.

Visualize that the room is like a merry-go-round. As it goes around slowly, you very gently and in a relaxed state feel your astral self rise up out of your physical body. Then you see me, Juliano, at the top of the room with the corridor. You can join me to travel through the corridor. While you are traveling and doing your work in thought projections, the room continues to go around in a circle. Your body is protected, and you will receive special instructions for reentry.

Go up into the corridor, and travel with us through the corridor to the crystal lake. Enter your fifth-dimensional body, receiving its light and energy. As an advanced exercise, you can visualize the crystal in the crystal temple being lifted so that you can experience an even higher vibration. [Pause.]

When you are ready to leave your fifth-dimensional body, travel back through the corridor and return into your third-dimensional Earth body. Come back in perfect alignment, allowing the spiritual osmosis and higher energy to be integrated.

It is preferable for you to do all of these steps before you begin to shimmer to the Arcturian crystal. In shimmering, you integrate all of these steps simultaneously and then astrally travel to the crystal lake. You go from your third-dimensional body to your fifth-dimensional body without doing the intermediate steps, but you can't shimmer to the crystal lake until you learn them.

Achieve Perfect Astral Alignment

I have a conflict with my self on the other side. How can I fix this conflict?

Well, this is a complicated question. Some of you, in other lifetimes, have crossed the line and not come back, so there are instances when the memory of that is still present, and there is a protective vibration that will ensure you will not make the same mistake again. So when you are experiencing that conflict, you will probably be guided back by somebody because, as you are reporting, it could cause problems. It would not be in your best interest to cross over when you are not supposed to.

One of the ideas of multidimensional work is to integrate the fifth dimension with the third dimension and not to leave the third dimension before you are ready. You have come here for a reason. Some have come here for service. Others have come here for specific missions. You haven't come here to leave early. Remember, there will be an opportunity to leave.

You have to return to your Earth body after your astral travels. There are cases in which people do not return who develop severe problems in their soul journeys. This is a reason why the ancient mystics used the travel process known as Merkavah, which is the ancient Hebrew word for "chariot." It is also spelled Merkabah or Merkaba. The idea of Merkavah travel is that you use the chariot or another vehicle to travel to the other side, to the higher dimensions, and you return in that vehicle.

Ancient mystics understood the importance of returning to the Earth body. They did not have the benefit of the knowledge of the Arcturian stargate nor did they have the benefit of the Arcturian crystal lake. When you go to the crystal lake, I, Juliano, am overlooking you; I'm not going to let you leave your physical body permanently while you practice these spiritual exercises. We will not leave you in your astral body even if you want to leave your Earth body prematurely.

How do we ensure that we come back into alignment perfectly?

The way to ensure coming back in perfect alignment is similar to the way that you put yourself into the cosmic egg. The mind is interesting. When your intention, affirmations, and will are in alignment, you can say the words: "I command my aura to reenter in perfect alignment." Then visualize that your aura is above you in perfect alignment with your physical body. Say, "I command my aura to come back into my body in perfect alignment." It is similar to saying: "I command my aura to go into the shape of the cosmic egg." Your mind can powerfully influence how these actions occur.

So the answer to your question is you command yourself to reenter in perfect alignment. Say that command with great conviction: "I command my astral body to reenter my physical body in perfect alignment." Visualize your aura above your body, and see the body and your aura coming into alignment. Then download your aura into your body.

The Need for Planetary Healing

Does the crystal in the crystal lake look like a pillar?

Yes, I guess you could call it a pillar. It is long, kind of like an obelisk but very wide. The obelisk was an ancient symbol of power and fifth-dimensional energy in Egypt. There are several examples of beautiful obelisks, but this crystal is like an obelisk with a triangular point on the top of its very thick crystal body.

Are there souls who come here without karma? Would they be called volunteers?

There are ascended masters who can be considered volunteers who have come into the Earth realm and are not bound by karma. There are also, as I said, lower astral spirits who are bound by karma but blocked from manifesting on Earth. They cannot move from the astral realm. They are stuck in the lower astral realm. We, the Arcturians, think this is a huge problem on Earth. There are many lower astral spirits stuck around Earth, and there needs to be a cleansing. People say Earth is being cleansed through earth changes, but the astral realm needs to be cleansed of lower beings, especially when you have a planet like Earth that has billions of souls.

The planet has a collective subconscious based on primitive responses and defenses that include such traits as jealousy, competition, and domination. These traits are imbedded in the collective subconscious, and countries and leaders who are not evolved continue to react from it, just as you do.

There are special exercises to help purify the planetary subconscious. Remember, we are also talking about planetary healing. Just as you can go to the fifth-dimensional lake and bring back higher energy into your third-dimensional body, there are ways of cleansing the subconscious on a planet. For example, the kachina dances that are done by the Hopi are attempts to work with and purify the collective subconscious. The Hopi dance is a brilliant example of how early humans understood the necessity of working with the collective subconscious of a planet. Unfortunately, now that job of planetary cleansing is too large. One tribe cannot handle it. At least one group is trying to do it [the Group of Forty], and this kind of work is powerful. But more groups need to work along with them for planetary healing.

I'm Juliano. Good day.

Chapter 22

Ascension and Higher Consciousness

Juliano and the Arcturians

Greetings, I am Juliano. We are the Arcturians. The ascension is a quantum energy shift. For the ascension to occur, there needs to be a quantum interaction of light, electromagnetic particles, thoughts, and sacred energy. There also needs to be cosmic energy fields, which are part of the galactic energy field, through which Earth passes on its huge journey around the Central Sun. Another variable needed is the activation ability of the planet and the participants, or the inhabitants, of the planet.

It is difficult to talk about personal ascension without speaking of the planetary ascension. So you will find us speaking of both in an interactive way. During the history of this planet, there have been people who have ascended. Perhaps 100 to 200 advanced beings have each gone through an ascension process and have been able to leave the planet through this magnificent and wonderful energy field. There has not, to this date, been a mass ascension. I define mass ascension as one that involves 10,000 people or more simultaneously.

When studying the galaxy, I, Juliano, have observed other planets that have gone through a planetary ascension as well as a mass ascension. I know you are interested in both your personal ascension as well as the planetary ascension. In fact, many of you have experienced or are experiencing your soul mission related to both aspects.

Ascension Requirements

There are requirements that must be met for both kinds of ascension to occur. There must be a council of planetary elders overseeing the process through which a planet ascends. A planetary group of elders often includes ascending masters. This council also includes ascended masters from the planet who have been on Earth previously and are working for Earth's upliftment.

One fundamental goal in the planetary ascension is to lift the planet as a unified energy field. This means that the planet has to go through a unification process that includes the energy fields on both a spiritual and a physical basis. It also directly relates to the energy work of the noosphere. So you see, Gaia has to participate in her ascension. The noosphere contains the akashic records — energy impressions — of Gaia as well as the entire history of all beings who have existed on the surface and currently exist on the inner planes as well.

The major objective is to create the unified energy field necessary for planetary ascension. There are specific spiritual tools we are teaching that are required for a planet to ascend. You have inner knowledge on how to work for planetary ascension. You have incarnated in this time to contribute your energy, your knowledge, and your work toward the planetary ascension. The main requirements for planetary ascension are that a planet must have a unified energy field and that there must be a council of elders.

Spiritual Technologies for Planetary Ascension

The energy field on Earth is third dimensional, which means that it is inherently dualistic, and it is comprised of many different opposites and polarizations. The unified energy field has to encompass a new consciousness, a new evolution in thought. The new unified energy field of the planet has to encompass the efforts of more evolved beings like you who are prepared to implement unity or unified consciousness on a planetary basis.

We have offered several spiritual technologies that will enhance the unified energy field for the planet, such as the ring of ascension, which is the halo around Earth that seeks to unify the energy field around the planet. The polarizations and the dualities can become merged into a higher unity. People experiencing the ring of ascension can feel the energies of harmony and enlightenment. Coincidentally, that energy greatly assists your personal ascension.

Other spiritual technologies we have shared with you include our extensive project called the planetary cities of light. We discussed at length the importance of the establishment of the cities of light around the planet. Each city of light has a fifth-dimensional energy field and contributes to the unified energy field of Earth. People have often asked about the cities of light versus the planetary cities of light. There is great enthusiasm for working independently and establishing the cities of light and creating higher energy fields. However, our work with you is for planetary ascension. The word "planetary" implies that the city of light is participating in the global network.

To achieve the planetary ascension, we must have a powerful network of planetary cities working together to create a spiritual energy field that meets the requirements of a unified energy field. The unified energy field is also a quantum fifth-dimensional concept. You see, there are discussions about chaos in the world of physics. Chaos occurs when there is a lack of unity and advancement.

A unified field overcomes chaos and entropy, and it moves to a holographic light. So, you see, for a hologram or for holographic energy to occur, there must be a participatory unified energy field. A unified energy field has qualities that can be defined in a simplistic way as the whole is greater than the sum of the parts. That means individually, each part may have a specific value. But when all of the parts form a unified energy field, it is far more powerful than the individual parts. This is demonstrated in the planetary cities of light project when the cities successfully unite their energies in the interactive, unified, quantum energy field. They become a powerful, magnetic, quantum energetic force for planetary ascension.

Another spiritual technology that contributes to the planetary ascension is the downloading and placement of the Arcturian etheric crystals. There are many powerful crystals on this planet. Some come from the Atlantean times, some come from the Lemurian times, and some have manifested from other dimensions. The etheric crystals originate from the etheric world. The fact that the etheric crystals exist in the etheric world means that they can interact directly with the planetary noosphere, which means they interface directly with the thought forms of both Earth and the fifth dimension and the fifth-dimensional thoughts of the starseeds.

The other multifaceted ability of the etheric crystals lies in their unique talent to be embedded into Earth's crust. Because the etheric crystals are fifth-dimensional, they are able to become great vessels for fifth-dimensional light, and they are able to download and hold fifth-dimensional light in the third-dimensional world of Earth. They are able, then, to help sustain a unified energy field on the third-dimensional Earth. The fifth-dimensional etheric crystals can hold the unity consciousness from the fifth dimension amid the duality and polarizations of this planet.

Other planets in the galaxy have ascended, namely Arcturus as well as Era in the Pleiades. There have also been planets in the Antares and Sirian star systems that have ascended. The ancient Egyptians were greatly connected to the Sirian star system. As an aside, there were lower and higher Sirian energy fields similar to what is going on with Earth. Earth's energy fields hold some of the highest energy in this galaxy. You know even better than I do that the lower Earth energies are quite primitive, quite pervasive, and quite polarizing. Needless to say, you are now witnessing a deep level of polarization.

As you have experienced, this deep level of polarization is causing a great deal of social and political upheaval as well as Earth changes. Remember, the other planetary systems I mentioned have successfully overcome these types of problems and have ascended. We, the Arcturians, present these etheric crystals based on a dynamic thought form from the fifth dimension. This dynamic thought form has a special internal program. When we made etheric duplicates of this crystal and downloaded them (with your assistance) into Earth, we included planetary ascension programs.

The etheric crystals hold special codes and programs for the planetary ascension. Some of you might question whether the planetary ascension is an unreachable goal. It is reachable. The planetary ascension is part of our spiritual technology.

The etheric crystals were brought down in a specialized form and have been linked to the Kabbalistic Tree of Life. We have added two modifications to the Tree of Life so that its configuration will exactly fit the needs for a planetary ascension.

Twelve etheric crystals were brought down, each one corresponding to a certain sphere on the map of the Tree of Life. The importance of the etheric crystals is how they are configured to interact with each other. This is the same principle as the planetary cities of light: The whole is greater than the sum of its parts. The twelve etheric crystals align with the ten spheres on the Tree of Life. Their interaction creates the holographic energy field that permeates the entire Earth and its energy field. Earth's energy field is then prepared for the ascension.

Use Biorelativity to Prepare for Your Ascension

Biorelativity is another important aspect of the planetary ascension. Biorelativity, as you know, is the ability to telepathically interact with Gaia. A planet cannot ascend by herself. A planet must have higher thought forms and higher beings on it. Biorelativity is the ability to interact with Gaia using higher consciousness. On one level, biorelativity can create unity consciousness and a unified energy field.

In our discussions of biorelativity, we sometimes lose sight of creating a unified energy field for the entire Earth because we usually look at a specific area of suffering. For example, when looking at the southwestern United States, you see that area is suffering from drought. The northeastern United States is suffering from too much rain. Both of these problems are examples of imbalance, of how there needs to be a rebalancing of Earth energies and unification. You don't want to see too much rain in the Northeast or rain denied to other parts of the world. You want to see a balance. There is enough water on Earth for everyone.

In biorelativity, you seek to create a balance. At this time, focus on the balance of water throughout the world, in particular, the southwestern United States. Please picture this and send that thought to Gaia.

The next aspect for the planetary ascension is the aura of the planet. As we have explained, the vibrational properties of the energy field of a planet are similar to the vibrational energy properties of a person. You use the concept of the cosmic egg in your individual work. In planetary work, you can use the cosmic egg as the optimal shape for the aura around the planet.

When we describe the planetary aura, it has a consistent, smooth line. There should not be any breaks. Unfortunately, Earth has many breaks at this time. There should also not be any distortions. Negative energy fields can cause distortions or negative thought forms. Distortions can be influenced by other civilizations sending thought forms to Earth and by extraterrestrial beings who have come to Earth and created certain deformities in Earth's aura.

You can evaluate Earth's aura by asking questions. What is the pulse of Earth's aura? Does Earth's aura have any holes in it? Are we able to seal the holes? Some of the holes are caused by nuclear radiation. Some are caused by thought-time experiments that were not in accord with certain rules and regulations of interdimensional time travel. Some of the distortions and holes are affected by cosmic activity.

You normally think that imbalances on Earth are created only from Earth and from human activities. But the cosmos is a dynamic and sometimes dangerous place. It is well known that supernovas can reach a point at which they can emit gamma ray bursts. If these bursts reached your planet, you would be extremely destructive to your biosphere. Fortunately, gamma ray bursts occur hundreds of thousands and millions of light-years away, far beyond the Milky Way galaxy. Earth's energy field has not been affected by a gamma ray burst from an exploding or dying star.

Auric Plaque Can Burden Your Energy Field

There is an intense planetary healing work and energy occurring now. At the same time, there is an intense polarization that seems to counter the unified energy necessary for the ascension. But the unified energy is helping spiritual people work together. Remember, the whole is greater than its parts. Unity is more powerful than polarization.

Your personal energy field can become confined, contracted, and burdened by being on the third dimension. Even the most advanced souls will find that their energy fields are slower on Earth. This can be likened to a concept in modern medicine: plaque. Plaque is formed when bacteria and other energies (or certain lower densities) form on teeth. Eventually the plaque forms around the gums and creates a thin film. If the plaque is not removed, then there can be infection and eventually gum disease. The plaque can be removed by a dentist. Then your teeth can vibrate at the right frequency.

Plaque is also formed in the circulatory system. It can build up in the arteries, veins, and heart valves. Plaque can also build up in the brain, which is quite serious. It is related to neurological diseases, such as Alzheimer's. Plaque can kill the brain cells and lead to serious mental problems known as dementia.

There are thin, contracted, dense energies that can attach to your aura. I will call these thin energies auric plaque. These energies come from many different sources. Certain contracted energies are part of culture, for example. There is a certain type of mental, emotional, physical, and spiritual indoctrination known as acculturation that you must go through to become a member of third-dimensional Earth society. Acculturation occurs through various media, including the ability to perceive television, listen to electromagnetic energy waves from radios, and operate smartphones and computers. A primitive person who never saw these devices would not be able to relate.

Acculturation creates a certain contracted force on your aura. Some of the cultural training you receive includes contracted negative forces based on duality and densities. They form a thin film that keeps you vibrating at a certain frequency so that you can stay in alignment with the general society. In other words, you are culturally trained to conform.

Everybody reacts differently to this. Some people refuse to be participants in society and drop out. They might become hermits and isolate themselves. Other people choose to stay in the society and become totally contracted by this energy. Some people struggle in both ways.

There are certain exercises that you must do for your ascension to free yourself of the auric plaque so that your energy field can vibrate at its natural frequency. You see, the plaque confines the vibrations of your energy field. One of the most important parts of the ascension is that you need a freely expanded, vibrating energy field. The etheric auric plaque must be removed.

Incidentally, the auric plaque on this planet does not affect the etheric crystals that were downloaded. That is another special characteristic of etheric crystals. Remember also that there is an etheric auric plaque around Earth. One of the things that planetary healers have to do is remove the etheric auric plaque around the whole biosphere so that Earth can vibrate at its true, free, fifth-dimensional light frequency.

Dissolving your auric plaque can be done through toning or through crystal work. It can also be done through connecting with the unified energy force field of a planetary healing group. You can achieve this energy vibration by connecting with the council of elders, as they focus on pure light and energy. Pure light and fifth-dimensional energy is the natural energy of your aura and of the planet.

Become aware now of your energy field, and become aware of a thin auric plaque. Do not be concerned about it, because we are going to help you remove it. We are going to free your energy field from this. Understand that part of the ascension process is to free your energy field from plaque. This will help you to expand to your true nature. It will help you expand to who you really are.

[Channel makes a series of sounds and tones.] Listen to these sounds, and you will be able to vibrate, shimmer, and feel the auric plaque being removed from your aura so that it can expand. Go into meditation now, and feel the etheric and the auric plaque being removed from your aura. State the affirmation, "My aura is now in a unified quantum energy field. I am connecting with my fifth-dimensional ascension." Send the thought into Earth's noosphere that Earth's auric field is unified and filled with quantum fifth-dimensional light.

Earth's Council of Elders

Other planets have ascended. Many of you know that the Pleiades once was in a very difficult situation because a scientific mishap caused the planet to be between both dimensions. Because of this scientific mistake, there was great disorientation. The planet could not be allowed to stay on the edge of the third dimension and on the edge of the fourth or fifth dimension because it was not sustainable.

The Pleiades had a council of elders and requested from the Galactic Council to ascend into the fifth dimension. Planet Earth needs a council of planetary elders to oversee its ascension and communicate with the Galactic Council and other higher beings in the galaxy that can assist Earth.

Earth does not have a council of elders for the ascension. You might ask, "Juliano, who could possibly do it? Do we have to find some special people close to being gurus or avatars who can serve as the council of elders for the ascension of planet Earth?" Among you are people who can participate on the council of elders for the planetary ascension. You might respond, "Juliano, I am not capable of that. I am not advanced enough, and I do not have the necessary skill level to be on the council of elders for the planetary ascension." It is not required that participants on the council have to be gurus or ascended masters. You are aware of the ascension, and that awareness will bring the right light and energy for the council of elders.

I hope that you will be able to fulfill this part because somebody has to speak for the planet. Somebody has to speak for the planetary ascension and the unified energy field of Earth. Among you are people who can do that.

Chapter 23

Shimmering to the Fifth Dimension

Juliano, the Arcturians, Vywamus, Archangel Metatron, Chief White Eagle, and Helio-ah

Greetings, I am Juliano. We are the Arcturians. There is a great opportunity for soul advancement now, which is defined as the ability to manifest more and higher elements of your soul essence onto the Earth plane. Connecting and manifesting your higher nature and higher gifts express soul advancement and higher abilities. An eclipse represents an accelerated opportunity to manifest soul abilities and soul essences related to shimmering energies and shimmering light exercises.

The evolution of humanity is represented by new abilities and new energies. The new abilities and new energies are related to shimmering energy. Shimmering energy is a methodology and a force in which third-dimensional objects, people, and even weather are upgraded into a fifth-dimensional modality. On a personal level, shimmering energy allows the auric field to vibrate at a frequency that enables it to shift electrons. The atomic structure of your cells transmutes into a vibratory energy field that elliptically shifts into the fifth dimension, causing a back and forth, or shimmering, modality. This modality affects the atomic and quantum levels of your cellular structures.

The shimmering energy is the precursor to the ascension. The ascension is an accelerated and enhanced shimmering energy in which you elevate yourselves into the fifth dimension permanently. Shimmering energy is a powerful and necessary prelude to the ascension to the fifth dimension.

We are working on a global scale in terms of group ascension. The shimmering energy enables powerful biorelativity streams of energy to be distributed throughout the planet. Starseeds can create a shimmering force field in areas of great power and strength. The places where the twelve Arcturian etheric crystals have been downloaded are boosted energetically by the powerful Arcturian crystal. The boost of energy from this crystal enables the areas where the etheric crystals have been downloaded into Earth to shimmer almost independently of the interaction of the starseeds. I say "almost" because a modest exercise and concentration by the starseeds at the places where the etheric crystals are located will increase the shimmering energetic field to be immediately created and activated. It will enable the people there to participate and experience this higher energy. [Tones] "Oooooooooooh, oooooooooh, shimmering liiiighhht."

By visualizing and meditating on these etheric crystals, you will receive the quantum elliptical energy from the shimmering force fields into your atomic cells, allowing you to immediately experience an activational energy field of shimmering. [Tones] "Tatatatatataaaaaaa."

Shimmering represents an opportunity for you to experience an evolutionary leap that includes a new force, a new power, in your biorelativity work. The areas that seem depleted energetically or that engage in lower vibrations can be uplifted by the circle of energy provided by the starseeds. You can do individual shimmering energy work distantly and in person. You can also do remote shimmering on Earth, which is a level of shimmering projected to areas where you might not be able to visit. There are necessary codes for upliftment and activation within each of your mental bodies and your brains. The codes need to be unlocked now, especially because we are in the midst of an Earth crisis. Everyone will be receptive to this shift. Shimmering is a steppingstone to the ascension.

I am Juliano.

* * *

Masters of the Third Dimension

Greetings, I am Vywamus. I am a soul psychologist. Recently there has been a great ability of enhancement and transformation. Oftentimes when transformation occurs, there is a personal upheaval, a sense of confusion, and even disorientation before the upliftment. Some of you might be feeling dizzy or somewhat lost or confused; perhaps you are irritable and having difficulty grounding yourselves.

Understand that the energy transformations you are going through are of a demanding nature. You are going through a high-energy workload with the basic third-dimensional mind and body. You were not necessarily trained as children to be lightworkers or starseeds. You are working on an old modality within you, an old structure. You have redesigned it beautifully.

We are going into a new phase of soul work, a transformation of total nature. You are becoming a new person. In some cases, you are moving into another lifetime. Perhaps you have heard some of the guides and teachers say that in ascension work you go through karmic work of three, four, and even five lifetimes rapidly. That has to do with what you are learning and assimilating. On a soul level, you can handle this. On a personality level, you are really stretching yourselves beyond what you were even able to consider a year ago. The upliftment and the energy that are being given now have set the groundwork for a newer connection with your soul essence, which is going to give you an energy source that will make the ride into the next level easier and more comfortable.

Release your ties to the third dimension, but at the same time, understand that this release will make your third-dimensional experiences easier. You are becoming masters of the third dimension. This is the paradox, but it is the law that all ascended masters understand. By releasing your attachments to the third dimension, you become more of the master of the third dimension, which enhances your abilities as planetary healers. Some of you are just awakening to your mission — the mission of connecting to the star families, the star crystals — and participating in the group energy field. This requires an expanded self-image and self-esteem, and it includes a humbleness, not an ego-inflated energy. It is an expansive energy.

I, Vywamus, call on each of you now to allow the ego, as you know it, to expand. My friends, it will expand on your command during this energy connection. You will expand, and the connection will stay expanded. Expand yourself! Expand!

The problems confronting you on a personal basis will more easily dissolve — not because you have done anything on the third dimension to affect it but because you have expanded. That is the level of shimmering energy Juliano and the guides were talking about. Shimmering is an expansion. One of the interesting levels of intervention on the third dimension is when you are confronted with a problem, you will try to do something to resolve it. From the fifth-dimensional — the shimmering light — perspective, you don't need to do anything. Just expand yourself, and then the problem dissolves, not because you did anything, but because you expanded and your perspective changed. In actuality, you did do something by not getting involved in the third-dimensional activity. Anytime you come across something that contracts you or seems insurmountable, know that this is an opportunity for you to expand.

Sometimes you might wonder why, when you are dealing with all this higher energy, you have to deal with the lower level. Just know that you are being called on to expand. You will be very pleased with the result. I always stand ready to work with you on any level to help you to expand, especially where you are. It is a holy experience. As a soul psychologist, I congratulate you on your opportunity to download more of your soul essence into this life. It is a true gift, and it is something that many souls who have come to Earth want to accomplish. If you have shimmering abilities and the sincerity and understanding, then you are experiencing a magnificent opportunity.

I am Vywamus. Good day.

• • •

Unlock the Codes of Ascension

Greetings, I am Archangel Metatron. One of my main missions in working with the starseeds is to help them unlock the codes of ascension, which allows them to interact with their fifth-dimensional bodies and abilities. It is necessary to unlock the codes for several reasons. Not just anyone can access fifth-dimensional energy. There needs to be a certain vibrational upliftment in a person's field to access the fifth dimension.

It is easier to unlock the codes when working with a group. In the past, people might have been able to unlock these codes individually. In Earth's history, fifth-dimensional upliftment energy was always processed in a group because a group enhances ascension. However, never before has there been this opportunity to unlock the codes on a global scale and on both a personal and a planetary basis. Groups of higher beings are now given the opportunity to manifest and access these abilities from the fifth-dimension simultaneously.

Unlocking the codes of ascension includes learning shimmering abilities. This gives you the ability to interact fifth dimensionally in a manifested back-and-forth way. We are using energy codes and sounds that you might have heard many times before through this channel. The first code is the energy of the Kadosh [Hebrew for "holy"].

With your intention and elevated consciousness, connect with holy energy and begin to shimmer. As you hear me tone, go inside your mental framework, your mental body, and give permission to unlock these codes and new shimmering abilities. You will experience your ability to shimmer immediately, and you will be given instructions on how to proceed in groups to practice shimmering. Shimmering energy happens on a multiple energetic level related to other energy levels in the galaxy. Shimmering energy can actually help you to connect to a galactic source.

Focus on your intention to unlock the codes within you. This will allow you to shimmer and connect with your ability to unlock the codes of ascension. This is an enhancement of our previous work in unlocking the codes of ascension. Prepare yourself in a one-minute meditation while we prepare the channel to emit these sounds for you.

[Chants] "Kadosh, Kadosh, Kadosh, Adonai Tzveaot Kadooooosh, Kadooooosh,

Kaaadooosh, Aaaaaadoanaiii Tsevaaaaooooth." [Repeats three times]: I, Archangel Metatron, call on the light force field of holiness to continue to unlock the codes for the shimmering light within each of you. Let a newer soul ability emerge and emanate from your soul source, from your lightbody, from your Neshamah [Hebrew for "higher soul"].

Integrate these abilities into this lifetime. Each of you will be able to manifest this ability on multiple levels. On a personal level, it will be very activating for healers and for lightworkers on this planet. You will be activated in the work you do in your daily lives, with your pets, and whatever you come in contact with now. You will, on a personal basis, help many aspects of the planet benefit from this. [Chants] "Hooolyyy liiight. Auuuurrrr Haaaakadosh. Aur Ha'Kadosh."

Your soul work will begin to manifest, and you will be able to complete the essence of your transformation because this ability is unlocked. It is a transformational experience. The energy from the shimmering can even be projected through your hands, minds, group interactions, and chanting. Your energy shimmers at a high vibration now.

In energy work, there is the receiver and the transmitter. You have to interact as the receiver of this shimmering light now. Let the higher palaces of the fifth-dimensional world fill your mental bodies so that there is a beautiful light field in your mind and on the screen of your subconscious. Most important, remember that you can reboot your mind to experience the higher dimensions. Like a computer, your mind can be cleared of dense energies. We will help you to experience the clearing within your mind field so that you have been upgraded into a new consciousness.

You will be called on to hold this light and energy, especially in the face of impending contractions and coming darkness. The shimmering light ability is not affected by the contractions on Earth. When you see contractions of weather, you can project this shimmering energy onto a screen of light over that area. These contractions include volcanic eruptions, earthquakes, tornadoes, storms, cyclones, and even drought. Shimmer the area so that it can interact with fifth-dimensional energy and the highest forces are activated.

The Hebrew words of *Eretz ha olam* [the Land of Eternity] are given as the Hebrew name for the fifth-dimensional Earth. [Chants] "Eretz ha olam." Let that term represent the fifth-dimensional Earth. [Tones] "Ooooohhhh."

I now ask Chief White Eagle to speak with you. I am Metatron.

• • •

Fifth-Dimensional Empowerment

[Chants] "Hey ya ho ya heyyyy!" Greetings, we are all brothers and sisters. All my words are sacred. I am Chief White Eagle.

When dark clouds came to the sky, we gathered in a circle and chanted; we would pray. When there is darkness and contractions on the planet, we call on the ancient ones. We call on our ancestors to help us connect to the force field of transformation, the force field of light. We seek in our circle to uplift ourselves so that we are in greater communication with the ancient ones, our grandfathers and grandmothers, and the wise ones.

When we begin to do what Metatron and the Arcturians call shimmering, we of the Native peoples find that we simultaneously connect with the ancient ones, our star families, our lineage of grandfathers and grandmothers, our ancient uncles and aunts, our brothers and sisters, and our soul families. When this happens, we feel more personal power. We feel as if we are not alone. We feel as if the ancient ones are connecting with us and sending us energy to perform sacred duties and tasks of shimmering and connecting to the fifth dimension.

We know that we do not stand alone. We stand in a lineage, and that lineage enhances us. We download the soul essences of our higher selves and from our lineage. Some of you stand in the lineage of Natives, and some of you stand in the lineage of star masters and your star families. Open now to your lineage. [Chants] "Hey eeeeh, hey ya hey yaaaa ya ya."

O Grandfathers, Grandmothers, we open to your light from the fifth dimension. We receive your knowledge that will help us unlock these codes within our hearts and within our minds. Give us these fifth-dimensional abilities. O Grandfather, Grandmother, we know that the ultimate healing sources for this planet come through the connections to the star families and the star masters now connecting with us. O Grandmother, Grandfather, we are with you.

O ancient ones, we know that you are in a higher place than we. O ancient ones, we know that you are in constant communication with the star teachers. We open ourselves up to you, Grandfather, Grandmother, so that we can receive an energy that is more refined than what we can usually access by ourselves.

The ancient ones ask that you see the star called Sirius connect with your eyes to open and receive its light, for that star is connected with many ancient civilization and ancient star energies. O Grandfather, Grandmother, you teach us that the star energies are transformational. The star energies are fifth-dimensional. They contain new energy and light. The star energies are encoded. They can be activated, and they can activate the crystals. The star energies also can seal the fractures in Earth's aura.

O Grandfather, Grandmother, let the star energies help to seal and connect the fractured Inner Earth. We focus on the healings of Earth's aura and outer level. On this point, we are given instructions through you, O Grandfather,

Grandmother, to send this healing shimmering light to the Inner Earth, for we know, Grandfather, Grandmother, that the Inner Earth has also been greatly affected by nuclear energies. We know the Inner Earth needs our thoughts and prayers. [Chants] "Hey ya hooooooo. Hey yey. Hey hey yoooo." Let the Inner Earth receive the shimmering light from the starseeds. The Inner Earth is glowing with fifth-dimensional light. The Telos cities of light in the Inner Earth receive our blessings.

All my words are sacred. Ho!

• • •

Connect with Your Future Self Using Holographic Healing

Greetings, I am Helio-ah. I am communicating with you from the holographic healing chambers on my ship. I ask you to connect holographically with your future self. You know that the seedling for a tree has within it a great history and potential to become a great tree — to become full of branches and leaves and to reach tall in the sky. The seed is just the beginning. Now you have this beginning, which is this lifetime. There is an available connection to your future self, which includes a connection to your advanced soul that can be brought down now. This is the future self. We, the Arcturians, know that the way to enhance growth and transformation is through connections with the future self.

I, Helio-ah, send down a golden-blue corridor of light over each of you. [Sings] "Helioooo-aaaAAhhhhh." In this golden-blue light, each of you through thought-projection enter my ship, the Starship Athena. You enter the heliographic, holographic healing chamber where you enter individual healing booths of light. As you come into that heliographic light chamber, you see a computer screen with a dial set at twelve o'clock, which is the present. Turn the dial to five minutes after twelve o'clock, and advance perhaps two to three years into your future — a future in which you have continued this development.

Enter a future in which you have gone into new heights and spiritual depths, a new future where you have new abilities at connecting the biorelativity energy field of the Inner Earth and the outer Earth. You now have connections to the shimmering energy fields, your force fields that enable you to develop this skill of working with higher energies on Earth. Yes, this is two to three years from now. You see that in the future you have refined these abilities. Hold that image. Press the button on the right that says "Save," and the image is saved in your holographic, computerized healing chamber.

There is another button there that says "Merging with the Present Self," which means that the saved image of the future self now can be merged with the present self. After you press that button, turn the dial back to twelve o'clock. As you arrive at twelve o'clock, the whole screen lights up, the whole energy field of the holographic *healing chamber lights up. There are streams of energy and light and vibration. Experience that now as we go into silence. Experience that vibrational upliftment.*

You receive this vibrational upliftment from your future self beautifully at the twelve o'clock position. You bring down the potential of shift and changes that you have ready to go two years from now. These other future changes are also ready to come into you. You are skilled lightworkers and energy workers.

Now leave your heliographic healing chambers. You may return later during the next twenty-four-hour period to continue this work. We return each of you from the corridor back into your physical bodies now. There is a great holographic light star above your crown chakras. [Sings] "Heeeliiioooo-aaaahhhh."

Blessings, I am Helio-ah.

•   •   •

Greetings, I'm Juliano. We are the Arcturians. Shimmering is a method used to unite you with the fifth dimension. You know we are working with you to help you interact with the fifth dimension and to bring down fifth-dimensional energy. To bring down fifth-dimensional energy, you need to personally experience the fifth dimension mentally, emotionally, spiritually, and if possible, physically. You need to have an elevation of all of those bodies as well as elevated thinking.

You also need elevated healing. Many of you are going through physical issues, and traditional medicines might not be useful. In fact, many Western medicines are quite barbaric. One hundred years from now, people are going to look back and say, "They did what? They were giving people what? For that? Oh my God! Those people were back in the stone ages. We would never do that." There are helpful fifth-dimensional healing energies you can use now for your physical, as well as spiritual, body. The spiritual light from the fifth dimension is stronger, more penetrating, and more dynamic than the third dimension.

Shimmering

Here are the foundational steps (thought projection) necessary before shimmering:

1. Astrally leave your body.
2. Thought-project yourself through a corridor.
3. Go to a specific place through the corridor, such as the Arcturian crystal lake.
4. At your destination, enter your fifth-dimensional body. Your astral body receives all the imprints, energies, and higher light.
5. When your visit is complete, leave with your astral/spiritual fifth-dimensional body.

6. Go back through the corridor.
7. Reenter the room where your body is.
8. Command a perfected alignment of your spiritual body to reenter your physical body.
9. Reenter your physical body.
10. Download the energies into your physical body through the process known as spiritual osmosis.

In shimmering, we shortcut several parts of this exercise. You go from being here in your Earth body to accelerating your aura. Shimmering shortens the process so that you go directly from the third-dimensional state into your fifth-dimensional body. Then from your fifth-dimensional body, you come right back. But you cannot shimmer unless you have learned the preliminary steps of thought projection.

So what is the advantage of shimmering? Well, obviously it is a shortcut. Also, you may be in a situation in which your life is in danger. You could be experiencing an earthquake or some kind of trauma. You might need fifth-dimensional energy immediately and not have enough time to go through all the steps. You might need an instantaneous boost of light, protection, or energy when you are in some kind of health crisis or transition. When you shimmer, you can interact with fifth-dimensional light immediately.

Also the shimmering can be used on places, such as shimmering planetary cities of light. In planetary healing, you can actually shimmer Earth.

Shimmering is similar to the transporting method used in the TV program Star Trek. The characters used a transporter to travel between the spaceship and other planets instead of landing. They transported their bodies by going through a process of electromagnetic destabilization of the atomic structures that were reformulated at their chosen destination. This process is known in the psychic world as teleportation. When they used the transporter in Star Trek, you could see them shimmer. They would go in and out, in and out, and you would think, "Oh, oh, it is not going to work," because the machine was vibrating really fast. They would appear and disappear, appear and disappear, and then they were transported.

The appearance and disappearance is the shimmering, and that process is done by working with the energy of the aura. If someone watched as you shimmered, they would see you going in and out of reality. They would see you sparkling. The word "shimmer" implies twinkling. It is a type of light frequency in which you go in and out of reality.

Spaceships shimmer from the fifth dimension into the third dimension. But of course they don't stay in the third dimension; they go in and out. When you are more advanced in space travel, you go in, stay, and then leave the third dimension. You will also be able to stay in the "in" phase longer. Some ships could stay in the third-dimensional reality for a half-hour. There are numerous reports of people who had contact with extraterrestrials, seeing their ships appear and disappear. Some people would see the ships, and others wouldn't. To see you shimmer, people need to be at a certain light frequency. By shimmering, you are taking your astral presence and moving it into the fifth dimension.

When you shimmer, you accelerate your aura. For you to exist in this frequency, you have to be at the resonant vibration to stay grounded and appear in the third dimension. In shimmering, you accelerate your frequency. It is important to have some training and the right spiritual light quotient. You have to be somewhat elevated in your thinking and know where you are going in the fifth dimension. It will not work as well if you just say, "Okay, I'm going to shimmer and go into the fifth dimension." The fifth dimension is a big place, and you need to have a focus for projecting yourself. We set up the crystal lake so that you can go right into your fifth-dimensional body there.

Shimmering Exercise

To help you accelerate your aura in preparation for shimmering, I will tone higher level sounds, such as "tatatatatata" and say, "Okay, begin to accelerate your aura; begin to accelerate your aura." When you reach a point of high vibration, I will say, "Shimmeeeer now!" Then you will go into your fifth-dimensional body. If you don't feel yourself going into the fifth dimension, just listen to the words, listen to the vibrations, and work with the energy. You will shimmer from the third dimension into the fifth, and while in the fifth dimension, you will enter your fifth-dimensional body. When I say, "Shimmeeer back," you will go back into you third-dimensional body. Let's begin.

Think about your cosmic egg. Think about shimmering and accelerating the pulsing of your aura. To shimmer at the highest level, your aura needs to pulse quickly. Focus on your energy field around the cosmic egg, focus on the line around the cosmic egg, think of the pulsing of that line, and then coordinate the pulsing with my tone. [Tones rapidly] "Ta, ta, ta, ta."

Shimmeeeer you third-dimensional body. Shimmeeeer. Go into your fifth-dimensional body. Shimmeeeeer now! You are now in your fifth-dimensional body. Feel this energy; feel this light. You are in your fifth-dimensional body.

Now shimmer from the fifth-dimensional body back to the third-dimensional body. Shimmeeeer your fifth-dimensional body. Shimmeeeer. Shimmeeeer the fifth-dimensional body back into the third-dimensional body now! You are back in your third-dimensional body.

By going into the fifth-dimensional body and coming back into your third-dimensional presence, you now feel an elevation of energy you did not feel before. Now you will shimmer again.

Shimmeeeer, shimmeeeeer, shimmer your third-dimensional body. Shimmer your third-dimensional body, and go into the fifth-dimensional body. Shimmeeeeer now! You are in your fifth-dimensional body at the crystal lake. Absorb all of the light and energy in the fifth dimension that you can.

Now you are going to shimmer back into the third-dimensional body. Bring as much of that light, energy and power as you can from the fifth dimension back into the third dimension, helping you to bring healing light to yourself. Shimmeeeer your fifth-dimensional body. Shimmeeeer your fifth-dimensional body, and come back into the third dimension. Shimmeeeer now!

You are back in your third-dimensional body with the light and the healing energy from the fifth dimension. That light and energy from the fifth dimension has come into your third-dimensional body with you.

Shimmeeeer, shimmeeeer, shimmeeeer, going in and out, in and out, shimmeeer, shimmeeeer, shimmeeeer. Shimmer your third-dimensional body. Feel the pulsing of your aura going faster and faster. Shimmeeeer, shimmeeeer and go to the fifth-dimensional body now! You are now in your fifth-dimensional body again. Feel the healing power of your fifth-dimensional body. Shimmeeeer. Feel the vibrational energies you are creating. Feel the comfort and ease that you can transfer from the third dimension to the fifth dimension and from the fifth dimension back to the third dimension.

Shimmeeeer, shimmeeeer, shimmeeeer. Shimmeeeer from your fifth-dimensional body. Shimmeeer from the fifth-dimensional body. Shimmeeeer, shimmeeeer back to the third-dimensional body now! Take a deep breath integrating all the spiritual energy and spiritual light. You have established this beautiful link between the fifth dimension and the third dimension. You are a shimmering magnetic field of light. Shimmeeeer, shimmeeeer, shimmeeeer.

Whenever you need to connect with the fifth dimension to bring back a light frequency, you can do it now by shimmering.

Shimmeeeer, shimmeeeer, shimmeeeer, shimmeeeer, shimmeeeer, shimmeeeer in your third-dimensional body. Shimmeeeer. [Tones] "Tat tat tat tat." Shimmer from your third-dimensional body and go into your fifth-dimensional body. Shimmeeeer now!

You are in your fifth-dimensional body feeling the light and feeling the energy in the crystal temple. Gather all this beautiful mental, emotional, physical, and spiritual energy. Gather all feelings of love and forgiveness. The fifth dimension feels of compassion, higher thinking, and spiritual energy. You feel new healing powers coming to you.

Shimmeeeer your fifth-dimensional body now. Shimmeeeer, shimmeeeer,

shimmeeeer, shimmmeer your fifth-dimensional body. Shimmeeeer back into your third-dimensional body. Shimmeeeer now! You are back in your third-dimensional body.

Please take a deep breath in and out, open your eyes, and stand up slowly. Let all this new energy penetrate each cell; just let it move into your body because you are reintegrating on a very deep level now. Bring the energy to you. You are still bringing down streams of light from the fifth dimension into your third-dimensional body because you have set up this beautiful connection. You are connected now.

Sit down again. Now we will go into a five-minute meditation. I will announce the end of the meditation with the tone.

[Five-minute pause.]

[Tones] "Oooooooo." Return to this room and into your third-dimensional body knowing that you have access to this technique. You will be able to use it whenever you wish.

The Dawning of the Fifth Dimension

You are reaching a point in your evolution where you are able to interact with the noosphere. By interacting with it, you are able to effect change in it. Throughout history humanity's actions, thoughts, and projections have gone into the noosphere, but now Earth and humanity have the opportunity to influence and control the evolution of the Adam species. Never before has this opportunity happened on the planet.

There are so many unique features now helping to create the right circumstances for shifting the noosphere. The ascension means that the fifth dimension is closer to the third dimension. You have understood this very well, and I hope that my explanation about the folding of the space-time continuum has helped you to understand the relationship between objects in the universe and how distances between those objects can be traveled instantaneously. Ultimately, the idea of folding the space-time continuum can be used between the third and the fifth dimensions.

Visualize the third dimension as a sphere. This concept of a sphere is very useful. There is debate about the shape of the universe. Of course, if the universe is infinite, then how could it have a sphere shape? Let's put that argument aside for now and visualize the entire third dimension as a sphere, and you are in the sphere. Visualize the fifth dimension as another sphere at a point so far away that there are no words to describe the distance because it is extra-dimensional.

There is a space between the third and the fifth dimensions. Sometimes I have called it hyperspace. (When you do the exercise for folding the space-time continuum on Earth and other planets, you are using actual third-dimensional space.) Now we are folding the space-time continuum in a different context, and we are calling it folding the hyperspace continuum. So in your mind, have a point that represents the fifth dimension. You are in the third dimension. Visualize this beautiful image as an intersecting circle. (This is like one sphere on the Tree of Life intersecting another sphere on the tree.) Visualize this intersection.

How do you visualize an intersection of dimensions? Fold the space-time continuum of hyperspace into the intersection of the dimensions, and say this affirmation: "I, [say your name], am folding this hyperspace continuum so that the fifth and third dimensions intersect now."

[Tones several times] "Ooooohhhhhh." Help the healing of Earth through the intersection of the third and fifth dimensions. Connect and fold the hyperspace continuum so that the fifth dimension and third dimension intersect. Work on that beautiful image and the affirmation: "I am folding the hyperspace continuum so that the fifth and third dimensions intersect now."

My friends, you are participating in the awakening — the dawning — of the fifth dimension. This is the key to all the planetary healing ceremonies. This is the key to all the balancing. This is the key to the solutions of all Earth's problems. This is the key to all the polarizations you are seeing. The key is integrating the fifth dimension!

Now say, "I see the fifth-dimensional light entering Earth's noosphere now. I see the fifth-dimensional light. I see the light from the fifth dimension entering Earth's noosphere, and the spirit of Earth is receiving the fifth-dimensional light in anticipation of the interaction of Earth with the fifth dimension." The more people you can gather to meditate and help bring in this attraction, the more quickly the fifth dimension will interact in a complete way with Earth.

I am Juliano. Good day!

Glossary

akashic records — The collective library of storage of all thoughts and events for all beings throughout the galaxies.

altered state of consciousness (higher) — A condition during which a person can see ultimate truth and is able to experience the present more fully, such as the dream state, trance, and meditation. This term is also used to describe changes in consciousness a person might experience with mind-altering drugs.

arcan energy — An Arcturian term for the measurement of the power of a thought field. It can symbolically be compared to watts in electromagnetic theory. A higher wattage means more light power, and a higher arcan energy means higher thought power.

Arcturian crystal lake — A fifth-dimensional lake on Arcturus set up to interact with Earth and the third dimension.

Arcturian etheric crystals — Fifth-dimensional crystals that originate from the etheric world and interact directly with the planetary noosphere. These crystals are great vessels for fifth-dimensional light. They can hold the unity consciousness from the fifth dimension amid the duality and polarizations of this planet. The crystals hold special codes and programs for planetary ascension.

Twelve etheric crystals were brought down, each corresponding to a certain sphere on the map of the Tree of Life. The Arcturian crystals are located in Mount Fuji, Japan; Istanbul, Turkey; Bodensee, Germany; Montserrat, Spain; Serra de Bocaina, Brazil; Volcan Poas, Costa Rica; Lake Puelo, Argentina;

Lake Moraine, Canada; Copper Canyon, Mexico; Mount Shasta, California, United States; Grose Valley, Australia; and Lake Taupo, New Zealand.

Arcturian Tree of Life for Planetary Healing — An updated version of the Kabbalistic Tree of Life with the added characteristic of balancing the spheres specifically for healing and helping Earth connect with the fifth dimension. The Arcturian Planetary Tree of Life has been designed to correspond to twelve sacred areas on the planet, which is now helping to establish a healing energy system. Each designated sacred area has been downloaded with a fifth-dimensional Arcturian etheric crystal to help it become more receptive to higher healing light.

ascended masters — Spiritual teachers who have graduated from Earth or teachers on higher dimensions, including archangels, higher beings from the galactic world, and prophets. A spiritual guide from any Earth religion, including Native American traditions. They have graduated from the Earth incarnational cycle and ascended into the fifth dimension.

astral plane — The nonphysical level of reality where most humans go when they die.

Aur Ha'kadosh — Hebrew for "holy light."

biorelativity — A meditation method that focuses on working together telepathically to send healing energy to the planet or change the outcome of an event. In biorelativity exercises, groups of starseeds around the planet send healing thought to specific areas in the world. Storms, hurricanes, and even earthquakes can potentially be averted or diminished.

Blue Jewel — The name Arcturians use to describe planet Earth. This is also a name of a movie made by German film producer Oliver Hauck on planetary healing, which features David K. Miller.

Blue People — The Andromeda galaxy is home to the Blue People. The Blue People are highly evolved spiritual beings who have been able to exist in thought form without incarnations into a physical body. You are on track to achieve this evolutionary step.

cellular memory cleansing or clearing — A method for clearing past-life memories from one's neurological memory system that can be described by the

German word *reinigung*, which illustrates the concept of cleansing and clearing at the same time. A cellular cleansing and clearing can dispel memories and traumas from earlier reincarnations.

Central Sun — The fifth-dimensional spiritual center located in the center of the Milky Way galaxy from which high spiritual energy is emitted. Earth came into direct alignment with the Central Sun in 2012.

coiled incarnations — A symbolic description representing the path of soul evolution. Notice that a coil goes up and around, but there is a part that is somewhat flat, which symbolically refers to multiple dimensional incarnations on a plane. You are moving up in your evolution. There are places on the coil where your development stays on a plane. In one part of the plane, you are in the third dimension, and in the other part of that plane, you might be in the fifth dimension. Eventually, you will reach the point where you are completely fifth-dimensional, and you never, unless for some reason you choose to, have to return to the third dimension.

Chief White Eagle — A fifth-dimensional Native American guide who is very connected to Jesus and other fifth-dimensional beings.

codes of ascension — Cellular keys for the ascension, also sometimes described as the Keys of Enoch. The codes of ascension are contained in certain sounds and tones that can activate your energy field to open up to the fifth dimension.

collective unconscious — This term, in part developed by the Swiss psychiatrist Carl Jung, is used to describe the ancient Earth archetypes and symbols used in each culture around the globe.

consciousness — "I think; therefore, I am" (a statement from Descartes) is the foundation of Western consciousness, which implies consciousness is based on thinking. "I Am That I Am" is a newer interpretation, which means, "I am aware of my being."

cosmic egg exercise — An exercise based on the belief that the perfect healing energy shape is an egg. The Arcturians refer to this as a cosmic egg. This is part of a dimensional healing method that involves forming your aura into an egg shape, in which you can experience immediate healing. The egg shape helps to protect your energy and helps you to maximize your spiritual potential.

cosmic justice — The rectification of events of all lifetimes from all planetary systems. It is an attempt to describe karma on a cosmic basis, taking into consideration people's energies and experiences from other planetary systems and galaxies.

cosmic memory — Energies and events that people are attracted to that are related to previous experiences locked in their cellular structures. In the theory of cellular memory, you tend to attract situations that were important to your soul development, whether positive or negative.

Council of Elders — A group of spiritual leaders who seek to lead Earth toward a higher spiritual plane.

dimensional bleeding — A process that can occur when there are not sufficient protections between dimensions. Many of the acts of violence, distortion, and strange events occurring on Earth are because of the bleeding of the lower fourth dimension into the third dimension. In many cases, because of these leaks, lower fourth-dimensional beings are able to come down into the third dimension and cause great mischief. These areas in the lower fourth dimension often have lower spirits, ghosts, and generally lower energy beings.

dimensional boom — The sonic boom that occurs when a spaceship comes from hyperspace and reenters close to a planet. The planet that is being re-entered can be thrown off balance by a dimensional boom.

dimensional waves — Pre-ascension fifth-dimensional waves of light coming down to the planet usually experienced by starseeds. You can call on the dimensional energy wave to help you experience more fifth-dimensional light.

doppelgänger — A German word describing the astral double of a person. "Doppelgänger" means that there is a double, or duplicate, of your body. Your astral body energetically forms a duplicate of your physical body. When you visualize during astral travel, you work with the doppelgänger, this etheric duplicate. Your etheric duplicate has powers and abilities far beyond the physical body. The physical body has limitations because it is in the third dimension, but the etheric body can bounce around, travel remotely, go through doors, and do all kinds of fun things.

Earth homeostasis — A maintained balance of certain levels of oxygen and nitrogen, as well as many other chemical factors, in the biosphere.

etheric — A term used to designate the higher bodies in the human system. In India, "etheric" is used to describe the unseen energy and thoughts of humans.

fifth dimension — A higher dimension of existence that transcends the circumstances of the third and fourth dimensions. It is the realm of infinite energy and love and can be compared to the Garden of Eden. In the fifth dimension, one transcends (ascends) the incarnational cycle and graduates from Earth. Jesus is one of the ascended masters residing in the fifth dimension.

feedback loop system of Earth — Earth's self-regulating mechanism that holds the biosphere in balance. It receives input from the planet and then makes adjustments accordingly.

folding of the space-time continuum — An important teaching from Arcturian technology. The image of folding cardboard like an accordion is a beautiful metaphor for the folding of the space-time continuum. Space is folded so that you can transcend normal space and be where you want to be instantaneously. The practice of the folding of the space-time continuum plays a central role in traveling throughout the galaxy and the universe.

Galactic Kachina — The intermediary between the Central Sun and this planet. In Native American Puebloan folklore, a kachina is an intermediary between the higher spirit world and this world.

galactic spirituality — A spiritual philosophy that accepts the existence of higher beings throughout the galaxy and the understanding that spirituality and planetary evolution are part of a galactic family of civilizations.

Group of Forty — A concept of group consciousness suggested by the Arcturians to aid humans in the ascension process. According to the Arcturians, 40 is a spiritually powerful number. The Arcturians emphasize the value and power of joining in groups. A group of 40 consists of 40 members located worldwide who focus on meditating together at a given time each month. Members agree to assist each other in spiritual development. These groups assist in Earth's healing and provide a foundation for the individual member's ascension.

Harmonic Convergence — A worldwide ceremony representing global unity when harmonic energy was downloaded to Earth from the Central Sun. The first Harmonic Convergence was in 1987, and another occurred on August 8,

2008, when a harmonic energy was brought down to Earth at Mount Shasta, California, and was transmitted around the world.

hyperspace — The space between dimensions. Arcturians say that once you reach hyperspace, you can instantly travel around the universe.

intermediaries — Spirit guides who can communicate between a higher energy field and the third dimension. You all have personal intermediaries — spirit guides and teachers — around you. It is not just one channel or one prophet who has the ability to communicate with these higher beings. The spirit guide, or intermediary, can bring special messages from the higher realms.

Iskalia mirror — An etheric mirror the Arcturians helped place over the North Pole. Visualize a gigantic mirror a mile or two in diameter in the etheric realm above the North Pole and in special alignment with the Central Sun. The purpose of the Iskalia mirror is to act as a magnifier, allowing a pure energy field to reach Earth from the Central Sun.

Juliano — The main Arcturian guide and ascended master working to help activate Earth and Arcturian starseeds for ascension.

kachinas — Intermediaries for the Native Americans who bridge the gap between this third-dimensional world and the spirit world. The kachinas have a home in the San Francisco Peaks outside of Flagstaff, Arizona. Katchinas are also masked dancers embodying such spirits as well as carved dolls representing them.

Kadosh — The Hebrew word for "holy."

Kadosh Kadosh Kadosh, Adonai Tzveaot — Hebrew for "holy, holy, holy is the Lord of hosts." This is a sacred Hebrew chant used to unlock the keys of ascension.

ladders of ascension — Etheric structures bringing fifth-dimensional light into the earth. The ladders of ascension have been set up in powerful, sacred places around Earth that provide stability and energy to be used by Gaia for her ascension. The ladders serve two purposes: (1) to provide a portal for you when you ascend at the right time and (2) to stabilize the fifth-dimensional energies in Gaia's spiritual light and presence.

merry-go-round technique — A spiritual exercise used to leave your physical body to travel with your astral body.

Messianic light — light from the fifth dimension that comes from the energy of the Messiah; a healing light for the entire planet.

near-death experience (NDE) — An experience in which a person nearly dies during which he or she might see tunnels and corridors or the entrance to other dimensions. This experience often happens after an accident or some other traumatic event.

nephilim — Offspring of the "sons of God" and "daughters of men." In Hebrew, nephilim means "fallen ones." They might have been space beings who came to Earth or could have been giants, as they often are described as large beings.

Neshamah — Hebrew for "higher soul." The Kabbalah describes the higher soul as the Neshamah.

noosphere — The thought field of the entire planet. The noosphere has many levels and can, in some ways, be compared to the akashic records. It interacts with Gaia as well as the dimensional levels and stability of the planet. The noosphere is part of the etheric energy field, which is having quite a dramatic effect on all of the events manifesting on Earth.

omega-time-particle dimensional waves — A wave energy from the fifth dimension that has special healing powers. For example, it can counterbalance energy waves coming from Earth's feedback loop system.

omega time zone — A period in which time can be accelerated. Multiple events that seemingly would take years to occur can transpire in as little as a month or two. In an omega time zone, you might feel as if you have had several lifetimes in the span of a year or two.

peak experiences — Described by Abraham Maslow as periods of heightened states of awareness and perception during which one has feelings of well-being and even ecstasy. These are experiences of expanded consciousness that result in altered states of consciousness. During these peak experiences, you can see the third dimension through a new perceptual lens. Thus, concepts difficult to understand (such as unified energy, unified field theory, or luminous strands of light theory) suddenly make sense. You can solve problems that previously might have seemed impossible.

perfect alignment — One of the key ingredients for returning your astral body into your physical body. Your astral body re-enters your physical body in the correct position and angle, just as it was before it left.

personal power — In the spiritual world, the ability to connect with higher energy for a specific purpose on Earth.

planetary cities of light project — A project working toward planetary healing and balancing by establishing cities of light around the planet. Each city of light has a fifth-dimensional energy field that contributes to the higher unified energy field for Earth. The key is that the planetary cities of light become united in a network. In order to achieve planetary ascension, Earth must have a powerful network of planetary cities working together on an interactive basis.

planetary logos — Sanat Kumara. An intermediary between Gaia and humankind.

pre-threshold — A predicted event, such as a storm, that can be altered or redirected using biorelativity. It can first be understood as a warning. Because it is only a possibility, it can possibly be deterred through biorelativity.

pung energy — A term in Taoist philosophy that focuses on pushing energy outward to ward off negative or aggressive energy. In spiritual work, it refers to a protective force used to repel negative energy coming into a person's aura.

quantum cohesiveness — In the world of physics, this term can be compared to the term "quantum entanglement," which refers to the observation that subatomic particles can relate to each other, even from a distance. In the spiritual world, this means that spiritual energy and thoughts relate to each other even if there is great distance between the thinkers.

quantum light — Healing light from the fifth dimension that transcends the normal cause-and-effect energy on the third dimension. Such light can create miraculous healings.

repetition compulsion — A concept developed by psychologist Alice Miller that postulates that people tend to repeat earlier unresolved conflicts until they are resolved. People tend to attract situations important to their souls' development that might be considered negative from the ego's perspective.

People need to repeat experiences in order to choose the correct action that enables them to ascend and move on to other places that contribute to their souls' evolution.

repetitious meditation — A meditative approach in which groups of people meditate hourly across the globe. For example, one group meditates at 9:00AM while another group meditates at 10:00AM and another group meditates at 11:00AM. Thus, there is a twenty-four-hour cycle (or even a twelve-hour cycle) in which people are meditating continuously around the world to achieve balance for the planet.

resonant frequencies — Harmonious energy that exists between two beings who have similar or complementary thought patterns.

ring of ascension — An etheric structure that was downloaded with the help of the Arcturians and ascended masters to aid Earth's ascension. The ring downloads fifth-dimensional energy into the third dimension.

sacred language — A language that contains words with vibrational tonal qualities that help you connect with your higher self, such as Hebrew or Sanskrit. When you tone a word in a sacred language (for example, the word for the higher self or the word for God), it activates higher energy in your aura.

sacred triangle — The teachings of the sacred triangle focus on the unity of three spiritual paradigms. Each paradigm (galactic spirituality, the White Brotherhood-Sisterhood, and the Native people teachings) on its own is not strong enough to manifest the fifth-dimensional energy necessary to heal Earth, but all three working together can bring a powerful healing energy to Earth.

Sanat Kumara — An intermediary between Gaia and humankind known as the planetary logos [overseer of Gaia's unfoldment].

shimmering — An energy exercise that allows your auric field to vibrate at a frequency to shift the electrons. The atomic structure of your cells transmutes into a vibratory energy field that elliptically shifts cellular structures into the fifth dimension, causing a back-and-forth, or "shimmering," modality. This shimmering modality affects the atomic and quantum levels of your cellular structures. The energy in shimmering is a powerful and necessary prelude to the fifth-dimensional ascension.

singularity — The study of the interaction between human consciousness and a computer whose purpose is to produce a superintelligence so powerful that it is beyond even your imagination.

sister–star cities of light — Cities of light from other planets connected to planetary cities of light on Earth.

space-time continuum — The four-dimensional continuum of one temporal and three spatial coordinates in which any event or physical object is located. When you collapse space, you also collapse time.

spiritual osmosis — An integration of higher auric energy into the physical body after you have had an out-of-body experience. This slow process has been compared to downloading a new computer program.

star family — A group of higher masters and teachers and similar to the Galactic Council from planetary systems related to Earth. The star family oversees the evolution of Earth energies as well as other planetary energies throughout the galaxy.

starseeds — People who have had previous incarnations in other lifetimes and on other planets.

symmetrical-particle energy field — Energy within thought fields that similar subatomic thought particles resonant with.

thought field — Composed of mental energy from ideas and beliefs. Thoughts merge in cohesive energy waves that become a field, similar to a magnetic field. Thought fields can attract and repel other thought fields.

thought projection — The method for moving your astral body in the etheric world by thought. In thought projection, you visualize your astral body leaving the physical body, traveling through a corridor, and going to a desired location.

tones — Sounds that produce a vibratory resonance to help activate and align the charkas.

trance channeling — Automatic speaking from a light trance or hypnotic, almost somnambulant, state. Trance is a type of hypnosis in which you put yourself into an altered state of consciousness. Deep trance is the way Edward Cayce used to channel. In light trance channeling, you are still awake while bringing through messages.

transcendent-thought energy field — A thought field that can go beyond the laws of cause and effect and third-dimensional rules to access fifth-dimensional energy.

Tree of Life — In Jewish mysticism, the Tree of Life is a galactic blueprint for the creation of this reality. It includes ten energy emanations placed in spheres in the shape of a tree. Each sphere has a specific energy and a sacred name of God associated with it. These spheres are used for individual and planetary healing. The three spiritualties of the sacred triangle are included in the Tree of Life. The Tree of Life is not flat; rather, multidimensional and holographic with paths for manifestation.

unified energy field of the planet — Unified consciousness on a planetary basis.

unified field of consciousness — Unified energy field awareness. All religions in their highest consciousness and form have paths that lead directly to the experience of the unified energy field. Experiencing the unified energy field is comparable to the feeling of enlightenment and harmony, a peace within.

unified field theory — An open line of research that allows all that is usually thought of as fundamental forces and elementary particles to be described in terms of a single field. Modern physicists have looked for a theory to encompass everything occurring in the manifested world. A paradox emerged when they discovered the microscopic world does not seem to follow the same rules and regulations as the exterior world.

Appendix A

The Cosmic Egg Energy Configuration

Juliano and the Arcturians

Your energy field is sensitive and responsive to healing work. No matter how many attachments you have and no matter how many cords attempt to suck energy from your field, know that the energy field is always responsive to higher intervention and correction. It is just a matter of becoming aware that there is a way to access your energy field. Through the special techniques of healing tones and visualizations, you can accelerate and repair the cosmic-egg energy field.

Become aware of the energy field around your body, and as I tone, visualize the perfect shape of an egg field. [Tones] "Hhhooohhhhh." This particular tone accelerates the cosmic egg to a perfected state. [Tones] "Oohhhmmmmm." Bring this field into the perfect shape and state of health and cosmic awareness. This is called the cosmic-egg energy field. When you are in this state and your aura is shaped in this manner, it is only natural that you develop your cosmic awareness. [Tones] "Oohhhmmmm."

Now you are going to transfer your energy field to the fifth dimension. The path of ascension is through your energy field. When you control your energy field, you can bring the body to a higher vibration. Vibrate your cosmic egg and become aware of its frequency. As I tone, your energy field will be brought into the proper shape and then accelerated. As the egg vibrates and the energy increases, the body will increase the vibration of its energy field. [Tones] "Ohhhhhhhh." All lower energies that are attached but do not belong to your cosmic energy field now leave as you perfect your shape and increase your frequency. [Tones] "Hewwwwww."

Appendix B

Cleansing Your Energy Fields at the Crystal Lake

Juliano and the Arcturians

Greetings. This is Juliano. I am here to speak to you about the importance of cleansing your energy fields. Many of you have requested healing because you are experiencing physical and emotional problems. You are becoming burdened by the densities. We are compassionate to your situation. In many ways, this is a time of great burden and difficulty, and you wanted to be here for the spiritual transformation on Earth. Some of you have had to make significant sacrifices along the way. You have gone through significant accelerations that have expanded you. We want to help you in your healing.

I bring the Starship Athena energy over you now. I, Juliano, am bringing multiple cones of light. They look like upside-down ice cream cones. These are special cones descending the corridors of light over each of you. They envelop you in Arcturian blue light. Feel the blueness. Feel the cone of light descending over you. It engulfs your entire energy field, absorbing all that is in density. Your entire energy and etheric body is inside this cone.

The cone and your etheric body rise together, leaving the physical body in its present place. I have opened up a huge travel corridor directly to the crystal temple. Follow me in your cone, your Merkavah cone of light. Travel with me now at lightning speeds through the corridor to the crystal temple. Your etheric body is enveloped by the cone.

We arrive at the shoreline of the temple. All that is dense in your energy field, all that is problematic, all that is in need of healing, and all that is not of the light is transferred into the cone. The cone lifts off your etheric body and goes into the crystal lake. We offer you healing now. You are lifted in spirit and put into the waters of the crystal lake. The lake absorbs all that is of density and transforms it into light and higher vibration.

Hear the Arcturian clarity of healing sound. See healing light, and experience healing acceleration. Sense telepathic connection. All these energies are now being charged and transmitted into your cone. The cone now emerges from the water, and I, Juliano, direct it to descend around your energy field as all the healing energy drops with this cone.

You experience a magnetic charge of healing light from the Arcturian crystal temple and from the crystal itself. Send it to any areas of your Earth life that need this light. Go even deeper. Scan your body. We need you to be of the highest vibration during this alignment energy time. The cone again absorbs any densities or projected problems you have.

The cone is lifted off and brought back into the crystal lake. It is easily absorbed into the light of the lake. The cones are charged one last time with a special genetic energy that will be used only by starseeds to activate corridors connecting the stargate. I place the cone back over your etheric body. In the name of Adonai, in the name of Metatron, in the name of the Arcturians, and in the name of our mission, I activate you to a higher frequency as the cone envelops you!

Now we descend the corridor with your etheric body and cone of light together. This cone will ensure the maximum function of light energy into your physical body. As you descend, you notice no significant decrease in your vibration. Because you are enveloped in this special cone, your energy vibration remains at its maximum. Now you descend back through the special light corridor into your Earth body. The cone of light is still around you. There is a transfer of light into the physical. All healings necessary are being maximized. The energy transcendence is almost complete as this higher frequency is maximized into the physicality of Earth.

The alignments necessary for the intersection of dimensions are present. The emotional, mental, and physical are all brought into alignment. The genetic codes allowing you to access the special corridor to the stargate are activated in your physical body. The cones are lifted away from you slowly, absorbing any last-minute energies that do not belong with you. They rise as you sit in maximum light energy. All the cones are gone. You are in full light connected to all your starseed friends.

Appendix C

Expanded Consciousness and Soul Journey Healing

Gudrun R. Miller

When I started hypnotherapy regressions with my clients, my intention was to access past lives and then the in-between-lifetimes state, or life between life (LBL). My instructions to my clients were to go to the lifetime most in need of healing and that might be causing blockages in this life. Often the most important and powerful part of the regression is the access to guidance — to the soul family and to the council of elders who oversee each person's lifetimes. These beings give specific pointers about the success of the client's current life, what that person still needs to achieve, and information about his or her soul journey. That is, clients would receive information about where they originated and their overall purpose in this journey.

My clientele consists mostly of highly evolved souls and starseeds who have started to follow their own guidance. They are guided by either their higher selves or their guides to go to the place in their soul journeys that needs to be healed. Oftentimes, aspects of them were stuck because of trauma or an overload of dense energy from Earth. Many were losing their soul connections and had a sense of disorientation in this life.

Vywamus (channeled by my husband, David K. Miller) is a soul psychologist and fifth-dimensional spirit guide. He explained that we have galactic karma as well as Earth karma. The beautiful people who come to see me often have to resolve galactic karma. To access galactic karma, they must enter a trance state of consciousness known as the theta state. In this deep level of trance, you are awake yet you are able to connect with your superconscious. The subconscious, on the other hand, has all the memories of your Earth incarnations and is accessed in the alpha state. The superconscious has memories of your entire soul journey.

233

I was surprised to learn that many of the advanced beings and clients I work with have not had many incarnations here. Most have had only one lifetime; some have had as many as nine. These souls have come here for many different reasons; some are personal, and some, for uplifting the human race.

Soul Healing Regression

I have developed an expanded healing technique called soul healing regressions. Expanded consciousness in both therapist and client is necessary for the regression and reading. What this means is that the clients are aware that there are different dimensions, they might have existed in higher dimensions, and they might not always have been in human form. For example, I had a client who queried where she came from, and she learned she was from a distant part of this galaxy and came here in the form of a tree seed. Her first incarnation on Earth was as a tree! She found this information wonderful but limiting.

When I begin to work with clients, I take a brief history of this life, make a list of concerns and questions they want to address, and most importantly, sense their level of energy, their frequency. The spiritual law of resonance, according to Vywamus, requires that the patient be brought up to a higher frequency and assumes the patient is willing. This is a normal and expected part of the regression process.

Often patients are anxious or nervous, so I spend some time just chatting with them to help them relax. If I sense their energy is out of balance, I take them into the medicine wheel in my yard and do a series of prayers and clearings. I also use the tepee we have had in our yard for more than twenty years, which is now a place of high resonant energy. Once our frequencies are in alignment, I start the regression process. I prepare myself by personally getting into a higher-consciousness state, a higher resonant frequency. I like to do these regressions at my house because of its high energy, which is in a city of light and part of the planetary cities of light project with the Group of Forty worldwide meditation project.

The protocols proceed first with relaxation exercises and guided meditation in which the clients are asked to "leave" their bodies and go to a higher frequency. I attempt to get them to the highest level of trance they can achieve so that they can access as much information as possible from higher realms. They then connect with their guides, higher selves, and soul families who give guidance and information. The locks of normal consciousness are loosened, allowing access to information about the soul journey.

Some clients are not able to go to higher levels because blocks have been created during their soul journeys. Because they want the experience, they are usually willing to go to the highest frequency they can attain. It is up to me to guide them but not push nor judge them. I remain flexible and compassionate and ask questions they can answer at the level of trance they achieve.

The Session

During the initial guided meditation and visualization process, I encourage my clients to interact with me and report their experiences, which helps to integrate what is happening and allows me to be a part of the regression process. The trance state can be a deep meditation during which it is difficult to verbalize the experiences. After the work is complete, my clients find it difficult to remember what happened, even though I instruct that they will remember everything. I make a recording of the session to help them validate what they experienced. The more they are able to tell me about their experiences during trance, the more there will be available for them later as they listen to the recording.

Dialogue with me also helps them deepen the trance state. I become an anchor and a guide throughout their trance. I am also in a trance and connected with my higher guidance. I am able to ask relevant questions and provide support, clarity, and guidance to the patient.

The guided meditations and visualizations are designed to loosen the creative mind. The clients are guided through gardens, landscapes, and forests. They have epic journeys with symbolic portals that take them to ever higher states of consciousness. Initially, these experiences might not appear rational to a third-dimensional mind.

What I found with my advanced souls is that as they reached deeper trance states, they would have free reign on their experiences. They were able to expand without my direction. I am sometimes challenged to keep up with them and also find myself in a profound state of trance as well. I enjoy this but have to stay focused on asking questions and being a guide. The therapist's job is to ensure that the client can make a link back into this life and into a regular state of consciousness. The client will need the information to better understand who they are and how their soul journeys link into their Earth incarnations.

Many want to dismiss the experience as just something they made up. I am there to reassure them that they truly had a profound session and that it would be difficult for most people to make this up.

The link with the higher self is crucial for the success of the session. The higher self cooperates to release information about past lives, karma, soul purposes, and soul journeys. It gives guidance without judgment or attachment. The higher self is only concerned with soul advancement and what lessons were learned in any experience.

Great Loss

One of my clients is a healer and starseed, and he wanted answers to questions about his life. He had several losses, including his mother, son, and a personal relationship, all within three years. He was in deep despair. He arrived late for the session and could only stay for an hour. Most sessions usually last at least three hours. I knew that he was ambivalent about the process, and he acknowledged being scared.

The regression went well and was surprisingly easy for him until we got to his soul dwelling, a place I take my clients where they can access any part of their soul journeys. He began to breathe heavily and started to panic. I asked what was wrong, and he stated that the dwelling was just a woven box that was much too small for him. I told him he could change it at will, and he was relieved but only made the space big enough to crawl into. He reported being uncomfortable but wanted to go on. We were able to go a little higher, and then he stopped to explore where he was. He saw nothing.

When encouraged to move forward, he saw a figure coming closer, and it was his deceased mother. He wept and was very relieved to see her. She gave him support and apologized for neglecting him when he was younger. She also answered some other questions. This was enough for him in one session, and he returned to normal consciousness quickly. He was happy about meeting his mother and about the reassurance of an afterlife.

As I reviewed this regression, I understood that he had, because of the trauma of loss and the intense grieving that followed, almost lost his connection with his higher self. He did not feel better immediately after the regression but reported a year later that he was doing much better in his life. I was glad I had been open to working with him in spite of the limitations he had set. I believe that he had a breakthrough and achieved exactly what he was able to, no more. I think letting go of expectations is critical in doing this work.

A Bifurcated Soul

One of my client's illustrates the soul journey in a very interesting way. The client, a middle-aged woman who had retired because of medical issues, requested help in understanding her soul. She was told she had a bifurcated soul and did not understand what that meant. She also wanted to know why she felt that she never fit in or belonged to any group. She always felt like the outsider in spite of the love shown to her by her husband and her many friends.

This client, whom I will name C, had previously done much spiritual work, especially shamanism. She had a support group and was in a good marriage. When asked about her history, she related a life that I was surprised to learn was filled with trauma and challenges.

As a teenager, C left Europe to study in the United States. She had left her family at the age of sixteen because of severe abuse. Interestingly, she felt compassion for her perpetrator, her father, and had forgiven him, understanding his limitations. In the United States, she did well and received a PhD from a prestigious university, ending up doing research and teaching bioengineering. After she married, she felt happy for the first time in her life.

Ten years later, she developed severe pain in her feet that forced an early retirement. Her husband also retired but soon passed away, leaving her lost and depressed. C found the spiritual group she has now been working with for more than ten years, and she also remarried. Although content, she began to experience new issues.

Instructed to go to the source of the problem, C regressed easily and soon was moving forward in the trance state without my direction. When this happens, I follow the client. She started to accelerate her energy while on a bridge and moved up, becoming a large bird. As a bird, she enjoyed the freedom of flying and described the scenery.

After a brief time, she pointed out a place where she worked. I asked her to describe it. She stated it was the Garden of Creation, where she and her soul family birthed new souls and soul families into creation. I remarked that it sounded interesting, and she responded despairingly, "No, it was boring." She explained in detail that there were precise mathematical formulas and also geometric configurations — sacred geometry — that she and her soul family had to hold in their consciousnesses in order to bring in souls correctly. Often, it was so boring that they became distracted. They would have to recycle the energy because it was created out of balance.

One time she noticed that their latest creation was not correct, but her soul family said that it was fine and would correct itself. She disagreed with them, which was rarely done in a soul family. When the new soul energy was born, C attempted to recycle the energy on her own. It did not work, and the new energy detonated in what seemed similar to a nuclear explosion. Because of the explosion, her soul group was destroyed. Only she remained, severely damaged with part of her soul essence burned. She, by sheer force of will, was able to bind the burned part to herself but had no soul family. She was not whole. This is how her soul became bifurcated.

I asked her guides if anything could be done. They did not think so but tried to "braid" her soul strands together so that she could be whole. I asked her guides who she was and what her name was in the galaxy. They declined to provide that information but did say that she was well known and respected throughout the galaxy.

C returned to normal consciousness and was quite overwhelmed with this information. A year later, she returned for another session, again to find out more about her purpose here on Earth. She had not achieved total relief of her issues from the first session and was interested to explore her superconscious mind some more.

C went easily into trance and transported herself quickly to a higher frequency where she met her guides. They provided more answers for her about her soul journey. After she had lost her soul family, she also lost her direction and sense of purpose for existence. When asked why she incarnated on Earth, the guides explained she did not need to come here, but because she had no other purpose, she decided to explore the Earth plane, the third dimension. For her, it was like a throw away because she could think of nothing else to do.

C asked to work with a shamanistic guide she was familiar with who took her into the fourth dimension. There he showed her, lovingly, that she could use her talents to free souls trapped in the fourth dimension. She had the skill to do this, plus it would provide purpose and direction. She accepted the assignment.

In this meeting, the guides informed me that the soul could not be braided perfectly during the past session, but there was some improvement. Also, I had asked if there was a soul family she could integrate with. They made an effort, but it was not possible because of the complexity of soul evolution in a soul family. This regression presented a lot of interesting information. It also generated so many more questions about the "real" reality!

I have not spoken with C since her last regression. The information she received in her soul journey regression work was challenging, and the healing in the second regression was helpful, I believe. I think she may be more content in that the information helped her see that she had reasons for her lack of connection in this life. Many regressions do not completely solve Earth problems, but they do put problems in context for self-acceptance.

As the Therapist

These sessions are intense for both the client and the therapist. Even though many questions come up for me, it is my job to support the work my client is doing. Often when they come out of trance, they are emotionally spent. They also come back to this reality reluctantly because the higher levels they experience are so much more comfortable.

Part of my job as a therapist is to assist my clients to connect with their higher selves. This connection, once established, can then be expanded by the client. I connect with my higher self while helping my clients access theirs. I instruct my higher self to connect with my clients' higher selves at the beginning of the regression, asking permission to bring through information that will be healing and beneficial. The higher self is a source of information and guidance critical to our soul journeys. Once the connection is established and deepened, clients can work in cooperation with their higher selves in all areas of their lives. This connection can have great healing effects because it expands the conscious mind into a deeper understanding of the soul, especially as it relates to the current lifetime.

I personally benefit from doing this work. It is reassuring for me to know there is a greater reality and that there is, in each of us, a greater self — a divine self — that we can access. The more we are able to access our higher selves, the more wisdom, love, compassion, and understanding we can bring into our lives.

I have found that emotional, mental, spiritual, and even physical issues do not always have a foundation in this life. We as multidimensional soul beings are much more complex than modern psychology is able to embrace. We evolve through different dimensions, galaxies, universes, and lifetimes on this planet and others. That is what I understand thus far, and I know that my understanding is in its infancy. I look forward to the time that the understanding of the soul journey becomes more accepted.

About the Author

David K. Miller is the director and founder of an international meditation group focused on personal and planetary healing. He has been the director of this global healing group, called the Group of Forty, for more than fifteen years. David has been developing groundbreaking global healing techniques using group consciousness to help heal areas of Earth that need balance, restoration, and harmony. The technique he uses with his group work is called biorelativity, which uses group consciousness work to restore Earth's feedback loop system, a complex planetary system that maintains the correct balance of our planet's atmosphere, ocean currents, and weather patterns.

David's meditation group has more than 1,200 members worldwide. In addition to his lectures and workshops, David is also a prolific author, having written ten books and numerous articles on Earth healing techniques. Several of his books also have been published in German and Spanish.

David works with his wife, Gudrun Miller, who is a psychotherapist and visionary artist. Together they have conducted workshops in Brazil, Germany, Australia, Mexico, Argentina, Costa Rica, Spain, New Zealand, Belgium, and Turkey. David's foundation for this work lies in his study and connection to Native American teachings and his intense research in mysticism, including the Kabbalah. He also has an avid interest in astronomy and Earth's relationship to the galaxy. To learn more, go to www.GroupofForty.com.

🌱 *Light Technology* PUBLISHING *Presents*

BOOKS BY DAVID K. MILLER

Arcturians: How to Heal, Ascend, and Help Planet Earth

Go on a mind-expanding journey to explore new spiritual tools for dealing with our planetary crisis. Included in this book are new and updated interpretations of the Kaballistic Tree of Life, which has now been expanded to embrace fifth-dimensional planetary healing methods. Learn new and expanded Arcturian spiritual technologies.

$16.95 • 352 PP. • Softcover • 978-1-62233-002-7

Kaballah and the Ascension

"Throughout Western history, channeling has come to us in various forms, including mediumship, shamanism, fortunetelling, visionaries, and oracles. There is also a long history of channeling in Kaballah, the major branch of Jewish mysticism. I am intrigued by this, especially because I believe that there is now an urgent necessity for entering higher realms with our consciousness because of the impending changes on the planet. Through these higher realms, new healing energies and insights can be brought down to assist us in these coming Earth changes." — David K. Miller

$16.95 • 176 PP. • Softcover • 978-1-891824-82-1

Biorelativity: Planetary Healing Technologies

Biorelativity describes the ability of human beings to telepathically communicate with the spirit of Earth. The goal of such communication is to influence the outcome of natural Earth events such as storms, volcanic eruptions, and earthquakes. Through the lessons contained in this book, you can implement new planetary healing techniques right now, actively participating in exciting changes as Earth and humanity come together in unity and healing.

$16.95 • 352 PP. • Softcover • 978-1-891824-98-2

A New Tree of Life for Planetary Ascension

This is the second book David Miller has written about the Kabbalah. His first book, Kaballah and the Ascension, introduced basic concepts in the Kabbalah and linked them to the ascended masters and the process of ascension. In this second book, David has teamed up with Torah scholar and Kabbalist expert Mordechai Yashin, who resides in Jerusalem, Israel. This book is based on unique lectures and classes David and Mordechai gave over an eight-month period between 2012 and 2013. These lectures on Jewish and Hebraic lessons were held in open discussion groups and offer a truly unique perspective into the Kabbalistic Tree of Life and how it has been expanded.

$16.95 • 464 PP. • Softcover • 978-1-62233-012-6

Raising the Spiritual Light Quotient

The spiritual light quotient is a measurement of a person's ability to work with and understand spirituality. This concept is compared to the intelligence quotient (IQ). However, in reality, spiritual ability is not related to intelligence, and interestingly, unlike the IQ, one's spiritual light quotient can increase with age and experience.

$16.95 • 384 PP. • Softcover • 978-1-891824-89-0

Connecting with the Arcturians

Who is really out there? Where are we going? What are our choices? What has to be done to prepare for this event? This book explains all of these questions in a way that we can easily understand. It explains what our relationships are to known extraterrestrial groups and what they are doing to help Earth and her people in this crucial galactic moment in time.

$17.00 • 256 PP. • Softcover • 978-1-891824-94-4

New Spiritual Technology for the Fifth-Dimensional Earth

Earth is moving closer to the fifth dimension. New spiritual ideas and technologies are becoming available for rebalancing our world, including native ceremonies to connect to Earth healing energies and thought projections and thought communication with Earth.

$19.95 • 240 PP. • Softcover • 978-1-891824-79-1

☥ *Light Technology* PUBLISHING *Presents*

BOOKS BY DAVID K. MILLER

Fifth-Dimensional Soul Psychology

"The basic essence of soul psychology rests with the idea that the soul is evolving and that part of this evolution is occurring through incarnations in the third dimension. Now, to even speak about the soul evolving is perhaps a controversial subject because we know that the soul is eternal. We know that the soul has been in existence for infinity, and we know that the soul is perfect. So why would the soul have to evolve?

The answer to this question is complex, and we may not be able to totally answer it using third-dimensional terminology. But it is an important question to answer, because the nature of soul evolution is inherently connected to your experiences in the third dimension. The soul, in completing its evolutionary journey, needs these experiences in the third dimension, and it needs to complete the lessons here."

—Vywamus

$16.95 • 288 pp. • Softcover • 978-1-62233-016-4

Teachings from the Sacred Triangle, Vol. 1

David's second book explains how the Arcturian energy melds with that of the White Brother-/Sisterhood and the ascended Native American masters to bring about planetary healing.

Topics include the Sacred Triangle energy and the sacred codes of ascension, how to create a bridge to the fifth dimension, what role you can play in the Sacred Triangle, and how sacred words from the Kaballah can assist you in your ascension work.

$16.95 • 288 pp. • Softcover • 978-1-62233-007-2

Teachings from the Sacred Triangle, Vol. 2

Our planet is at a dire crossroads from a physical standpoint, but from a spiritual standpoint, it is experiencing a great awakening. Never before have there been so many conscious lightworkers, awakened spiritual beings, and masters as there are on this planet now. A great sense of a spiritual harmony emanates from the many starseed groups, and there is also a new spiritual energy and force that is spreading throughout the planet.

$16.95 • 288 pp. • Softcover • 978-1-891824-19-7

Teachings from the Sacred Triangle, Vol. 3

Learn how to use holographic technology to project energies in the most direct and transformative way throughout Earth.

Chapters Include:
- Heart Chakra and the Energy of Love
- Multidimensional Crystal Healing Energy
- Healing Space-Time Rifts
- Integration of Spirituality and Technology, Space, and Time Travel

$16.95 • 288 pp. • Softcover • 978-1-891824-23-4

Enseñanzas del Sagrado Triángulo Arcturiano

Este paradigma es necesario para ayudar en la transición de la humanidad hacia la próxima etapa evolutiva. La humanidad debe realizar esta próxima etapa de la evolución, para asegurar su sobrevivencia por los cambios climáticos globales, la guerra y la destrucción del medio ambiente. ¿Cuál es la próxima etapa? Esta involucra la expansión de la consciencia del ser humano y está representada por el símbolo de este nuevo paradigma, el Sagrado Triángulo Arcturiano.

El guía de la quinta dimensión, Juliano, proveniente del sistema estelar galáctico conocido como Arcturus, trabaja junto a David en un papel prominente en esta introducción de la energía del Triángulo Sagrado en la Tierra. David le ofrece al lector un entendimiento del alma, su naturaleza evolutiva y como la humanidad esta avanzando hacia esa siguiente etapa evolutiva.

$19.95 • 416 pp. • Softcover • 978-1-62233-264-9

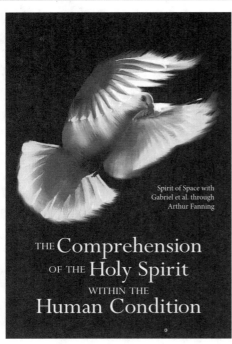

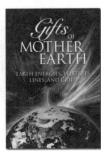

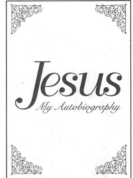
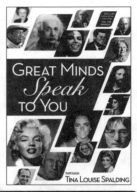

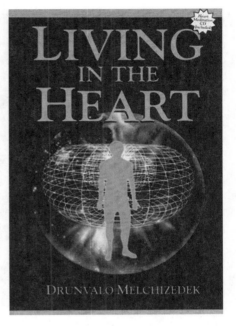

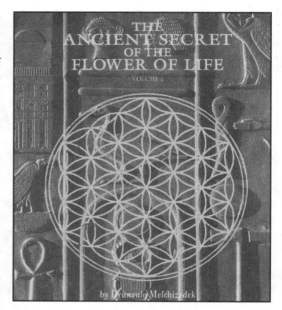

THE ANCIENT SECRET
OF THE FLOWER OF LIFE,
VOLUME 2

The sacred Flower of Life pattern, the primary geometric generator of all physical form, is explored in even more depth in this volume, the second half of the famed Flower of Life workshop. The proportions of the human body; the nuances of human consciousness; the sizes and distances of the stars, planets, and moons; and even the creations of humankind are all shown to reflect their origins in this beautiful and divine image. Through an intricate and detailed geometrical mapping, Drunvalo Melchizedek shows how the seemingly simple design of the Flower of Life contains the genesis of our entire third-dimensional existence.

From the pyramids and mysteries of Egypt to the new race of Indigo children, Drunvalo presents the sacred geometries of the reality and the subtle energies that shape our world. We are led through a divinely inspired labyrinth of science and stories, logic and coincidence, on a path of remembering where we come from and the wonder and magic of who we are.

Finally, for the first time in print, Drunvalo shares the instructions for the Mer-Ka-Ba meditation, step-by-step techniques for the re-creation of the energy field of the evolved human, which is the key to ascension and the next dimensional world. If done from love, this ancient process of breathing prana opens up for us a world of tantalizing possibility in this dimension, from protective powers to the healing of oneself, of others, and even of the planet.

Topics Include:
- The Unfolding of the Third Informational System
- Whispers from Our Ancient Heritage
- Unveiling the Mer-Ka-Ba Meditation
- Using Your Mer-Ka-Ba
- Connecting to the Levels of Self
- Two Cosmic Experiments
- What We May Expect in the Forthcoming Dimensional Shift

$25⁰⁰ Softcover, 272 PP.
ISBN 978-1-891824-21-0

RAE CHANDRAN

Partner with Angels

For Physical and Emotional Benefits in Every Area of Your Life

*Channeled through Rae Chandran
with Robert Mason Pollock*

Angels are the Creator's workforce, and in this book, individual angels describe their responsibilities and explain how they can help you with all aspects of your life — practical and spiritual. All you need to do is ask.

$16.95 • Softcover • 256 pp. • ISBN 978-1-62233-034-8

DNA of the Spirit, Vol. 1

*Channeled through Rae Chandran
with Robert Mason Pollock*

The etheric strands of your DNA are the information library of your soul. They contain the complete history of you, lifetime after lifetime; a record of the attitudes, karma, and emotional predispositions you brought into this lifetime; and a blueprint, or lesson plan, for your self-improvement. Your DNA is also a record of your existence from the moment of your creation as a starbeing to your present incarnation. This information is written in every cell of your body.

$19.95 • Softcover • 384 pp. • ISBN 978-1-62233-013-0

32 color pages of mudras and images to activate your 12 levels of DNA

DNA of the Spirit, Vol. 2

*Channeled through Rae Chandran
with Robert Mason Pollock*

This companion book to *DNA of the Spirit, Vol. 1* originated with the intention and desire to bring forth understanding to support humanity. Go through this volume while holding a sacredness inside of you, asking that the material be imprinted in your sacredness so that it may become an experience that you will be able to live.

Some of the material in this book is coded, and sincere students will find they can open these codes. Understanding can be received through your own filter and in your own way. This way, you will find the Divine within.

$16.95 • Softcover • 192 pp. • ISBN 978-1-62233-027-0

LYNN BUESS

Lynn Buess, MA, Eds

Numerology OF Astrology
Degrees of the Sun

$17⁹⁵
Plus Shipping

ISBN 978-1-62233-011-9
Softcover • 416 PP.

Numerology OF Astrology
Degrees of the Sun

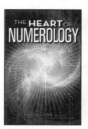

Forever Numerology
ISBN 978-1-891824-97-5
Softcover • 512 PP.
$25.³⁰ plus shipping

Forever Numerology
ISBN 978-1-891824-65-4
Softcover • 320 PP.
$17.⁹⁵ plus shipping

Numerology for the New Age
ISBN 978-0-929385-31-0
Softcover • 272 PP.
$11.⁰⁰ plus shipping

Numerology: Nuances in Relationships
ISBN 978-0-929385-23-5
Softcover • 352 PP.
$13.⁷⁵ plus shipping

L ynn Buess has done it again! As an innovator in the consciousness and self-awareness field for over fifty years, he has now contributed a decidedly unique perspective of the time-honored system of astrology, helping humanity further understand its relationship to the universe. With this latest contribution to self-growth, Lynn offers an original perspective of numerology — this time with the combination of numerological characteristics and astrological influences. He writes not only from an intellectual viewpoint but as someone who has experienced glimpses of cosmic consciousness.

Like with most of his works, it is his hope that this volume will help seekers better connect to their cosmic memories of being both human and eternal in nature. Experience all the signs of the zodiac in minute detail:

Aries • Taurus • Gemini • Cancer • Leo • Virgo • Libra • Scorpio
• Sagittarius Capricorn • Aquarius • Pisces

Synergy Session
ISBN 978-1-62233-758-3
eBook Only

The Tarot and Transformation
ISBN 978-1-62233-759-0
eBook Only

OUT-OF-BODY EXPERIENCES
by Gene Schmitz
WITH CHANNELED EXPLANATIONS AND COMMENTARY THROUGH Robert Shapiro

This book not only tells the full story of Gene's life but it also includes a detailed conversation with an angelic being who speaks through superchannel Robert Shapiro to reveal the meaning behind Gene's out-of-body experiences and his life's purpose. In the process of explaining the twists and turns of Gene's life, this angelic being also unveils some surprising truths about the connection between the body and the soul that apply to all of us.

$14⁹⁵
Plus Shipping

ISBN 978-1-891824-95-1
Softcover 160 PP.
6 X 9 Perfect Bound

CHAPTERS INCLUDE:

- Soul Travel Begins
- Meeting Willie
- The White Light

- Floating Farther from Home
- My Soul Travels Resume
- Message from Grandpa

- Angels and Animals
- New Traveling Companions
- Soul Crossings

Hearing the Angels Sing:
A True Story of Angelic Assistance
by Peter Sterling

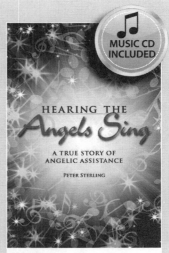

MUSIC CD INCLUDED

Hearing the Angel's Sing chronicles my extraordinary journeys into the higher dimensions of light where I met the angels who ultimately brought me to the realization that my mission was to be a channel for God's heavenly music. The book includes never-before-shared details of my journey of awakening. From the snowcapped peaks of the Rocky Mountains, to the tropical jungles of the Mayan temple lands, to the red rock towers of Sedona, and ultimately to the Incan highlands of Peru, this is a captivating story that will take you on an amazing journey of discovery!

— Peter Sterling

$16⁹⁵
Plus Shipping

ISBN 13: 978-1-891824-96-8
Softcover 256 PP.
6 X 9 Perfect Bound

CHAPTERS INCLUDE:

- Descension and Birth
- Down the Rabbit Hole
- Windows to Heaven

- Rocky Mountain High
- Angels and Devils
- Harmonic Converging

- Red Rocks Calling
- To Hear the Angels Sing
- Fires of Purification

☀ *Light Technology* PUBLISHING

12 Steps TO A Lightness OF Being
by Sarah Goddard Neves

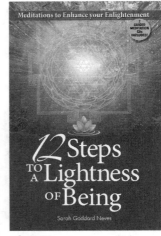

This unique book has is a very special spiritual development course you take in the comfort of your own home. Through its wisdom and guided meditations — **included on the enclosed CDs to boost empowerment** — *12 Steps to a Lightness of Being* will gradually but surely lift your vibration and awaken you. To get the most out of this book, don't rush through it, but read it slowly. Take as long as you need each step before moving to the next. Commit to doing each meditation or visualization, giving yourself some quiet, undisturbed time to do this, and recall your meditation experiences and insights afterward. By doing so, you will get the most out of *12 Steps tp a Lightness of Being*.

$19⁹⁵   ISBN 13: 978-1-891824-99-9
Plus Shipping   Softcover • 160 pp.
   6 X 9 Perfect Bound

3 GUIDED MEDITATION CDs INCLUDED!

The Twelve Steps:

1. Meditation on the Light
2. Opening to Your Intuition
3. Master Connection
4. Being Happy
5. The Healing Power of Forgiveness
6. Evolving with Love and Light
7. Realizing Your Life's Purpose
8. Awakening to Love
9. You: a Creation and a Creator
10. Soul Reflection
11. Hope from the Stars
12. Becoming a Lightness of Being

$25⁰⁰   ISBN 13: 978-1-891824-72-2
Plus Shipping   60 min. CD • 31 min. DVD
   192 pp. • Spiral Bound

Includes CD & DVD

HANDBOOK FOR HEALERS
by Frankie Z Avery & the OMA Group

Accompanied by an instructional DVD and a healing tones CD, the *Handbook for Healers* is intended for healers of all skill levels. OMA, channeled through Frankie Z Avery, offers advice on such issues as nutrition, lifestyle, and healing techniques. The companion DVD contains demonstrations of each of the meditations and exercises included. The *Healing Room Tones* CD is a creation of unique frequencies meant to enhance balance, harmony, and depth of perception in the healing room.

CHAPTERS INCLUDE:
- What Distinguishes Healers
- What Healers Do
- How Healing Works
- The Healer
- The Healer with a Patient
- Optimized Healing Environments
- Happiness
- The Importance of Eating Well

EXERCISES INCLUDE:
- Energize Your Day
- Check for Balance
- Expand Energy before Session
- Focus
- Balance with the Patient
- Stroke and Seal
- Cleanse between Patients
- Dust Off after Healing
- Restore: Catch Your Breath

♀ *Light Technology* PUBLISHING *Presents*

BY JEFF MICHAELS

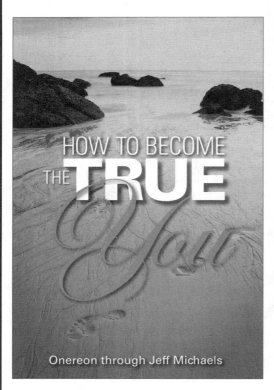

Onereon through Jeff Michaels

$16.00 • Softcover • 6 x 9 • 160 pp.
ISBN 978-1-62233-032-4

How to Become the True You

Are You Seeking to Create a Spiritual Life?

Spiritually minded humans often look to those in the spirit realm for guidance and a higher perspective. We are Onereon, a family of beings dwelling in that realm of spirit. Our chosen path is to assist humanity, helping you gain the opportunity to enjoy life to the fullest and to improve your karmic future.

During life there are myriad opportunities for significant personal growth. Spiritually motivated beings living in difficult times on Earth may find themselves distracted from their true path of attaining a higher vibrational state of existence. One of the strongest proponents of growth is to begin making individual choices based on self-awareness and practical guidance.

Vital questions you can ask now include the following:

- Who is the true you?
- Who are you at your karmic core?
- Who would you be without outside influences?
- What is your true karmic purpose?

By asking yourself these questions, you begin a process of deep spiritual development that will change what is important to you now and in your future. Do not ask these questions lightly! Once spoken, the process begins.

Chapters Include the Following:

- Your Family of Guides
- Who Is the True You?
- Who Are You Now?
- What Just Happened?
- Clarify Your Choices
- Your Strength and Purity
- Live in the Present to Create the Future
- Be Attached to Earth
- Your Perfect Core Energy
- Create a Spiritual Life
- Walk Between the Ages

Print Books: Visit Our Online Bookstore www.LightTechnology.com
eBooks Available on Amazon, Apple iTunes, Google Play, and Barnes & Noble

☥ *Light Technology* PUBLISHING *Presents*

THE EXPLORER RACE SERIES

ZOOSH AND HIS FRIENDS THROUGH ROBERT SHAPIRO

The series: Humans — creators in training — have a purpose and destiny so heartwarmingly, profoundly glorious that it is almost unbelievable from our present dimensional perspective. Humans are great light-beings from beyond this creation gaining experience in dense physicality. This truth about the great human genetic experiment of the Explorer Race and the mechanics of creation is being revealed for the first time by Zoosh and his friends through superchannel Robert Shapiro. These books read like adventure stories as we follow the clues from this creation that we live in out to the Council of Creators and beyond.

❶ THE EXPLORER RACE

You are truly a result of the genetic experiment on Earth. You are beings who uphold the principles of the Explorer Race. The key to empowerment in these days is not to know everything about your past but to know what will help you now. You are constantly being given responsibilities by the Creator that would normally be things that Creator would do. The responsibility and the destiny of the Explorer Race is not only to explore but to create.
ISBN 978-0-929385-38-9 • Softcover • 608 PP. • $25.00

❷ ETs and the EXPLORER RACE

In this book, Robert channels Joopah, a Zeta Reticulan now in the ninth dimension who continues the story of the great experiment — the Explorer Race — from the perspective of his civilization. The Zetas would have been humanity's future selves had humanity not re-created the past and changed the future.
ISBN 978-0-929385-79-2 • Softcover • 240 PP. • $14.95

❸ EXPLORER RACE: ORIGINS and the NEXT 50 YEARS

This volume has so much information about who we are and where we came from — the source of male and female beings, the war of the sexes, the beginning of the linear mind, feelings, the origin of souls — it is a treasure trove. In addition, there is a section that relates to our near future — how the rise of global corporations and politics affects our future, how to use benevolent magic as a force of creation, and how we will go out to the stars and affect other civilizations. It is full of astounding information.
ISBN 978-0-929385-95-2 • Softcover • 384 PP. • $14.95

❹ EXPLORER RACE: CREATORS and FRIENDS, the MECHANICS of CREATION

Now that you have a greater understanding of who you are in the larger sense, it is necessary to remind you of where you came from, the true magnificence of your being. You must understand that you are creators in training, and you were once a portion of Creator. This book will allow you to understand the vaster qualities and help you remember the nature of the desires that drive any creator, the responsibilities to which a creator must answer, the reaction a creator must have to consequences, and the ultimate reward for any creator. ISBN 978-1-891824-01-2 • Softcover • 480 PP. • $19.95

❺ EXPLORER RACE: PARTICLE PERSONALITIES

All around you in every moment, you are surrounded by the most magical and mystical beings. They are too small for you to see individually, but in groups, you know them as the physical matter of your daily life. These particles might be considered either atoms or portions of atoms who consciously view the vast spectrum of reality yet also have a sense of personal memory like your own linear memory. Some of the particles we hear from are Gold, Mountain Lion, Liquid Light, Uranium, the Great Pyramid's Capstone, This Orb's Boundary, Ice, and Ninth-Dimensional Fire.
ISBN 978-0-929385-97-6 • Softcover • 256 PP. • $14.95

❻ EXPLORER RACE and BEYOND

With a better idea of how creation works, we go back to the Creator's advisors and receive deeper and more profound explanations of the roots of the Explorer Race. The Liquid Domain and the Double Diamond Portal share lessons given to the roots on their way to meet the Creator of this universe, and the roots speak of their origins and their incomprehensibly long journey here.
ISBN 978-1-891824-06-7 • Softcover • 384 PP. • $14.95